The Fool of God
JACOPONE DA TODI

The Fool of God

JACOPONE DA TODI

George T. Peck

Opposite:
Portrait of Jacopone by an
unknown
fifteenth-century artist,
fresco in the Cathedral of
Prato *(Photo by
Alinari/Editorial Photocolor
Archives)*

KEFA NE·DO
RAI·F·R·SE·CI
RATE·VИTO·
J·ADO·ALPARA
ORE

BEATO·IACOPO·DA·TODI·

The University of
Alabama Press
University, Alabama

Library of Congress Cataloging in Publication Data

Peck, George Terhune, 1916-
    The fool of God, Jacopone da Todi.

    Includes bibliographical references and index.
    1. Jacopone da Todi, 1230-1306.   2. Authors, Italian—To
1500—Biography.   3. Franciscans—Italy—Biography.   I. Title.
PQ4472.J3P4   851′.1 [B]   79-16713
ISBN 0-8173-0022-8

Contents

Illustrations

to Annie

Preface

The study of Jacopone da Todi is rewarding.

Partly because of the novelty of the act. Though an outstanding poet and "one of the two major [literary] personalities of the end of the thirteenth century"[1]—the other being, of course, Dante—it is astonishing how little attention has been devoted to him. A cursory perusal of the learned periodicals of the last ten years will reveal nearly a hundred articles on Dante for each one on Jacopone.[2] And the case is the same in the area of printed books; no substantial treatment is in print at the present time, though a fine edition of his *Laude* and a profound analysis of his style and the corpus of his work are both available.[3]

Several reasons for such neglect spring to mind. There are those who don't like his poetry, those who overlook him because he lies outside the mainstream of Italian literature, and the students of medieval intellectual traditions who can afford to skip Jacopone, because medieval thinkers themselves—no less than Plato—hardly expected wisdom from a singer. There are the students of the bright, bustling, and rich world of the Italian communes who may never have considered Jacopone, since he rejected that world with a passionate fervor. Finally, there are the orthodox Christians who look on Jacopone's criticism of the hierarchy with even less sympathy than they look on Dante's, for Jacopone was a friar. In the words of Salvatore Quasimodo: "He is a perennial exile, a defeated man condoned because of his immortality."[4]

Being a strong personality, Jacopone has been cordially condemned by some of his critics. The seventeenth-century compiler of a dictionary of Franciscan writers has this to say of him: "Affecting wretched clothing both for his body and his verse, he composed many rhymes and poems in a rough Tuscan language mixed with grosser words from the dialects of Todi, Calabria, Siena, and Naples."[5] In the early nineteenth century, a French critic referred to Jacopone as "the fool in the same category as Dante was the true poet."[6] Even some contemporary critics find him less than attractive. Eugenio Donadoni, the author of the most widely used college text on Italian literature wrote:

> although Jacopone is sporadically a poet, he is never an artist; he lacks the sense of fitness, propriety, and restraint. He passes from the delicate to the coarse with no intimate fusion of the two elements. At times his mystical language is an ardent stammering which expresses nothing. He repeats the same themes endlessly and becomes lost in interminable sermons. From this "madman of Jesus Christ," as he was called, a work of art is not to be expected. Art is the product of the most exquisite spiritual balance.[7]

As if this kind of evaluation were not enough to discourage the student, Ernest Hatch Wilkins in another well-known text described the *laude* as "hard reading, partly because of the difficulty of the thought, partly because of the extensive and apparently deliberate use of dialectical forms, and partly because the phrasing is highly laconic."[8]

If one had not read Jacopone, such comments might well be off-putting. To one who has read him, they serve mainly to describe the aesthetic criteria of the reviewers, who seem to share a high regard for the elegant, the moderate, and the classical—in short, official Tuscan Italian.

Perhaps the most imposing answers to Jacopone's critics come from other poets. The revered Giosuè Carducci proclaimed: "I have passionately studied Jacopone da Todi and announce to all his great superiority to Manzoni [as a religious poet], and I salute him as the Christian Pindar."[9] Giovanni Papini, one of the most prominent writers on religious themes in modern Italy, called him "the greatest religious poet of the Italian middle ages and one of the greatest in the world. . . . An instinctive artist, warm and sturdy, Jacopone is a great poet in spite of little critics." Then there is Gabriele D'Annunzio, who like Bernard Shaw was rarely known to praise other writers: "I have a predilection for this book. . . . No poet has a full-throated song like this Minorite brother. If he is crazy, he is crazy like a lark."[10]

Clearly Jacopone either does not speak to one's condition or he does. If he does, it is because he projects his own spiritual experience with force and directness. The use of words from local dialects is an integral element in the poet's plain honesty—an element welcome to the ear of D'Annunzio, who knew so well the accents of his native Pescara, and abhorrent to the upholders of intellectual respectability. (Florence, Edinburgh, and Boston are the three great capitals of linguistic correctness—and the greatest of these is Florence.) Rarely has a poet revealed the marrow of his inner life with more precision and more passion.

It is true that between Jacopone and us hangs a veil spun by the distance in time and space that separates us. This distance is a great challenge to the historical imagination, for the symbols by which he grasps the universal realities of pain, fear, guilt, love, and peace are those of his time on earth, and not ours. His language, despite the complaints of classicists, is no more opaque to the reader of modern Italian than Chaucer's is to the reader of modern English. As Ernst Robert Curtius has written:

> To transmit tradition is not to solidify it into an immovable body of doctrine or into a fixed choice of canonical books. For the letter killeth, but the spirit giveth life. The study of literature ought to be conducted in such a way as to give a student joy and to make him marvel at beauties which he did not even suspect. Devotion and enthusiasm are the keys which will open these hidden treasures. I believe that wide stretches of mediaeval

literature are still waiting for the divining rod which will point to sources of beauty and truth.[11]

Knowing a little of Jacopone's time and place and the forms that had meaning for him gently draws the veil aside, and Jacopone is present. His immediacy is overwhelming. We have learned to draw the veil from Cimabue, Giotto, and Duccio—not to speak of Dante—to our great enrichment. Have we yet learned to do the same for Jacopone?

Paradoxically such an unveiling is easier now than it was fifty years ago. The only extended treatment of Jacopone in English dates from 1919. Written by Evelyn Underhill,[12] a true and sensitive mystic, the work shows deep understanding, but it is overlaid by its own rather sticky patina of Tennysonian gentility. The patina of Jacopone is hard enough to penetrate without adding to it that of Edwardian England; few would use Wedgewood ware to study Greek urns.

Since 1919 much has changed in our spiritual climate. The poetic lexicon has been considerably broadened by such poets as Eliot and Pound; hence, many of Jacopone's words, considered "unpoetic" fifty years ago, are now not only acceptable but strongly meaningful. Several wars have finally got into our consciousness, and violence and insecurity are as much a part of our lives as they were of Jacopone's. Apocalyptic visions of the Last Judgment have a new reality for us who live in the shadow of the mushroom cloud. Our streets are occasionally crowded with idealistic revivalists as were his. We have, as he did, a deep longing for a better life unencumbered by wealth and power. We live, as he did, in an aggressively materialistic community. In short, once the veil of time is drawn aside, he speaks to our condition.

Underhill's study has been accepted as the standard work in English by a historian writing as recently as 1968,[13] and so it is. Strangely enough, it has had little effect in Italy, where Mario Casella, the author of what is still the most substantial work on Jacopone, was quick to point out its historical inaccuracies.[14] The understanding of Jacopone's work in Italy has been hindered by a curious critical phenomenon—the separation of mysticism and poetry. Benedetto Croce wrote: "Religion, if it is religion, is not and cannot become poetry, just as criticism and morality cannot either. . . . The reason for excluding it is entirely in its didactic, pedagogical, and practical goal. . . . Poetry, however, by its nature . . . is skeptical of all faiths and incentives to action, because it is fixed, victorious and serene in the drama of the soul, in the suffering and joyful life of the cosmos, with which it is identified."[15] This preposterous notion was put forth by one of the most profound thinkers of our century and so received and still receives careful consideration. Upon examination, it will be seen to be true for vast stretches of Italian literature, though not for that of other countries like France, Spain, Germany, or England. In the Italy of Petrarch, Tasso, or d'Annunzio, one was either a poet, for whom religion was a nearly meaningless form, or a professional religionist—not both. Unfortunately Croce's exclusion of mysticism from poetry bars from the canon of Italian literature not only the *Paradiso* of Dante but also all of Jacopone. It has marred the work of a substantial student of Jacopone, Natalino Sapegno, whose attempt to apply Crocean aesthetics to Jacopone has been described as a "desperate labor with an absurd goal."[16] Despite such critical blocks, scholarship in the last fifty years has very much broadened our knowledge of Jacopone both by the increasingly secure definition of the corpus of his work and by the truly penetrating analyses of his style and thought.

To those specifically interested in Renaissance Italy the study of Jacopone is also rewarding. Though he was part of a counterculture standing aside from the main currents of humanist literature and scholarship, it is a counterculture of considerable substance continuously interacting with the mainstream. From a broad historical perspective, Bernardino of Siena, Antonino of Florence, and Girolamo Savonarola are representatives of this counterculture in later generations. And how much the study of these later figures has added to our grasp of the spirit of their times! The view of Italy from the age of Dante to that of Machiavelli is incomplete without an intuitive understanding of its great mystics.

In a like manner, the study of Jacopone can be greatly rewarding to those who are primarily interested in political and economic history. A whole battery of eminent historians have devoted themselves in recent decades to the study of the political and economic conditions of thirteenth-century Italy. So our knowledge of the life of later medieval communes is considerably more detailed and profound than it was only a short time ago, and we now know more clearly the sort of society against which Jacopone was in rebellion. After such research, it seems no longer possible to analyze Franciscan poverty, as was done quite recently,[17] with scanty reference to the actual economic conditions under which it developed. The fact of Jacopone's rebellion does not place him beyond the ken of those who are involved in the things of this world, but adds a new dimension to their thinking. For whether one considers men today or men in 1300, it is not cold and partial abstractions like "economic man" or "political man" that are under examination, but whole man.

In the last analysis Jacopone speaks most directly to the faithful—those who have themselves, however fleetingly, stood in the presence of God. As Émile Durkheim demonstrated many years ago,[18] such experience happens to men in all ages, places, and conditions; and those who are versed in mysticism will find that Jacopone shares the "perennial philosophy"[19] of all mystics and will discover in him echoes of other great souls from Lao-Tsu to Teilhard. Yet here the veil that hangs between Jacopone and us is perhaps the thickest. There are many today for whom even the word "God" is a stumbling block; to them God is a prisoner of the ecclesiastical establishment. So how could a Franciscan, immersed in the rich symbolism of the church, speak to them?

Difficult as it may seem, this veil too can be drawn aside by the working of the spirit. If indeed some can find revelation through Buddha and Krishna, how much easier it might be to find revelation within a tradition that is much closer to us. One would have thought that Roman Catholics would have accepted Jacopone long since as a hero and saint, as in fact many did during the Renaissance; but the Reformation brought a stop. They found Jacopone's invective against the hierarchy uncomfortable in a world that also contained Luther. Now that the spirit of "aggiornamento" has grown so big and so fast, Christians are discovering that they are separated less from each other than they are from unbelievers.

It is time to unveil Jacopone.

Acknowledgments: The writer wishes to thank Professors Felix Gilbert of the Institute for Advanced Study and Carolly Erickson of the University of California at Berkeley for their careful reading of the manuscript and their many constructive criticisms. My gratitude also extends to the Italian Cultural Institute of New York City for their many kindnesses and assistance. Needless to add, the author takes full responsibility for the work.

The Fool of God

JACOPONE DA TODI

I ∞ *Jacopo dei Benedetti*

S ometime in the 1230s—perhaps 1236—Jacopo dei Benedetti (or Benedettoni) was born at Todi. Like most men of his century, the year of
his birth is not known, because chroniclers of that time were not interested
in recording the exact ages of their contemporaries. In the case of Jacopo it
does not matter exactly when he was born, for all his spiritual journey—
and the poetry through which he expressed it—took place between 1268,
when he was already a mature man, and his death in 1306.[1] A difference
of five or ten years in physical age is of importance to a youth or a very old
man, but not to one in his middle years. Interestingly enough, the exact
age of Jacopo's great and worthy antagonist, the irascible Pope Boniface
VIII, is of importance. Estimates of the latter's birth year vary from 1220 to
nearly 1240,[2] and when we contemplate that scene in 1303 in which the
great pope was brutally dragged from his throne in full regalia, it makes a
great difference if we visualize a doddering and helpless old man or a
terrifying monarch in full possession of his powers.

For the first fifteen years of his life Jacopo did something that would
nowadays be taken for granted but that could not be taken for granted in
the thirteenth century. He survived. Death, and especially that most
unsettling of all forms of death, the death of children, was commonplace.
Infant mortality must have been appalling, though there is no way of our
knowing how great it was, since baptisms were usually performed only
once a year. The bishop baptized the survivors. Probably one out of two
children died before reaching the age of ten—a higher rate of mortality
than that recorded for the ancient world of the *pax romana* or for modern
India before the introduction of widespread medical care.[3] Of these
survivors only one out of three lived to be fifty.[4]

The omnipresence of death was a fact of life. During much of his
spiritual journey, Jacopo was obsessed by the fear of death, and it is not
surprising that death took such a large role in the thought and feelings of

the thirteenth century. The lament for a dead mistress is a powerful theme in the hands of the Sicilian poet, Giacomino Pugliese:

> Morte, perchè m'hai fatta sì gran guerra,
> che m'hai tolta madonna, ond'io mi doglio?
>   La fior de le belezze mort'hai in terra,
> per che lo mondo non amo nè voglio.

> Death, why are you warring so greatly against me that you have taken away my lady, for whom I mourn? You have killed in the ground the flower of beauty, so that I neither love nor wish the world.[5]

The entire life of man is considered in the light of his imminent death by Lothario dei Conti (Pope Innocent III) in his somber moral tract, *De Contemptu Mundi*, which was one of the most widely read books of the time.[6] Modern men are apt to conclude that such a vivid realization of the presence of death was morbid. It was, on the contrary, factual. In the same way a thirteenth-century man would be astounded at the degree to which death is buried in our consciousness today and would have thought it ludicrous that doctors and nurses must take special courses to learn how to deal with such an obvious fact.

Jacopo not only survived but was among the elite who were educated. Only one child in ten got an education beyond the elementary three "Rs," even in such a cultural center as Florence and in the next and more literate century.[7] In a market town such as Todi the proportion of educated children must have been even smaller. Normally the favored child went to study with a tutor, often a layman, several of whom were probably available at Todi. The name of one, a certain Filippo, has come down to us, together with that of his brother Bartolo, who taught canon and civil law.[8]

The whole body of knowledge was guarded by a foreign language, so that in effect all learned men had to be bilingual. The ancient Latin had to be mastered to an extent that made it still a living language. In the process not only was the classical idiom tortured to fit the new needs of medieval men into forms that would have been unrecognizable ten centuries earlier, but also the new realities of thirteenth-century life could reach only approximate and frequently obscure verbalization. It was an unhandy mechanism at best, despite its obvious advantages as the lingua franca for the intellectual elite of western Europe.[9]

The *Ars Grammatica* of Aelius Donatus, written in the fourth century, was the accepted text, and the scholar set about learning it by rote. From this study he progressed to a wide selection of fables, saints' lives, biblical texts, and such theological works as the *Consolations of Philosophy* of Boethius. Medieval Latin could be mastered relatively easily by the student, since it used word order to determine the relationships between words, just like the native dialect. Then came the writers of the classical period: Virgil, Cicero, Statius, Juvenal, Ovid, Cato, Sallust, Lucan, and Persius—with their thoroughly haphazard word order and tricky word endings defining grammatical relationships.[10] Such archaic constructions had long been abandoned by the dialects of Italy. It was hard work, and Jacopo hated it. Later he wrote:

> Poi venne el tempo mio pate è mosto,
> a leger m'ha posto - ch'emprenda scrittura;
> se non emprenda quel ch'era emposto,
> davame 'l costo - de gran battetura;
> con quanta paura - loco ce stetti,
> sirìan longhi detti - a farne contata.
>   Vedea li garzoni girse iocando,
> ed io lamentando - che non podea fare;
> se non già alla scola, - gìame frustando
> e svincigliando - con mio lamentare. . . .

Then came the time when my father was moved to put me to learning to read and write; if I didn't learn what was put in front of me, he gave me a big beating as reward; with what fear I stayed there would be too long to tell.

I saw the boys going about playing and I was sorry that I couldn't do it; if I didn't go to school, I was whipped and whipped to my sorrow. [*Lauda* XXIV, lines 45–54]

Whipping and all, it was a successful education, for young Jacopo was linguistically gifted and became a competent Latinist. Later on he wrote a short treatise, *Il trattato,* in workaday Latin prose, and a number of his sayings, *I detti,* were taken down by his admirers.[11] Latin became such an intimate part of his make-up that Latinisms tripped off his tongue in a completely unselfconscious manner. For example, "nichilitade," "prelio," "domo," etc., are Latinist inventions that never survived into Italian; at other times pure Latin words like "omnia," "vale," "magno," etc., appeared quite naturally.[12] He was so much at home in the language that one does not feel that his Latinisms are used for rhetorical effect, as they are for instance in the intensely self-conscious style of Machiavelli, who expresses his inner tensions by weaving between the poles of dialect and Latin.

Yet Latin remained a foreign language for Jacopo. It was the official language of the learned world against which he was later to revolt with deep revulsion. It was not the language of the heart and soul.[13]

In his youth, however, Jacopo was not concerned with such matters. *La Franceschina,* a legend compiled many years later from the sayings and

traditions of the friars for the edification of the faithful—very much like
the sayings and traditions of Jesus set down many years after his
death—reports:

> This man, being in lay garb, was a complete man of the world and tasted
> the essence neither of God nor of the saints. . . . He was one of those
> unbridled lovers of the world, proud, greedy, and all involved in the
> concupiscences of this miserable world, which held him in such blindness
> that rather than knowing God and the things of God, he was for the
> opposite—an enemy of those who wished to walk in the ways of God.[14]

What were the concupiscences of the world that were available to
Jacopo in the rather isolated hill town of Todi? Objectively and by
modern standards, they might seem very tame indeed, and this has led
some modern critics to believe that the pious friars have exaggerated
them in the effort to magnify the depth of his conversion.[15] But such
criticism misses the essential point: that the strong, sex-driven desires of
the worldly life can and do exist in the minds and spirits of people
regardless of the opportunities for their expression in external behavior.
The thought, as the Sermon on the Mount teaches, is as important as the
deed.

That Jacopo had concupiscences cannot be doubted; he was of a violent
and emotional nature. He speaks in his penance:

> Poi che fui preso a far cortesia,
> la malsanìa - si non è peggiore;
> l'auro e l'argento - che è en Surìa
> non empierìa - la briga d'onore;
> moriva a dolore - che non potea fare;
> el vergognare - non già en fallata.
>   Battaglia continua del manecare,
> pranzo, cenare - e mai non ha posa;
> se non è aparechiato - co a me pare,
> scandalizare - sì fa la sua osa. . . .
>   Mai non se giogne la gola mia brutta;
> sapor de condutta - sì vol per usanza,
> vina exquisita - e nuove frutta. . . .

> Then I was taken to follow the life of courtesy; there is no worse sickness;
> all the gold and silver in Syria does not assuage the cares of honor. He who
> can't do it dies of sadness; shame is never absent. A continual battle to eat,
> to dine, and to sup, which never let up; if the meal was not prepared to
> please me, I berated the cook's way of doing things. My ugly appetite was
> never sated; I wanted as a matter of course tasty dishes, exquisite wine, and
> new fruit. . . . [*Lauda* XXIV, lines 69–74, 109–112, 115–117]

The pleasures of the flesh were certainly attractive to the young Jacopo, but it can be seen that these pleasures were not so much to be enjoyed for their own sake as to be flaunted as symbols of his social status, his "onore." For the nobility and commercial middle classes of Todi, the firm foundation of status was money. A consuming passion for money engrossed Jacopo; he was a notary. His pious biographer wrote: "And it is no wonder [that he had no feeling for God]; but his occupation led to the opposite; that is, he was a procurator, which occupation is dangerous for one who does not have a very tender conscience and leads man to eternal damnation."[16] The "famous procurator of the city of Todi" was a member of a profession that, together with the moneylenders, composed the most aggressively upward mobile social class in the Italian communes. And these communes themselves were engaged in tearing apart the traditional fabric of medieval society with their revolutionary commercialism.

It is not known how Jacopo became a notary or procurator or judge—at Todi, as at Florence, no great distinction was made between the various types of men of law.[17] Perhaps the most common way of entering this profession, as any other medieval occupation, was to follow in the footsteps of one's father, and in the case of notaries, this practice was very common because of the nature of the work. Not only did a notary have a proprietary interest in his clientele, which he would like to keep in the family if possible, but also in the absence of communal archives, he was himself the keeper of a mass of legal documents, which his clients, their descendants, and any other interested party might have to consult. Such notarial chartularies were also kept in the family if possible; if not, they had to be turned over to another notary on the death of the first under the careful supervision of the commune or the guild, which were vitally concerned in the preservation of these practical records.

Jacopo's uncle may have been a certain Benedetto—the geneology of the family is not clear—who was the notary for an important transaction in December, 1218.[18] The deed involved the count of Coccorone, a member of the same family as that which held the county of Foligno, who bought the village of Foscano in the contado of Todi. In the usual manner, Benedetto kept the deed of title, turning over to the parties drafts or copies of it.

On the other hand, Jacopo may have come to the notariat by another route. His family was prominent enough so that it was considered "noble" and so that the name of, his father, Iacovello, and those of his two brothers, Andalò and Rinaldo, have come down to us.[19] Such a family with substantial properties in the country or in town might have a son trained as a notary to prepare for the administration of these holdings, much as a modern businessman would encourage his son to go to law school or business school. There may have been as many as sixty-five notaries in Todi, though some may never have practiced their profession.[20]

That the Benedetti or Benedettoni were a prominent family in Todi seems likely from the documentary references to them. In 1232 one Rainaldo dei Benedettoni was among the leaders of the commune who received the homage of the lord of Alviano, and the names of several Benedetti—Giovanni, Rainaldo, Benedetto, and Todino—appear frequently in the episcopal registers of this period. The latter fact has led to the supposition that the family was Guelph; certainly it had frequent contact with the chapter of the cathedral, a not unusual channel of family progress regardless of political sympathies. Unfortunately the notarial chartularies as well as most of the communal documents of thirteenth-century Todi have not survived; so we do not know the relationships between these different Benedetti. What we do know is that it was a family of sufficient prominence that it was beginning to acquire a patronymic like so many other rising bourgeois families. Later in the century the Benedetti were able to buy a house in the Colle quarter close to the main square, and this was in the upper town, where members of the ruling class lived in fine houses made of stone.

Whatever the route by which Jacopo came to be a notary, he probably studied in his native town, either with Bartolo, the teacher of civil and canon law, or with another teacher or with another notary. Most notaries were trained locally, though some went to the great center of notarial and legal studies at Bologna. At this time even nearby Perugia was beginning to develop the *studium*, which was to become its university in the next century. However, in the absence of any evidence, it is an unlikely supposition that Jacopo went away to either city.[21]

In his whole lifestyle, Jacopo was an up-and-coming young businessman—"a noble citizen very learned in law and poetry. . . . of sharp intelligence, of fiery spirit and free speech, eager for gain, a successful and thorough lawyer, and also proud and splendid in his dress and way of life."[22] In short, he was, as a modern psychologist would say, normal. At the age of about thirty, in 1267, he decided to marry and chose for his wife a beautiful young girl Donna Vanna, the daughter of Bernardino di Guidone of the counts of Collemedio (or Coldimezzo). The Collemedio family had a strong religious tradition and was of the Guelph party. One member, a certain Francesca, had joined Clare at Assisi in the first enthusiastic flush of the Franciscan movement and was beatified on her death in 1238. Her brother Pietro rose to be the Cardinal Bishop of Albano. The fief of the family lay near Casalta, where the boundaries of the territories of Perugia, Assisi, and Todi came together. In order to protect it from the ambitions of these powerful communes, it was given to the monastery of St. Peter in Perugia and received back in *enfiteusi;* thus the family bought protection by paying a nominal rent under a long-term contract. Though there is no record of the marriage agreement, it is likely that the Benedetti could not obtain a large dowry, as they were probably not so "noble" as the counts of Collemedio.[23]

Jacopo really loved Donna Vanna. He wrote later:

> Volea moglie bella che fosse sana
> e non fosse vana - per mio pacire;
> con grande dota, gentile e piana,
> da gente non strana - con lengua a garrire. . . .

> I wanted for my pleasure a beautiful wife who was healthy and not vain—with a large dowry, kind and even tempered, from a family that was not foreign, with a ready tongue. . . . [*Lauda* XXIV, lines 91–94]

On another occasion, probably thinking of Donna Vanna, he wrote:

> Recordo d'una femena - ch'era bianca, vermiglia,
> vestita, ornata, morbeda, - ch'era una maraviglia;
> le sue belle fateze, - lo pensier m'asutiglia;
> molto sì me somiglia - de potergli parlare.

> I remember a woman who was white and rosy, beautifully dressed and soft—she was a marvel. The thought of her lovely ways torments me; I should like so much to speak with her. [*Lauda* III, lines 63–66]

The young couple lived a fashionable life in Todi. As the Franciscan biographer reported,[24] Jacopo

> lived with much vanity and took great pleasure and delight in his wife's going about well adorned. So he led her to this much against her will. But she, who truly feared God, showed to the eyes of her husband and the world every vanity she could in her clothes and every other curiosity and adornment, and within herself secretly did severe penance.

Tragedy was to interrupt their lives. The chronicle continues:

> One time at the wish of her husband, Ser Jacopo, she went to a party, a usual one in that town, adorned as always to honor those who had invited her and her husband. A very strange accident occurred. While they were dancing and having a good time, the balcony on which they were dancing suddenly fell, and every one fell down with it in such a way that all were injured, some in the head, some in the body, and some in other members. But no one was killed, except only the wife of Ser Jacopo, who as it pleased the great God was cut off in this way and almost immediately passed from this life.
>
> When this was reported to Ser Jacopo (who by the will of God was not

there, having been called away by the podestà to a certain judgment),[25] he quickly ran to that place and had her carried home with great bitterness because he loved her tenderly. And after they got home, he had those vain vestments taken off her to prepare her for burial. Finally he found on her bare flesh a harsh hair-shirt; seeing which the husband, Ser Jacopo, was much astounded and stupefied. He considered the vain life which she had shown in appearance and how he had never known such a thing by the least act. So from the strange and unforeseeable accident of her death or from the secret and virtuous life of his wife, Jacopo was struck in his mind and stricken in his heart and deprived of his senses, so that from that time forth, he never really seemed a reasonable man as before, but went among folk as crazy and stupefied.

This traumatic experience started Jacopo on his spiritual journey. Jacopo, the notary, was transformed into—and ever after known as—Jacopone.

II ∞ The Prime of Todi

Many Italian towns today convey to us through their buildings that once in the course of the centuries they were in their prime. Even the dead cities of Paestum and Pompeii carry still the aura of ancient Greece and imperial Rome; the age of Justinian lives on in the mosaics of Ravenna; the stone of the old city of Bari projects the rugged brutality of the Norman conquerors of the eleventh century. The prime of Todi coincides with the lifetime of Jacopone. In those seventy years the commune achieved the peak of its power and vitality, and at the time of Jacopone's death in 1306, the wars with Perugia that clipped Todi's wings broke out. Jacopone shared fully in the civic and cultural life of Todi, and after his conversion, in the religious life of this home town, which he rarely left. Though no records at all have survived of his notariat, it would not have been possible for an ambitious and prominent young man to have lived in the Todi of the thirteenth century without being influenced by the social and political atmosphere of the commune.

The Polis Like the ancient Greek *polis* of the age of Pericles, the thirteenth-century commune commanded an allegiance that went far deeper than what we are accustomed to think of when using the word "political." It took a positive and active role in conforming the intimate details of family, social, and economic life to the requirements of community development. At Todi everyone knew everyone else, and so the Aristotelian requirement that a *polis* should be small enough so that the citizens would be capable of decision-making based on firsthand observation was fulfilled. Just as the concept of the Greek *polis* was firmly embedded in the world view of Hellenism, so communal loyalty developed in the matrix of Christianity. Echoing Aristotle, the Dominican preacher Remigio di Girolami told the Florentines: "If you are not a citizen, you are not a man, because man is naturally a civic animal."[1]

The glory of the communes is memorialized in stone from Todi near the southern boundary of communal civilization to Verona on the northern. Each had its piazza, to perform the function of *agora* or *forum,* and each, its palazzo communale—many built like those of Todi in the thirteenth century, but few surviving so nearly unchanged as at Todi. One walks up the narrow streets from the piazza to the acropolis of Todi, crowned then by the rich abbey of San Leucio and now by the ruins of a later papal fortress. To the east, south, and west stretch the tumbled hills and to the north winds the valley of the Tiber 900 feet below. Almost as far as the eye can see, for ten or fifteen miles on every side, lies the contado or territory of Todi. This is the world of the thirteenth century— small perhaps by the standards of other ages, but remarkably self-sufficient, homogenous, and vigorous. It bred a hardy race of men, and the courage of such a one as Jacopone was not unusual.

Like the *polei* and other communes, Todi had its tutelary divinity, San Fortunato, whose shrine was immediately below the acropolis in a small eleventh-century church, next to a Franciscan house in which Jacopone was to spend many years. The building one sees today is the great Gothic Church of San Fortunato, the construction of which was begun towards the end of Jacopone's life. Here on October 14 of each year all the citizens proceeded, led by the podestà, the bishop, judges, and syndics to do honor to patron and protector. Fortunato's miracles, recorded by Gregory the Great, may well not have passed muster in a later age, but in the sixth century they symbolized the hopes of the Italic population of Todi threatened by heroic Gothic power. A story, known to Jacopo as to all citizens of Todi, illustrates precisely the juxtaposition of Catholic spiritual power and Gothic force. The Gothic chieftain Vitiges, being driven by the Byzantines from Todi, wished to take with him two Todian hostages despite the pleas and threats of Fortunato. He set the boys on a horse. The horse broke its leg. In superstitious fear Vitiges returned the hostages, and Fortunato cured the horse's broken leg with holy water. Such a saint-bishop was a fit protector of the commune.

The closeness of later bishops to the commune was indicated when the diocese of Todi became almost identical with the contado of Todi. An act of 760, in the "time of the [Lombard] king Desiderius," defined the boundaries of the diocese in all directions except the south; these became the boundaries of the contado and remained those of the diocese down to the present day.[2]

During Jacopo's lifetime, Todi entered a sort of golden age. Secure in the government of the contado, she was in practice independent of the two great international powers of the age, empire and papacy. From the acropolis of Todi, the view of the world was orderly and complete. Only when one thinks in terms of the aspirations of emperor and pope can one speak of anarchy, defeat, and disillusion. Both contemporary chroniclers

and later historians are much concerned with the struggles of the mighty
to establish real control over the communes of central Italy; when they
failed to achieve anything but a vague general suzerainty, the result is
conceived of as anarchical. The "anarchy" of the papal states is merely a
backhanded way of describing the independence of the communes.[3] The
rule of Todi and her sister communes may well have been turbulent,
involving on some occasions considerable military activity, but it was far
from anarchical.

The imperial threat to Todi was less effective, though more dramatic,
than the papal. On the tide of his victory over the Lombard communes at
Cortenuova in 1237, Frederick II of Hohenstaufen turned to subdue
Tuscany and the papal states. Todi allied herself with Perugia, Foligno,
Gubbio, and Spoleto to meet the danger. Mostly by diplomacy the
emperor was able to gain entrance into Spoleto, long the seat of an
imperial duke,[4] and into Foligno, always at odds with its neighbor
Perugia. In 1241, Frederick was also able to capture Todi's little subject
ally, Amelia, by knocking down its ancient Roman walls, but he could
not even take Narni and made little headway in several seasons of
warfare against the walls of Perugia. He did not have the resources to take
on both Todi and Perugia at the same time, and so Todi was left un-
molested. After the death of Frederick's opponent, Gregory IX, in 1241,
and during the ensuing interregnum, Todi was led to swear fealty to the
emperor. Almost as though to indicate the emptiness of this act, the
commune decided in 1244 to build its second series of walls, enclosing
the Borgo Nuovo. Such walls made the town virtually impregnable at the
then state of military science, and when Frederick left in 1246, the danger
passed.[5]

Later attempts to reestablish the imperial power by Frederick's succes-
sors, Conrad and Manfred, scarcely affected Todi at all; so the young
citizen, Jacopo, probably did not go to war at all.[6]

Independence from effective papal control was much more difficult to
maintain and involved complicated and continuous diplomatic negotia-
tions throughout the century. Despite the persistent efforts of the popes,
it is astonishing to see how little the papal *plenitudo potestatis,* claimed
since the eighth century, meant in actual fact. The great Innocent III tried
to build a real administrative system for the lands secured to him in 1201
by the emperor, Otto IV; in that year he visited Todi as part of a progress
to most of the towns of Umbria and northern Latium, collecting communal oaths of allegiance as he went. He was finally able to establish
rectors for the provinces of the Patrimony of St. Peter in Tuscany and the
Duchy of Spoleto. Todi was on the border between the two, but most of
her troubles arose with the rector of the Patrimony at Montefiascone.
There Todi joined the other communes and feudal lords in the first
parlamentum (1207), at which the papal allegiance was reconfirmed; but

Todi, together with Perugia, successfully maintained their rights to hear appeals from their own judges without reference to the papal curia. Occasionally the pope, as in 1207 and again in 1232, intervened in the life of the commune to mediate between opposing local groups, but increasingly even this function was performed either by the podestà or by one commune for another. For instance, in 1276 Todians were called in to arbitrate in Perugia, and Perugians performed the same service for Todi—two examples of a widespread practice.[7] The pope was never able to challenge the right of the commune to elect its own podestà and make its own *statuto* covering almost all the legal needs of the contado. There is little evidence that the papacy ever derived considerable income from the traditional census tax on the commune; when Todi supplied military contingents, like the 800 horsemen sent in 1288 to aid Perugia in its war with Foligno, it was in answer to local ambitions rather than papal policy. Todi hoped to gain some of the lands of Bevagna in the contado of Foligno.

Even in ecclesiastical affairs, which we are inclined to think of as distinct from lay politics but which the thirteenth century did not, the *plenitudo potestatis* was a weak abstraction. Accusations of heresy were indeed brought by the clergy, but the podestà of Todi, as defender of the citizens, presided at the trials—a privilege that even Venice did not gain until 1289. It often occurred that political rebellion was allied to heresy, as the later conflict between Jacopone and Boniface VIII was to show. Florentine experience was similar. The pope at this time was not even able to enforce his decision on the appointment of an abbot in Florence or to force the commune to persecute heretics, despite an interdict and all the machinery of papal pressure.[8] At Todi the Rector of the Patrimony repeatedly tried to establish his authority (in 1258, 1268, 1274, and 1282), but the bishop joined the commune in resisting the encroachments. Both fell under an interdict, and both claimed that their allegiance was directly to the pope regardless of the rector. The commune often elected as podestàs relatives of the reigning pope, either a Savelli or an Orsini, to present its case at the curia. In the end the threat from the rector was effectively parried.[9]

The real business of thirteenth-century Todi was the control and expansion of the contado. In the first half of the century Todi was surrounded by a whole ring of tiny "buffer states" between herself and the neighbors, Orvieto, Perugia, Spoleto, and Narni, and its control of the contado was far from complete. In these circumstances intercommunal war broke out when the neighbors pressed too close. Such was the case with Orvieto, with whom Todi was intermittently at war from 1207 until the final resolution of the conflict at the end of the century. The main bone of contention was the castle of the counts of Montemarte, who changed sides with feudal abandon; Todi finally bought the fortress in

1291—a rather bourgeois solution.[10] Another source of conflict was the territory of Lugnano, an Orvietan enclave within the sphere of Todian influence. In 1237 Todi tried to take it from Orvieto, but the army was defeated with a loss of 600 prisoners. Encouraged by this defeat and by the growing power of Frederick, the Guibelline nobles revolted. The lords of Collazzone, Iovolino, Paragnano, Avigliano, Monte Marchiano, and Mogliemala in the contado of Todi joined with six of the leading families in the contado of Amelia; but the commune defeated them all in the next year at Ponte del Paglia. It was the last serious challenge by the feudality to the power of the commune. Peace and the prisoners were restored after an ineffectual intervention by Gregory IX.

By 1256, when Jacopo was becoming interested in the affairs of the commune, Todi had succeeded in gaining secure control of the two nearest communes to the south, Amelia and San Gemini, forcing them to accept Todians as podestàs. Further expansion in this direction was blocked by Cesi, the fortress of a papal castellan that Todi feared to attack, and by Narni. To the west the power of the commune was growing in the "buffer states," the lordships of Alviano, Baschi, and Titignano. On the north Todi was dealing by the end of the century with such powerful nobles as the counts of Marsciano through peaceful negotiation rather than war. A survey of the contado, done in 1294 for tax purposes,[11] determined the effective dimensions of the contado. Though it was not a large state, it was a compact one, reasonably well regulated.

Only, to be sure, reasonably well regulated, for a phenomenon characteristic of the contemporary Romagna was in evidence also at Todi. The feudal nobility were only partly tamed by the commune, for though they moved to town, they brought with them the boisterous and aggressive independence of feudal lords.[12] Thus conflicts that in earlier days led to battles in the open country were metamorphosed into party strife within Todi. Such a development was characteristic of many communes, and violent strife arose at Todi from 1257 to 1269, during the youth of Jacopone.

Vendettas made the life of the young blade a dangerous one. As Jacopone wrote:

Se era constretto a far vendecanza
per soperchianza - ch' avesse patuta,
pagar lo bando non era in usanza
e la briganza - non c'era partuta;
la mente smarruta - crepava a dolore,
che 'l descionore - non era vegnata.

Se l'avea fatta, giàmene armato,
emparaurato - del doppio aravire;

e stavame en casa empregionato
e paventato - nel gire e venire;
chi el porrìa dire - quant'è la pena
che l'odio mena - per ria comenzata.

I was forced to take vengeance for insolence which I had undergone. It was not the practice to pay the fine, and the enmity was not reduced; I was out of my mind with grief that the dishonor was not avenged.

If I had taken arms and avenged myself, I would have been afraid of having it paid back double, would have stayed imprisoned in my house and have been fearful of going abroad. Who can say how much pain hate brings from a wicked beginning? [*Lauda* XXIV, lines 79–90]

Tempers were short, and little effort was made to suppress their expression. The son of the Florentine banker, Simone di Ranieri Peruzzi, took money from the family safe and caused the firm to lose an important loan. His father exploded: "May my son be cursed for eternity by God and by me. So be it! And if he is still alive after my death, so that I cannot punish him as he deserves, may the justice of God punish him for his infamy and his treachery."[13] The power of party strife and the brutality of vendettas form major themes for Dante's disdain in the Inferno: he condemns ferociously the violence in the Romagna, where murders, especially among members of a family, were common; and the story of Ugolino dramatizes the sheer horror of civil war. Many years later Machiavelli was to remark wryly: "But in republics there is greater life, greater hatred, and more desire for vengeance. . . ."[14]

Mainly in order to keep party strife and the aggressive antagonisms of the ruling classes within bounds, the communes developed the institution of the podestà in the early years of the thirteenth century. Prior to that time, the town consuls, elected by the Great Council and working in conjunction with the bishop, had been able to keep the peace; but as the bourgeoisie and urbanized nobility grew in power, they also grew in unruliness. Hence, following the custom of other communes, the Great Council of Todi, consisting of 300 members of the leading families, began to select a special chief executive to serve under its supervision for a limited period of time. This executive, the podestà, was expected to stand above local rivalries and did in fact introduce enough surcease of internal conflicts as to permit a rapid increase in the wealth and power of Todi. In order to ensure his impartiality, the podestà was always a foreigner, and as a leading public figure in his own city, was an expert in municipal affairs. He quite often made a career of his work, being elected by the town councils of one town after another. For example, Jacopino dei Rangoni, a native of Modena, came to Todi as podestà in 1234 as a young man starting his career in a smaller center. Thence, he went on to become podestà of Siena, Foligno, Bologna, and Rimini, and in 1260 led the forces of Florence in the disastrous defeat at Montaperti. However, this defeat did not ruin his career, and he later served in Reggio, Cremona, Modena, and Parma—an active professional life covering a span of forty-four years.

At Todi this official had a term of office of one year (up until 1270 when it was reduced to six months) and brought with him a whole official family: three judges, seven notaries of whom two served each judge and one was town recorder, and a number of minor household retainers.[15] So each town had its own little court comfortably ensconced in the palazzo del commune.

Every one who like Jacopo had a legal business and was a member of the small municipal elite could not fail to come into almost daily contact with this "international" court and be influenced by it. This situation goes far to explain the remarkable similarity of communal institutions all over north and central Italy. The podestà even went so far as to introduce new political forms, despite the fact that the latter might not suit the needs of a particular commune.[16] More importantly, the entourage of the podestà arrived with books and frequently contained individuals who were interested in literature and history as well as law. Here was a cultural center that Jacopo must have frequented. From 1221 to 1270 Todi drew its podestàs mostly from the more prominent communes. Rome headed the list, as Todi's foreign policy was primarily involved with the papal power and it was helpful to have a friend at court. Florence and Bologna supplied a goodly number each, while Modena, Perugia, Spoleto, Milan, and Parma were represented. Only occasionally, in periods of Guibelline power, was some local noble, like the lords of Baschi, Alviano, or Titigano elected to serve.[17]

Despite the undoubted effectiveness of the podestà, vendettas and party strife remained harassing problems. Local police powers, though they were to develop later, were virtually nonexistent.[18] In practice vendettas formed part of the legal system. The *statuto* of Todi, though it gave little attention to criminal law, which was generally covered by standard Roman law, did contain an extraordinary provision testifying to the strength of the practice of vendetta. Any crime could be followed by a peace between the two parties, and the prosecution would be dropped on payment of one quarter of the fine to the court. As Jacopone remarked, it was not the custom to pay the fine. Law reflected a strong class bias; powerful nobles and high churchmen were effectively beyond its power, no matter what crime they committed. In 1272 a podestà of Orvieto exiled all the members of the powerful Filippeschi clan, because they had arranged the murder of the capitano del popolo and had killed many of their adversaries in numerous street fights; then he fled town in fear for his own life. Todi employed as its podestà in 1227 the notorious Mosca dei Lamberti, who had been exiled from Florence for the vendetta murder of Buondelmonte dei Buondelmonti. Dante placed Mosca deep in Hell—among the hacked-up schismatics in the ninth ditch of the eighth circle (*Inferno*, XXVIII, 103–111).

Party strife between the Guelphs and the Guibellines was intense at Todi during Jacopo's life in the world. The parties were primarily defined by local cliques, even though the Guelphs had originally been the party of the pope and the communes, and the Guibellines, that of the emperor and the feudality. This situation is illustrated by the action of Boniface VIII at the end of the century; the pope, who knew his Todi well, wished to control the town through the Guibelline party then in the ascendency, and so he created a new party, the "Guibellines of the Church Party." In general the Guibellines drew their strength from the rural nobility, and the Guelphs, from the bourgeoisie. The Benedetti have generally been considered Guelphs, in part because they rose to prominence as bourgeois in the service of the bishop and in part because Jacopo married into one of the prominent local Guelph families.

Between the death of Frederick in 1250 and the battle of Montaperti in 1260, the Guelphs tended to have the upper hand in Todi as elsewhere in Tuscany and Umbria. Podestàs were mostly chosen from the Guelph communes, and two institutions of these great communes were introduced at Todi: the *capitano del popolo*, named probably to organize the citizen militia in 1255, and the *anziani*, a council of leading guild members. Neither institution obtained a firm foothold in Todi, since they presupposed the existence of a ruling class based on the greater guilds as was the case in Florence, Pisa, and Bologna; whereas at Todi only the guild of the merchants took a role in government. By and large Todi did not have greater guilds because it had little industrial and only regional commercial activity. Even the notaries were not organized into a college until 1289.

A Guibelline revival seems to have taken place after 1260, as the Guibelline victory at Montaperti made it politic to be on friendly terms with the victor, Manfred, and the rural nobles, impressed with the power of the commune, became interested in using it for their own ends. The office of podestà went one year to one party and the next to the other, while skirmishes took place in the contado for several years as each contended for power.

A virtual civil war broke out in 1269 and reveals a state of political insecurity that forms a meaningful background for the emotional tension of Jacopone's early poems. The Guelphs made an intensive effort to gain control of the administration. They named the commune of Bologna podestà, and the latter sent as its agent a certain Comaccio accompanied by thirty Bolognese soldiers. Expecting trouble, the Guelphs recruited 135 more men from neighboring towns to add to the dozen or so retainers that the podestà normally had. The Great Council passed a series of laws prohibiting the bearing and keeping of arms and meetings in churches, to be backed up by the reinforced constabulary. For forty days the Guibellines were forced to keep the peace, and then a great riot, featuring stone throwing, broke out in the piazza. Some Guelphs were killed and others fled. Comaccio and his retainers were cornered in the Palazzo del Commune, and the situation appeared critical, when Bishop Pietro Gaetani rang the bells of the cathedral across the piazza and sallied forth at the head of his clergy and the Franciscan friars. One wonders if the newly converted Jacopone was among them. Comaccio was rescued and brought to sanctuary in the Church of San Fortunato, but he could not recover his powers and left town, to be succeeded as podestà by a Guibelline noble, Count Ugolino di Baschi.

As the parties were evenly matched, the office of podestà became a partisan office, thus defeating its original purpose. In 1274 two podestàs were elected, one from each party, obviously an untenable situation. Hence, the parties came to a pact: the *Statuto* of 1275 provided that the podestà should be elected by an even number of partisans from each side, the deciding vote in case of a draw being cast by the bishop. Such a provision indicated how tightly the party lines were drawn. Excessive partisanship was not only a feature of communal politics but also something that infected religious life—especially in the conflict between the spirituals and conventuals of the Franciscan Order in which Jacopone was later to take a prominent role. The sharpness of Jacopone's fight with Boniface VIII can be attributed in no small measure to the pervasive atmosphere of political partisanship.

The Boom   If the power of Todi must have been attractive to a young notary like Jacopo, its wealth was perhaps even more attractive. Even though it was only an agricultural market town, there is much evidence that Todi shared in the economic boom that swept the communes in the latter half of the century. The Florentine chronicler, Giovanni Villani, said of his thirteenth-century forebears: "With their simple life and poverty, they did greater and more virtuous things than are done in our time with more luxury and riches."[19] Similarly Ricobaldo da Ferrara, writing around 1300, referred with disdain to the poor living conditions of fifty years earlier. Within this time span, the period of the adult life of Jacopone, all of the basic patterns of consumption in food, clothing, and housing were revolutionized.

In Jacopone's youth, according to Ricobaldo, the members of a family had to share the few dishes and cups, and the house was lit, if at all, by torches and not by candles. Towns were crowded and dirty, with unpaved streets that were little better than open sewers; while by 1300 many towns, including Todi, had paved streets, some sewers, and adequate supplies of pure water. In 1250 little wine was consumed, and dowries were small. People wore coarse linen undergarments, leather tunics, and rough sheepskin capes—instead of fine linens, woolen tunics, and furs lined with wool. To anyone interested in material things—and Jacopo the notary was—it must have been perpetually stimulating to live in the midst of this unparalleled economic expansion. It was also, as the sumptuary laws show, disturbing to one's conscience; communes like Perugia and Florence passed laws limiting the luxury of weddings and the ostentatious elegance of dress. To the converted Jacopone, in love with Franciscan poverty, the consuming interest in the material things of this world was not only an inversion of priorities clearly condemned in the Gospels but also evidence of the decline of righteousness prior to the last judgment.

At Todi the foundation of prosperity was agriculture, since the contado of Todi provided a terrain admirably suited to the capabilities of thirteenth-century peasant technology. About 80 percent of the land was in hilly country between 500 and 1,500 feet above sea level, hills blessed by the vine and the olive. General crops like wheat, barley, fruit, and vegetables were also raised on small peasant holdings. If the pattern at Todi was similar to that at Pistoia, San Gimignano, and Orvieto—and it almost certainly was, as otherwise the land could not have supported the dense population that it did—a large class of small farmers derived a substantial living from lands that yielded best after inputs of vast amounts of peasant labor—intensive cultivation through the use of ter- racing and contour plowing. Medieval and renaissance art gives a vivid picture of the gardenlike appearance of the Tuscan and Umbrian coun- tryside.[20] Many rubrics in the Todian *statuto* deal with agricultural con- tracts; other provisions controlled the activities of millers and bakers, the holding of fruit and vegetable markets, the operation of inns, and the hygiene of butchers.[21] Clearly the town was the center of food processing and marketing for the contado. Like Padua and the towns of the Romagna, Todi prohibited the export of foodstuffs in order to concen- trate trade in the town. Though Padua had an entirely different type of contado, both Padua and Todi grew rich through agriculture.[22]

Prices showed a steady rise throughout the last half of the century, that of wheat increasing by at least 25 percent. Even in small rural settlements, the opening up of agricultural markets not only provided a great incen- tive to produce more than for mere subsistence but also led to the increase of seigneurial dues. Landlords, whether noble or bourgeois, insisted on their share of the profits. The latter have been estimated at as high as 10 percent a year, an astounding return when one considers that land was the safest form of investment.[23]

Historians like Henri Pirenne thought of medieval communes as primarily merchant and artisan centers;[24] thus it comes as a surprise to realize that most Todians then as now were cultivators of the land.

Economically speaking, Todi was more like a modern Italian agricultural town than it was like a thirteenth-century industrial center such as Florence. (The wool business that was creating a population boom in Florence did not exist at Todi.) Then as now, peasants descended in the early morning from the acropolis to farm most intensively the nearby lands, which formed a crown of gardens around the walls. Some went three or four miles to their more distant fields and returned every evening to the shelter and comfort of the town. Such a pattern of cultivation can be deduced from the fact that, according to the tax survey of 1294, there were only six hamlets, having from 250 to 500 inhabitants each, within five miles of Todi. Farther out, six to eleven miles from Todi, lay a ring of eleven larger settlements with populations ranging from 500 to 5,000, each with its own area of intensive cultivation. From these subsidiary towns and their neighboring seventeen hamlets, it was an easy day's ride to bring the produce to Todi and get back by nightfall. Such was the efficient pattern of rural settlement.[25]

Remarkably little of the contado was agriculturally unproductive in the thirteenth century. Unlike Pisa and Pistoia, Todi had practically no plains, that is, land lying below 500 feet in altitude, for the Tiber valley above the town is rarely as much as 2,500 yards wide and narrows below it to a wild gorge, now a lake. Such land was subject to both floods and malaria—factors that much hindered the growth of both Pisa and Pistoia—and in the thirteenth century was almost uninhabited. It contained only one hamlet, Ponte Cuti, established to protect the bridge over the Tiber, and one Franciscan house at Pantanelli, where Jacopone probably spent several years.

Of relatively unproductive mountainous country, land above 1,500 feet in altitude, Todi also had little: a spur of the Appenines that ran along the eastern border, culminating in the 3,500-foot Monte Martano, and a few scattered mountains to the south and west near Canònica and Toscolano. Such regions were normally devoted to forestry and animal raising and were probably able to supply Todi's needs for wood, meat, and leather.[26]

Long-distance trade and high finance were not of much importance. Not for Todi were the extensive travels and long residence abroad of the saffron merchants of San Gimignano or the almost incredible voyages of the Polos of Venice.[27] Yet the merchant community did provide an important channel of cultural contact with the capitalist world in its heroic stage. As was usual in communes, Todi's merchants formed the first guild to be organized (1223) and made it the most prominent throughout the thirteenth century. They traded in the cities of Tuscany and the Romagna, where the communal officials occasionally had to protect their interests. In addition, Todi had a small banking community consisting of both Christians and Jews, the survival of Jews indicating that Todian banking had not developed to the extent of that of the great communes to the north.[28] Elsewhere great fortunes were rapidly amassed through loans to the papacy and to high churchmen by such families as the Tolomei of Siena, the Peruzzi of Florence, and the Scrovegni of Padua. By comparison Todian bankers dealt in the small change of ecclesiastical banking; the Todian Cardinal Bentivenga d'Acquasparta did some of his banking locally with one Nardo di Todino. Since Jacopone was later in close relations with Cardinal Bentivenga, he no doubt was thoroughly acquainted with papal financing and particularly with the shady deals of Boniface VIII.

The going rates for money, as indicated by the loans floated by the commune in this period, varied from a low of 20 percent to a high of 42 percent per year, the term of the loan usually being two years. A banker could quickly build a fortune, whether he lent to cardinal, commune, or private entrepreneur. It has been acutely observed that the church was caught in a paradox; while on the one hand it condemned usury, it provided on the other hand one of the major reasons for the rapid rise of Italian banking through its pressing and continuous need for capital. English observers like Matthew Paris constantly refer to the greed of the Italian clergy, leading a recent historian to state: "The secularism of these mundane Italian bishops was both petty and grand."[29] Financial requirements took precedence not only over ecclesiastical law but also over political considerations; the papacy continued to do most of its banking in Florence, even when that city lay under an interdict.

Such venality was later to be castigated by Jacopone:

> Piange la Ecclesia, piange e dolura,
> sente fortura di pessimo stato.
>   Veggio esbandita la povertate,
> nullo è che curi se non degnetate. . . .
>   Auro e argento on rebandito,
> fatt'on nemici con lor gran convito,
> onne buon uso da loro è fugito,
> donde el mio pianto con grande eiulato.

> The church laments, laments and cries and feels pain at its most evil state. I see poverty banished; no one cares for aught but offices. . . . They have scattered gold and silver, have made enemies with their great banquet, have abandoned every good custom. So I grieve with great wailing. [*Lauda* LIII, lines 1–2, 19–20, 23–26]

Communal affluence expressed itself at Todi as elsewhere in ambitious building programs during the latter half of the century.[30] Though Todi did not strain to create the towered masterpieces that grace Siena, Pisa,

Florence, and Bologna, she did create a piazza that for its rugged simplicity and classic restraint was and remains today a near-perfect example of communal architecture. On the southeast corner rises the Palazzo del Commune on an open-vaulted base dating back to the last years of the twelfth century and used then as now for a market. A wide, unbalustraded staircase leads up to the second floor, built in 1213; a third floor, tower, and battlements were added in 1228. Abutting it stands what is now called the Palazzo del Capitano; here in 1267, the second and third floors were combined to form a large meeting hall with a handsome bank of three mullioned Gothic windows. The 300 members of the Great Council, 50 from each quarter, met in this hall, and a large picture was commissioned for it by the podestà Pandolfo Savelli, senator of Rome and brother to Pope Honorius IV.

The south side of the piazza is enclosed by the solid bulk of the Palazzo dei Priori, begun in 1288 and completed in 1297; its six-storied tower and crenelated walls dominate with classical moderation the whole piazza. At the opposite end stands the Romanesque cathedral on a raised platform reached by a broad staircase almost as wide as the piazza. In 1246, a severe earthquake damaged the building and also knocked down many of the wooden houses in the Borgo Nuovo behind the cathedral. Substantial funds were provided for the rebuilding of the church in 1256, 1261, 1262, and 1269.

Towards the end of Jacopone's lifetime in 1297, the Church of St. John and St. Paul was torn down on the initiative of Boniface VIII and the land given to the commune for a marketplace. It is now the Piazza Garibaldi and near it stood the solid stone house of the Benedetti. The church had apparently not been much used, for a specific regulation of the *statuto* punished defecating in or near its porch. Its removal opened out the piazza behind the communal buildings and gave it a roomy and airy atmosphere.

Continued prosperity is indicated by the considerable building after another earthquake in 1298, which, however, did not harm either the piazza or the homes of the wealthy in the Colle quarter. Again at the initiative of Pope Boniface VIII, the foundations of the great Church of San Fortunato were laid, and construction continued on it for the next 150 years. Probably during Jacopone's time much of the earlier wooden residential houses were replaced by new stone palazzi, some with porticoes and balconies. The commune laid down precise regulations on the manner of building, and the podestà was required to inspect the plans and edifices in person, so as to be sure that the public ways were not encroached upon.[31]

Todi was among the first of the Tuscan and Umbrian towns to pave its piazza and streets—in 1262–1263. The commune made strict laws against dumping refuse in the streets and began building sewers in the 1270s.

The piazza of Todi: on the left the Palazzo del Capitano del Popolo, completed in 1267; in the center the Palazzo del Commune, built between 1190 ca. and 1228; and on the right the Palazzo dei Priori, 1288-1297 *(Photo by Ed. Foglietti Zenone, Todi)*

Windows of the Hall of the Great Council in the Palazzo del Capitano del Popolo, 1267 *(Photo by Alterocca, Terni)*

Aerial view of the Church of San Fortunato, begun in 1298 and completed in the fifteenth century *(Photo by Alterocca, Terni)*

The great portal of the Church of San Fortunato, fifteenth century
(Photo by Alterocca, Terni)

The water supply was important for reasons of both health and defense. So the Scarnabecco fountain was built in 1244, at the same time as the new walls; in 1288, the cisterns on the Rocca, which had been in use since Roman times, were considerably enlarged. All in all, Todi achieved in the thirteenth century many of the urban amenities that it still enjoys today. In this achievement it was no different from most of the Italian communes, but it would be centuries before northern towns were to progress as far.

In all likelihood the economic prosperity of Todi was accompanied by a burgeoning growth of the population. Such was the experience of San Gimignano, which doubled in size from 1227 to 1277. At Todi the walls of 1244 enclosed an area more than twice the size of the old city—82 acres as against 37. In 1268 the town population was probably around 11,000.[32] More impressive was the population of the rich contado. The survey of 1294 lists a total of 6,888 hearths or a population of about 32,000, affording a density of 60 per square kilometer, including the town population. This population compares with a density of 38 per square kilometer at Pistoia and 74 per square kilometer at San Gimignano. Like other communes Todi probably reached a peak of population in the early fourteenth century, to be followed by a long decline. It is interesting to note that while Todi was only one among about thirty substantial communes in Italy north of Rome, there were only six towns in all of Britain larger than Todi. Central Italy as a whole did not surpass its late medieval population until about the middle of the last century, and even today the population of Todi is only 24 percent greater than it was in 1300.[33]

The Notary   No group stood closer to the center of action in Todi than the notaries. Together with merchants and bankers, they took leading parts in both the economic and political growth of the town, and no doubt the young Jacopo spent many a morning in the piazza discussing the latest mercantile reports from abroad, exchanging gossip about current land acquisitions, and airing opinions on the docket of cases in the municipal courts. Knowing that Jacopone had been a notary not only defines the social class from which he sprang but also explains certain patterns of thought that appeared later in his poetry.

By the time Jacopo came to study for the notariat, the course had been highly developed mainly through the work of Rainierio da Perugia and Rolandino Passageri. The former, after having qualified under papal appointment in his native city, went to settle in Bologna, where he spent the rest of his life and opened a school. In order to systematize the instruction, he wrote the *Liber formularum et instrumentorum* in about 1215 and then a much more complete work, the *Ars notarie*, in 1240. The basis of all instruction was, of course, Roman law. Among other Bolognese teachers who published similar handbooks, by far the most influential was Rolandino Passageri, whose books remained standard for the profession until the seventeenth century. These were the *Summa ars notarie* of 1255, frequently glossed by later teachers, the *Tractatus de notulis*, an abridgment of the *Summa*, and the *De officio tabellionatus in villis*, which covered the special requirements for notaries involved in communal government.[34]

The range of subjects treated indicate the range of the notary's activity—which was very wide indeed. For the notary in private practice the bulk of the business was in contracts of all sorts, mainly marriages, deeds of sale, and title deeds. Wills and estate matters of every kind form another whole section in Rolandino's work, and judgments, in which the notary was called upon to register the agreements of contending parties in civil disputes, made up a third section. It can be seen that the notary performed many of the services of an attorney of today, and a good deal more.

The dignity and importance of the profession reached a peak in Jacopone's lifetime, a state that can be deduced from the forms of notarial documents. Originally a mere scribe—and such he remained in country districts—the notary of the eleventh century required the signatures of witnesses in order for an act to stand up in court. Then the *carta compiuta* or full document written on parchment, signed and kept by the notary alone, became adequate legal evidence. About 1200, many clients were willing to dispense with the fully written-out act, which cost more, and rely on the rough draft of the notary. Despite town statutes that insisted fruitlessly on the prompt presentation of a *carta compiuta* in court, rough drafts gradually became accepted as legally binding. Then a third step was made: by 1270 both clients and courts were willing to accept even the notary's notes, still signed and kept by him; and few contracts at this period passed through the three stages from notes to rough drafts to *carta compiuta*.[35]

The reason for the streamlining of legal procedure was the enormous increase in business. Jacopo was in a highly prosperous calling. It has been estimated that the busy port of Genoa produced 56,000 documents in 1265 and 80,000 in 1291. Such was the passion for defining *mine* and *thine*; a notary might write four or five documents a day. It was by far the largest single profession; in 1293, Pisa had 232 notaries, Genoa about 200, and Florence about 600. The *matricola* or list of guild members of Verona contained the surprising total of 589 notaries in 1302, and Prato, with an estimated population of only 7,500, had no less than 102 notaries and only 9 teachers and 3 medical doctors in 1339. After this time the number of notaries began to decrease all over Italy as merchants came more and more to rely on their own records without feeling the need to go to notaries. However, in the thirteenth century the notary still remained supreme, and the forms of notarial science took precedence even over the laws of individual communes. In the words of one historian: "The appearance of a universally valid notariat contributed inestimably to the commercial revival, serving as a kind of international currency which did much to balance the political fragmentation of the time."[36]

The business of the notary was by no means confined to private practice, either among businessmen or church officials, since the growing communes required a rapidly expanding bureaucracy heavily staffed with notaries. Padua employed 14 judges and 86 notaries in 1254 and perhaps 100 judges and 500 notaries by the end of the century. The *statuti* or codes of communal law were often drawn up by notaries, as for example that of Bologna by Rolandino. In the case of Todi, the *statuto* was composed in 1275 by a commission of twenty-four citizens assisted by two notaries.[37] In it the large role of notaries in the life of the town was defined; not only were the three major judges attended by notaries but also the several minor ones, the *sindaci* or town overseers, and the arbitrators. All records of meetings, communal contracts, feudal oaths, and public correspondence were written by notaries. Unlike larger towns that had guilds of judges and notaries,[38] Todi put the control of its men of law directly under the podestà. Their regulation must have been as strict as that of the guilds, for Todi's notaries became famous in the next century. Florence during the period from 1345 to 1400 obtained 46 town notaries from Todi—more than from any other single town, and many of the judges and podestà serving Florence in this period also came from Todi.

Perhaps the most important qualification of the notary was his ability to write precise documents in a correct and brief form, and such was the teaching of Rolandino. The extremely condensed character of much of Jacopone's poetry probably reflects this early legal training. Certainly legal terms appear in his work, and it may be that his favorite dialogue form of expression derives just as much from the arguments of pro and con in court as it does from the Provençal *tenson*.[39]

As a class notaries were interested in writing in general. It has been said that writing was a secondary activity of the legal profession, and more writers came from this stratum of society than any other. The most common form of writing was the composition of chronicles for the communes. Several notaries succeeded each other as writers of the quasi-official chronicle of Genoa covering the years 1174 to 1250. Milan, Florence, Bologna, Naples, Treviso, and other cities produced chronicles written by notaries. Furthermore, some of the more famous writers were trained as notaries, notably Brunetto Latini, Cino da Pistoia, and Boccaccio. The great Florentine chancellor, Coluccio Salutati, began his career as an humble village notary in his home town, progressed to be chancellor of Todi and then Lucca, and ended his full life as a leader of the humanist circle in Florence.[40]

As a class, too, notaries were moneymakers—or greedy, as Jacopone was to come to think. The Paduan chronicler, Da Nono, thought of them as being in the same category as usurers, both having a "propensity to rapid advancement."[41] Time and again in the biographies of notaries one reads of individuals who made a lot of money and invested it in land or urban properties. It is not that their profession was in itself lucrative, since fees for drawing documents were exactly fixed at a low level by communal statute, but moneylending was the passion of the age. Not only bankers but also nobles and notaries engaged in it. Notaries were in a particularly good position to take advantage of profitable deals when they came along because they knew both the affairs of the town and those of many private citizens.[42] As a prominent notary of Todi, Jacopo must have dabbled in moneylending. Since the mechanics of the money market were imperfectly understood, the profits to be made from this novel activity appeared little short of miraculous, the return on investment hovering around a mouth-watering 35 percent per year. And if after a lifetime of vigorous acquisition, one felt the pangs of conscience, one could follow the example of the banker, Enrico Scrovegni, who squared accounts with Paduan society and with God by giving the commune a fine chapel and hiring Giotto to paint it.[43]

Jacopone wrote that he was always in need of money and cut corners to get it:

Passato el tempo, empresi a giocare,
con la gente usare - e far grande spesa;
mio pate stava a dolorare
e non pagare - le mie male emprese;
le spese commese - stregnème a furare,
lo biado sprecare - en male menata.

As time passed, I took to gambling, going about in society, and making great expenditures. My father mourned over it and would not pay for my bad activities; the expenses I incurred forced me to steal, and I wasted the harvest in a bad way. [*Lauda* XXIV, lines 63–68]

With the rise of the money economy, well oiled by notaries, the sin of greed began to take on an importance even greater than that of pride, the besetting sin of the old nobility.[44] Jacopone's later espousal of the Franciscan ideal of poverty grew out of the reaction against his own experience as a rich young man.

Notaries were patriots too. Rolandino Passageri spent a lifetime in the service of Bologna from 1238 till near the time of his death in 1297. A leader of the Guelph party, he filled the highest offices, defending the rule of the popolo against both emperor and feudal nobility. In 1249 after the Bolognese had captured and imprisoned Re Enzo, Frederick threatened to demolish the city and free his son. Rolandino composed the proud answer of the independent commune:

> May God arise and all his enemies be scattered, who rely on their own strength rather than on justice. These are now excited with great fury and think that they can subdue others with terrors and threats, but may it not always happen so, for neither the arrow strikes the target, nor the wolf his intended prey. Therefore, we do not wish to be frightened with windy words, for we are not reeds of the swamp which the slightest wind bends, nor feathers, nor dew which is dissolved by the rays of the sun. Therefore, we advise you that we hold Re Enzo prisoner, have held him and will hold him as long as we believe in our law. So we will take our swords in our hands and wield them so that your hostile fighting lions will be wiped out. Let not your magnificence have faith in your unnumbered multitudes, for where a crowd is gathered, there is to be found confusion. As it is said in the proverbs of the ancients: "A small dog knows how to hold a boar at bay."[45]

Prominent Todians   In its prime Todi produced a generation of outstanding men who grew up together between 1250 and 1270. Perhaps the surest way to achieve a European reputation was through the church, and these ambitious young men were all churchmen. Surely the most ambitious and the most successful was Benedetto Gaetani, who as Boniface VIII was to become Jacopone's great antagonist. Not by birth a Todian, Benedetto came from a powerful Roman family, whose feudal estates centered in the southern Campagna at Anagni. There Benedetto spent his early years and was given a church benefice though he was not ordained. He came to Todi shortly after 1250 in the train of his uncle, Pietro, a bishop who had been transferred from the diocese of Sora to that of Todi. Pietro remained at Todi until 1276 and in the manner of the Roman nobility, took care to bring his young nephew forward in order to increase the fortunes of the house. First, Benedetto was sent to study grammar and canon law with Dr. Bartolo of Todi and then in 1260 was granted a canonry in the cathedral by Alexander IV, whose niece was Benedetto's mother. In addition he collected a sinecure, the priorate of Santa Illuminata di Collarezzo, an almost abandoned Benedictine house on the Foligno road.

What the relationship between Benedetto and Jacopone was at this stage of their lives can only be surmised. They were probably about the same age and so studied law at the same time. They may even have studied under the same master, as Dr. Bartolo taught both canon and civil law. While Jacopo was probably a Guelph, Benedetto was a Guibelline and was wounded in 1267 during the civil strife between the parties. It has been suggested that personal animosity existed between the two in these years and that their later conflict thus reflected a long-standing grudge.[46] Such a suggestion is, however, superfluous because the contrast between the ruthlessly worldly Gaetani and the saintly Jacopone after his conversion could in itself hardly be greater. Jacopone before his conversion must have had much in common with Benedetto, as both were intensely ambitious and completely worldly. That they knew each other, perhaps well, can hardly be doubted, for they passed fifteen years of their youth together as members of the Todian elite, which could not have consisted of more than forty or fifty families.[47]

Though Benedetto kept his connections with Todi all his life (his aunt lived there) and during his pontificate showered the town with patronage, his ambition and the support of his uncle soon brought him to the papal court. As a well-connected member of the Roman nobility, he was frequently sent on diplomatic missions and moved in the highest circles. In 1264, he was in Paris with Cardinal Simon de Brie, later Martin IV, and in the next year went to London on a mission that included three who were later to become popes—Honorius IV, Gregory X, and himself. After 1268, he represented the commune and diocese of Todi in their running conflict with the Rector of the Patrimony. Such representatives, called proctors, were retained on an occasional or regular basis by all sorts of institutions both lay and clerical. Todi paid him 1000 florins, a very considerable sum, for his services, and in 1289 he received a like fee from Bologna. Legal business at the curia increased enormously during the entire course of the century and gave employment to crowds of notaries and proctors. As a contemporary sarcastically observed: "One would be more likely to find an infant child deserted by its mother, pasture grasses by their herds, green waters by their fish, a pond by its croaking frogs, a bride by her young husband, a mother's breast by the suckling babe than find the Sacred City deserted by its proctors."[48] No doubt Benedetto was helped in his work for Todi by Cardinal Matteo Rosso Orsini, who at the height of the conflict with the rector was chosen podestà of Todi for two years in a row (1278–1279), an unusual procedure. The latter sent a vicar to Todi, since his presence was much more valuable at the court of his uncle Nicolas III.

At this point it is clear that the Gaetani and the Orsini were on friendly terms, much to the advantage of Benedetto. The Orsini pope, Nicolas III, was among the first to practice nepotism in a thoroughgoing manner, and he sent his nephew Matteo Rosso together with Benedetto to Germany on an extremely important diplomatic mission, the reconciliation of the emperor Rudolph of Habsburg with Charles of Anjou, king of Naples and Sicily. It is a tribute to the adroitness of Benedetto that his connections with the Orsini did not hinder his career during the reaction against that family which occurred during the pontificate of Nicolas III's successor, Martin IV. On the contrary it was Martin who finally absolved Todi from its dependence on the Rector of the Patrimony in 1284, and it was Martin who made Benedetto cardinal as a reward for his extensive diplomatic activity during the Franco-Aragonnese war in Sicily.

Benedetto's rise to the cardinalate came at a propitious moment for the building of the power of his family, for the cardinals were becoming increasingly influential not only because the volume of papal business was growing but also because cardinalates often lasted thirty or forty years whereas pontificates rarely lasted ten years. Benedetto used his newly gained power to the utmost; it has been said that his relentless pursuit of family gain was brutal and peasantlike. His portrait statue on his tomb at Orvieto shows a face full of dogged persistence; another statue, that of Arnolfo di Cambio in the Florentine Duomo, displays a bland grandeur. The two interpretations complement each other.[49]

Family aggrandizement through papal politics was in fact a requirement for the Roman nobility, and one amply filled by Benedetto. In the feudal territories of the Campagna, competition for lands and position was so strong that a family, like the Annibaldi, lost its lands when it failed to provide cardinals to protect them—in this case mostly to the Gaetani. The latter suffered from being parvenus and were faced with the entrenched power of the Conti, Savelli, Orsini, and Colonna, heritages of earlier pontificates. Near Todi Benedetto obtained in 1289 the fief of Sosmano, probably through the will of his uncle Pietro—a pleasant country castle where he liked to come to rest from his labors. Just as his uncle had built his career, Benedetto helped his elder brother, Roffredo, who was made podestà of Todi in 1282. However, the major achievements of Benedetto were registered in the southern Campagna, where Roffredo acquired by marriage the county of Fondi and eventually, through Boniface VIII's influence at the court of Naples, became in addition the count of Caserta. Gaetani lands finally stretched in a compact block from Caserta to Anagni; among them were the fiefs of Ninfa and Sermoneta, which are still in the possession of the family.

A curious story illustrates the close interrelationship of papal power and family aggrandizement. It concerns the lands of the Aldobrandeschi, a vast area comprising the eastern half of what is now the province of Grosseto. The fief descended in 1284 to a single daughter, Margherita, who was passed from one husband to the next in the fierce competition for her inheritance. The first was Guy de Montfort, who was captured by the Aragonese in 1287 and died in prison in Palermo five years later. In the meantime Margherita lived with and probably married a local noble and was given Benedetto as a guardian through the favor of Nicolas IV. However, the wardship of Margherita passed for some reason to Cardinal Napoleone Orsini. In these straits Benedetto made an agreement early in 1293 with the commune of Orvieto. He promised that if he were made pope, he would cede the Val del Lago, an important papal fief coveted by the Orvietans, to the commune in exchange for gaining the Aldobrandeschine inheritance for his family—"a scandalous proposal to alienate lands held by virtue of a spiritual office. . . . in return for a favor to the holder's own family."[50]

However, the Orsini won out, for Cardinal Napoleone married off Margherita to his brother Orsello. But only temporarily. Orsello died in 1294, and Benedetto, now Boniface VIII, married Margherita with great ceremony to his brother Roffredo. But even this fourth marriage of Margherita's did not last. There were no heirs. Roffredo was needed to marry the countess of Fondi, and so the pope dissolved the union on the grounds that Margherita was already married to the local noble—a fact that he must have known all along.

Of such stuff was Benedetto Gaetani, Pope Boniface VIII, the mighty enemy of Jacopone's last years.

Other ambitious young men who were to enter Jacopone's later life circulated in the society of Todi in the 1260s, especially the three brothers of the noble family of Acquasparta, Bentivenga, Angelario, and Matteo. All three were Franciscans and the first to achieve prominence was Bentivenga, who was made rector of the Ospedale della Carità in 1259. It had fifty-five beds, maintained nineteen more outside the building, and enjoyed considerable revenues, according to the inventory of 1280.[51] From this post Bentivenga was promoted to bishop of Todi, when Pietro Gaetani was transferred to Anagni in 1276, but he was not to remain long at Todi. Next we find him as confessor and chaplain to Nicolas III, who made him Cardinal Bishop of Albano, after that post fell vacant on the death of Bonaventure. He studied under Thomas Aquinas at Orvieto and Perugia, and Salimbene wrote that he was "a reader in theology, a handsome man, good and honest, and a dear friend of Pope Nicolas III."[52] In 1286, Cardinal Bentivenga made his will at Todi, and his fellow Franciscan and exnotary, Jacopo of Todi, was one of the witnesses. Under that will his valuable library passed to the Franciscan Church of San Fortunato on his death in 1289. It affords us a valuable list of books, some of which Jacopone may have read.[53]

The second brother, Angelario, was the least prominent; he succeeded to the diocese of Todi when Bentivenga left in 1278, and died young in 1285. But the third brother, Matteo, was the most prominent of all. Like Jacopone he was a member of the Franciscan community at San Fortunato. In 1281, probably because of the influence of Bentivenga, he was named lector of the papal palace by Nicholas III to succeed the Englishman, John Pecham, who became the highly controversial archbishop of Canterbury. From 1287 to 1289, he was minister general of the Franciscan Order, where he followed a policy of moderation during the raging conflict between the spirituals and the conventuals. He was a "man of easy nature, inclined to console the brethren, and who permitted the rule to be broadened."[54] His last years were passed as one of the main agents of Boniface VIII; his actions, as we shall see, much affected Jacopone.

Cortesia The cultural life of the *beau monde* of Todi in its prime was marked by *cortesia*, the formulas of courtly deportment imported from France. Looking back across the centuries of Italian primacy during the Renaissance, it comes as a surprise to discover that Italian upper-class life of the thirteenth century aped the manners of the French. Even the saintly Francis was enamoured of Provençal lyric poetry, and though he may have known the language only superficially, he surely caught the *joie de vivre* flowing from across the Alps and absorbed it into his own soul.[55] In the country castles and townhouses of noble and bourgeois, the heroic Roland was a regular visitor, as were the *preux* and *dames* of Chrétien de Troyes, Benoît de Saint-Maur, and Marie de France. That courtesy was an upper-class manifestation is dramatically illustrated in a bilingual poem dating from the first decade of the century, in which the noble courtly lover regales his lady on the joys of love in flawless Provençal, while the bourgeois girl successfully defends her virtue in the broad accents of her native Genoa—among the first verses written in Italian.[56]

Even late in the century on the eve of the explosion of genius in Italian literature, Brunetto Latini, the teacher of Dante, wrote his compendium of courtly information, the *Livre dou trésor*, in French, partly because he was in France at the time of its composition and partly because French "speech was more pleasing and more common to every one." And Dante shared this respect for the French language as "one of easier and wider acceptance."[57]

How deeply French penetrated into the provincial society of the contado of Todi is problematical, as Jacopone showed in his writing hardly a trace of its direct influence. But the case is far different with the courtly compositions of the Sicilian school, for they provided Jacopone with his poetical education. Between the years 1230 and 1250, the Sicilian poets produced the first substantial body of Italian poetry, under the dual impetus of Provençal inspiration and the imperial favor of the magnificent Frederick. The term "Sicilian" does not have a precise geographical reference, since many of the poets were not natives of the island, and the court of the "Sicilian" emperor, with which they were associated, was highly migratory. The Hohenstaufen power and court made a brilliant if transitory impression on all of northern and central Italy, including the very countryside in which Jacopo was growing up. Frederick spent the winter of 1239–1240 in Pisa. Advancing against the pope in Rome, he marched in the spring through the territory of Todi via Coccorone and

Acquasparta to hold a great court in the nearby city of Foligno. Wherever he went, Frederick impressed both friend and enemy alike with the splendor of his entourage.[58]

Dante, a convinced adherent of the Guibelline cause, wrote of Frederick:

> In effect, the illustrious champions, the emperor Frederick and his well-born [though bastard] son Manfred, manifesting the nobility and rectitude of their essence, followed human ideals and scorned to live like brutes. Thus, whoever had a noble heart or was gifted with talent forced himself to come up to the majesty of such princes, with the result that in their times whatever was best among the Italians showed itself in the first place at the court of these sovereigns.[59]

The poetry of the Sicilian school, for which Dante was showing his respect, reflected imperial dignity and elegance. Even the emperor himself dabbled in it.

The poets were either high court officials or distinguished feudal lords. There was Pier della Vigna, protonotary of Sicily and the chief minister of Frederick, who "held the two keys of his heart" for many years until his fall from favor, which led to suicide—and immortality as a tragic soul in the seventh circle of Hell (*Inferno*, XIII, 55–108). Others were Re Enzo, natural son of Frederick, who was captured by the Bolognese in 1249 and spent twenty-three years, the rest of his life, as a prisoner in the Palazzo Communale; Giacomo da Lentini, court notary, who was perhaps the earliest leader of the school, if such a group can be said to have had a leader; and Guido delle Colonne, high court judge. The feudal officials included Rinaldo Count of Aquino, perhaps the brother and certainly a relative of St. Thomas; Percivalle Doria of the distinguished Genoese family, who acted as podestà in many northern Italian cities and eventually became under Manfred, the imperial vicar for the Marches of Ancona and the Duchy of Spoleto; and about twenty others whose names have survived.

Though the names have survived, the personalities that went with them have not. What was said of the Provençal poets is even more true of the Sicilian: "One could think of this whole literature as the work of one poet, only expressed by different voices."[60] Yet the school as a whole did have a decided personality, even if it was only to express the main themes of Provencal poetry in what Dante was to call "volgare illustre." There can be but little doubt that the young Jacopo, engulfed as he was in the concupiscences of the world, learned what he knew of Italian poetry from the Sicilians and their Tuscan followers.[61] He learned the language of love—the love of women in which strangely enough women took almost always a passive role as mere objects of the passion of the poet. It was the poet's subjective state, closely analyzed and charmingly expressed, which held the center of attention. When Jacopone was later to write his own love poetry, it was no great step to replace women with God and draw upon the experience and style of the Sicilians in his own lyrical self-analysis.

Many of the major themes of Sicilian poetry were reflected in Jacopone's production. For example, love is a fire that burns. Guido delle Colonne developed the figure:

> . . . ma Amor m'ha allumato
> di fiamma che m'abbraccia,
> ch'eo fora consummato
> se voi, donna sovrana,
> non fustici mezzana
> infra l'Amore e meve,
> che fa lo foco nascere di neve.

> . . . but Love has lit me with a flame which embraces me so that I would be burnt up, if you, sovereign lady, did not set a shield between Love and me, you who made the fire to be born from snow.[62]

Another Jacoponian concept is: the heart of a lover is like a furnace. Giacomo da Lentini used the same thought:

> Foc'aio al cor, non credo mai si stingua,
>   Anzi pur si alluma:
> Perchè non si consumava?
> La salamandra audivi
> che 'nfra lo foco vivi—stando sana;
> eo sì fo per long'uso:
> vivo 'n foc' amoroso,
> e non saccio ch'eo dica. . . .

> I have a fire in my heart; I don't believe it will ever be extinguished; rather it will be lit again. Why am I not burned up? I have heard of the salamander who lives in the fire and survives; I have been like him for a long time. I live in an amorous fire and don't know what I say. . . .[63]

The fire of love melts the heart of the poet as wax or a candle is burnt—a theme relating to the fact that candles were just coming into general use:

> feristimi a la mente
> und' ardo come cera . . .
> [and]
> anzi distruggo come al foco cera
> e sto com'om che non si pò sentire. . . .

You wound my spirit so I burn like wax. [And:] Then I am destroyed like wax in a fire and am like a man who cannot feel.⁶⁴

Love is full of paradoxes. It is like peace and yet like a battle; it is wounded, but wounds—as this sonnet of Giacomo da Lentini illustrates:

> . . . e dui guerrieri in fina pace stare,
> e 'ntra dui amici nascereci errore.
>   Ed ho visto d'Amor cosa più forte:
> ch'era feruto, e sanòmi ferendo;
> lo foco donde ardea stutò con foco.

> . . . and two warriors stand in perfect peace, and between two friends conflict is born. And I saw a stronger thing in Love: that I was wounded and was cured being wounded; the fire with which I burned was extinguished with fire.⁶⁵

The service of love is like the service to a feudal lord, as Rinaldo d'Aquino explains:

> Signoria vol ch'eo serva lëalmente,
> che mi sia ben renduto
> bon merito, ch'eo non saccia blasmare;
>   ed eo mi laudo che più altamente
> ca eo non ho servuto
> Amor m'ha conizato a meritare.

> Lordship wishes that I serve loyally, and that I be given a good reward about which I can't complain; and that I am pleased that I have not served better than Love has begun to reward me.⁶⁶

Notice the neat point made by the word "begun"; Count Rinaldo expects more!

Love is full of joy, and Guido delle Colonne peals out all the changes of joy in his canzone, which begins:

> Giosamente canto
> e vivo in allegranza,
> ca per la vostr' amanza,
> madonna, gran gioi sento.

> Joyously I sing and live in happiness, since through your love, my lady, I feel great joy.⁶⁷

But love is also full of sorrow, the sorrow of separation and loss. This theme is expressed in one of the few canzoni of the Sicilian school that succeeds in bringing a woman to life by invoking scenes full of pictorial detail and letting her speak. It is the intensely human experience of the woman abandoned by the man who goes off to war—an experience repeated, it seems, in every generation. Rinaldo d'Aquino's poem should be quoted in its entirety:

Già mai non mi conforto
nè mi voglio ralegrare.
    Le navi son giunte a porto
e or vogliono collare.
    Vassene lo più gente
in terra d'oltramare
    ed io lasso dolente,
come degio fare?

    Vassene en altra contrata
e no lo mi manda a diri
    ed io rimango ingannata:
tanti sono li sospiri,
    che mi fanno gran guerra
la notte co la dia,
    nè 'n celo ned in terra
non mi par ch'io sia.

    Santus, santus, santus Deo,
ch' n la Vergine venisti,
    salva e guarda l'amor meo,
poi da me lo dipartisti.
    Oit alta potestade
temuta e dottata,
    la mia dolze amistade
ti sia acomandata!

    La croce salva la gente
e me face disviare,
    la croce mi fa dolente
e non mi val Dio pregare.
    Oi croce pellegrina,
perchè m'hai sì distrutta?
    Oimè, lassa tapina,
chi ardo e 'ncendo tutta!

    Lo 'mperadore con pace
tutto lo mondo mantene
    ed a meve guerra face,
chè m'ha tolta la mia spene.
    Oit alta potestate
temuta e dottata,

la mia dolze amistate
vi sia acomandata!

Quando la croce pigliao,
certo no lo mi pensai,
   quelli che tanto m'amao
ed illu tanto amai,
   chi eo ne fui battuta
e messa in pregionia
   e in celata tenuta
per la vita mia!

Le navi sono collate,
in bonor possan andare
   con elle la mia amistate
e la gente che v'ha andare!
   Oi padre crïatore
a porto le conduci,
   chè vanno a servidore
de la santa cruci.

Però ti prego, Duccetto,
tu che sai la pena mia,
   che me ne faci un sonetto
e mandilo in Soria.
   Ch'io non posso abentare
la notte nè la dia:
   in terra d'oltremare
sta la vita mia!

I will never be comforted nor wish to be happy. The ships are in the port and now wish to sail; the most gentle one is going overseas; and I, tired and grieving, what should I do? He is going to another country and will not write to me, and I remain abandoned; my sighs are so many that they besiege me night and day; I don't know whether I am in heaven or on earth.

Holy, holy, holy God, who came in the Virgin, save and guard my love, since you have separated him from me. Hear, o fearsome and high power, may my sweet love be acceptable to you. The cross saves men and ruins me; the cross saddens me and I cannot pray to God. O cross of the pilgrim, why have you so destroyed me? Alas, I am a worn-out wretch who burns and is all burnt up.

The emperor maintains the whole world in peace and makes war on me, since he has taken away my hope. Hear, o fearsome and high power, may my sweet love be acceptable to you. When he took the cross, he surely did not think of me—he who loved me so much and I, him, so that I was tortured for it, put in prison, held in a dungeon for my lifetime.

The ships have spread their sails and can go with good auspices, and with them my love and the men who are going away. O Father of Creation, bring them to port—those who serve the holy cross.

But I beg you, friend Rinaldo, you who know my pain, that you make me a sonnet and send it to Syria, for I cannot rest night or day—my life is overseas.[68]

All these themes of love expressed by the Sicilian school were to sound again in a very different context when Jacopone turned later in life to poetry as a means of expressing his love of God. Furthermore, the dramatic dialogue, the *tenson*, which was such a frequently used form in both Sicilian and Provençal poetry, was also one of Jacopone's favorite means of expression.

The other characteristics of the Sicilian school find little or no echo at all in the later work of Jacopone. Their love of nature, of the singing birds, and the gentle breezes of spring—so beautifully expressed by Francis of Assisi—find no echo in the tortured soul of the Franciscan, Jacopone. He did not use the sonnet form, which he probably felt was too confining and genteel for his muse. Nor did he retain the formal "voi" of the Sicilians; it would seem that the latter kept to their courtly manners even in bed, though, to be sure, being in bed with someone does not necessarily indicate either intimacy or even friendliness. Jacopone preferred the direct "tu," addressing everyone including the Virgin and the pope, with Quakerly simplicity. The pall of self-consciousness and strict adherence to foreign patterns, which shrouds the creations of the Sicilian poets and makes one wonder if they ever had any genuine feelings at all, disappears entirely from the work of Jacopone. Rarely, if ever, does Jacopone use the gallicisms with which the Sicilians indicate their membership in an international aristocracy.

In all likelihood Jacopone had plenty of opportunity to read or hear the work of the Sicilian poets. As we have seen, the imperial court passed close to Todi, and wherever it went in Tuscany, the court poets left behind them a host of imitators. The aristocracy of the growing communes admired the manners of the Sicilians and began to express them in the still rough Tuscan dialect. Among the first poets to flourish, perhaps as early as 1250, was the notary Bonagiunta da Lucca, who was much influenced by that other notary, Giacomo da Lentini. In the Guibelline city of Pisa, where Frederick had been a welcome visitor, a whole group of leading citizens came to write sonnets and canzoni; the names of at least eight have come down to us—judges, notaries, nobles, and members of the communal government. Pistoia, another Guibelline town, produced Meo Abbracciavacca and Paolo Lanfranchi. Florence, which after 1250 was rapidly replacing Pisa as the largest Tuscan center, was also beginning to show its cultural hegemony; her poets, the chief of whom in the generation before Dante was Chiaro Davanzati, were like the Pisans either nobles or members of the communal elite.[69]

Of all the imitators of the Sicilian school, Guittone d'Arezzo was the most innovative and became in effect the leader of the Tuscan group. He is credited with having been the first to develop the *lauda* into a genuine art form from the artless chants of contemporary zealots. It is hard to determine if Guittone had any direct influence on Jacopone; since except for the famous lament on the Guelph defeat at Montaperti (1260), it has not been possible to assign any clear dating to his work. Some elements they did have in common; both were at home in the ballad style. One of Guittone's best is the ballad that begins with the refrain:

Vegna - vegna - chi vole giocandare
e a la danza se tegna.

Come, come who wish to play, and join
the dance.[70]

As in any ballad, the refrain would be repeated at the end of every stanza, but to increase the lilting effect of the song, Guittone uses in each stanza rhymes that hark back to the refrain: "degna - degna," "tegna - tegna," "stregna - stregna," "regna - regna," and "stegna - stegna." Such repetitive rhymes were a mark of Jacopone's ballads, especially the "Amor de caritate."[71]

In little else did the noble of Arezzo and Jacopone resemble each other. Though Guittone like Jacopone underwent a conversion and joined the order of the Knights of the Blessed Virgin Mary, the "frati godenti" of which the Franciscan chronicler Salimbene had so little of good to say,[72] his religiosity expressed itself in a kind of municipal moralism. The Guelph noble longed for the good old days of his "dolce terra aretina" and looked with disdain at the corrupt upstarts in its civic life—"gente noiosa e villana."[73] Such was not the course of Jacopone's spiritual development.

If there was relatively little which Guittone and Jacopone had in common, there was still less contact between him and the poets of the *dolce stil nuovo*, the mainstream of Italian literature that flowed from Guinizelli to Dante. The new style grew up almost entirely after 1268, the year in which Jacopone entered upon his religious life. Though he certainly must have heard the soft cadences of the elegant Tuscans, he lived in another world. In the evolution of Italian poetry, his school branched off from the main trunk on the far side of the branch that bore Dante. The latter never mentions him in his critique of Italian writing, the *De volgari eloquentia*. Some have thought that this Dantean disdain resulted from a conscious position; if Dante despised Guittone as rough and vulgar, how much more would he have despised Jacopone![74] More likely the great Florentine did not even consider Jacopone a poet. The feeling was probably mutual; the aged Jacopone and the young Dante were worlds apart.

Popular Culture   Unlike Dante, Jacopone had a rich streak of vulgarity; one can easily see that he delighted in using the rough and expressive words of his native dialect. As a Franciscan he was eager to get his message across to the poor as well as the rich, the uneducated as well as the educated; it is this element of earnest plainness, in contrast to the snobbish artificiality of the Sicilian and Tuscan poets, which so captivated the democrat de Sanctis a hundred years ago. The great Risorgimento historian wrote: "There is in Jacopone a vein of frank, popular, and spontaneous inspiration which is not to be found in the cultivated poets which we have spoken of so far. If the thousand Italian troubadours had felt love with the warmth and affectiveness which roused such fire in the religious spirit of Jacopone, we would have had a poetry less learned and less artistic, but more popular and more sincere."[75] Jacopone's ear was attuned to popular culture.

For the common people also had their culture, growing up beside the courtly manners of the elite, and like the elite had many contacts with the wider world. Many in the artisan class lived almost migratory lives; for example, Perugia hired 100 Todian masons in 1289, perhaps to help build the great Palazzo dei Priori, which still magnificently dominates her main square.[76] The babble in the piazza included not only the news of merchants and notaries but also the latest stories of humble folk. There is every reason to believe that the folklore of the lower classes was common currency in Todi—a currency dealt in by crowds of traveling minstrels. If the great court of Frederick was graced by aristocratic poets, it was also disgraced, in the eyes of Salimbene at least, by a host of jugglers, minstrels, acrobats, cantastorie (storytellers), fools, and charlatans. As an old Florentine tale reports: "To Frederick came players, troubadours, good talkers, men of art, jousters, fencers, and all sorts of people." With the disappearance of the imperial court after 1250, these entertainers took to the roads of all central and northern Italy, bringing their wares to the new market provided by the wealth of the rising communes. They formed a bridge between the life of the courts and that of the merchants and artisans. To the more staid bourgeois they were a nuisance, and laws were passed to limit their activities—in Viterbo (1251), Siena (1251), San Gimignano (1258), and Bologna (1288). They were not to sing in the main square in front of the palazzo communale. They were not to cadge meals—apparently they were so insistent in this respect (it was probably their main source of subsistence) that the law had to be invoked to throw them out if uninvited. A case was brought in Siena by Ruggiero Apugliese, the well-known notary of the commune and a poet himself, against a minstrel who allegedly consorted with heretics, cadged meals, and satirized judges and bishops in private gatherings of gentlemen.[77] Perhaps he was a competitor.

The cantastorie or singer of tales became a fixed part of the town scene—to remain so until, within recent memory, he was finally driven out by radio and television. With the aid of a trumpet or lute he announced his presence and gathered a crowd. Jacopone was frequently to strike such a minstrel's pose and announce his *laude* with a verbal fanfare: "Audite un 'ntenzione - ch'è 'nfra l'anima e 'l corpo [Hear a *tenson* between the soul and the body]," (*Lauda* III); "Or udite la battaglia - che me fa el falso Nemico [Now listen to the battle which the false Enemy wages against me]," (*Lauda* XLVII); "Guarda che non caggi, amico, guarda! [Watch out that you don't fall, friend, watch out!]," (*Lauda* VI); and "O frate mio, briga de tornare - 'nante ch'en morte si' pigliato [O my brother, hurry to reform, before you are struck by death]," (*Lauda* IX). The main qualifications for the cantastorie were a good memory and the ability to spin off rhymes almost extempore. As Italian rhymes much more readily than English and ordinary Italians of today can compose rhymed toasts at parties while half seas over, these are not difficult acquisitions. Neither the cantastorie nor Jacopone was fussy about rhyme; assonance would do just as well in their urge to express themselves in common, racy dialect.

What the minstrels sang about is imposible to know; their art was by its very nature ephemeral. Much of it was probably humorous. As wit travels across centuries and national boundaries only with great difficulty, we are inclined to think of other ages and other peoples as unduly solemn. Sex, as might be expected, was a rich source of humor. Here is a rare example: A woman is suspected of adultery by her jealous husband, who disguises himself as a priest in order to trap her. She goes to confession, recognizes him, and confesses in the broadest dialect. The tricker is tricked:

> Ch'è sont inamorata d'un bel preyto.
> Con quel preyto è son zazuta
> mille volte sot un lenzolo;
> perzò l'amo e ll'o amato
> più che la madre lo fiolo.
> S'el meo marito lo savesse,
> el morirave del dolo!
> E' te llo digo, preyto, ella gran credenza
> de', tènime zellata la mia penetenza!

> I fell in love with a handsome priest. I have gone with that priest a thousand times under the sheets; so I have loved him and love him, more than a mother her son! If my husband knew about it, he would die of grief! I tell it to you, priest, in great confidence; you must keep my repentance secret![78]

Quite a few of such verses have been preserved on notarial documents in Bologna, where they were copied by the notaries to fill out the space and so prevent unauthorized additions to the contracts.[79] Probably the fullest source of popular tales comes from the collection called *Le cento novelle antiche*, or more casually, *Il novellino*. First printed in 1525, these stories of Florentine origin were written down in the last decades of the thirteenth century and were based on strong oral traditions.[80] They were a mine that Boccaccio worked to the full in his raising of the genre to artistic heights and that Chaucer, following Boccaccio, introduced to English audiences. Their most outstanding characteristic was their almost elliptical brevity (another of Jacopo's stylistic quirks). The minstrel knew that a story could be funny if it was rapid-fire enough. Many are built around a punch line, and the faster one gets to it the better.

The subjects that are covered in the stories provide an encyclopedic survey of popular culture—the concupiscences of the world in which Jacopo wallowed. Some stories are straight out of the Bible—slightly botched; some are short versions of saints' lives. Many of the heroes and heroines of the epics appear, such as Roland, Lancelot, the Lady of Shalott, Tristan, and Charlemagne. Mythical figures like Narcissus and ancient Romans like Cato and Trajan come to life again. All these are positive figures in which the people believed. So also the great feudal lords appear in a favorable light: Frederick, Henry II of England, Conrad of Hohenstaufen, and Charles of Anjou. The bourgeoisie respected their betters, but every other figure was the butt of satire.

The age of faith was also the age of anticlericalism. The rich bishop who has ruined his digestion from overeating will exchange his stomach with a poor friar—but not his office. A physician of Toulouse marries the archbishop's niece who has a child in two months; he returns her to her uncle with the comment that, rich as he may be, he is not rich enough to support a wife who can bear a child every two months. A countess and her ladies-in-waiting are caught in adultery; they are converted and become adulterous abbess and nuns. A bishop is caught in bed with a whore by a priest whom he has accused of whoring; case dimissed. When Jacopone came to write his anticlerical satires, he knew the people for whom he was writing and could enjoy bitter paradoxes of striking vulgarity.

The age of faith was also the age of blasphemy. In fact, without faith blasphemy is insipid. To turn for a moment from the *Novellino* to the stories that Salimbene is pleased to collect, consider Fra Detesalve of Florence, who on a visit to a Franciscan house in Puglia begged a piece of the habit of a holy friar to take home as a relic. Then he ate a big meal, relieved himself, and threw in the piece. He cried out lustily for help, and when all the friars were gathered over the hole, stirred up the contents, pretending to look for the piece, so that the stink was very strong. Coming home to Florence, the same Fra Detesalve slid on the ice and sprawled in the street. "Seeing the accident, the Florentines, who are great jokers, laughed heartily. And one asked the friar lying on the ground: 'Do you want something under you?' And the friar: 'For sure, your wife.' The Florentines were not scandalized by this answer but praised the brother, saying: 'God bless him. He is certainly one of us.'"[81]

As might be expected in a collection of Florentine stories like the *Novellino,* there are many tales of the fickleness and wit of women—to balance off the poetic tragedy of the Lady of Shalott. The learned are spoofed: an absent-minded astrologer comes out of his house at night to gaze at the stars and falls into a ditch. A scholar, pondering the infinite empyrean, asks what is over his head; the answer: his hat.

A surprising number of stories reveal an intense interest in justice and money and must have been especially fascinating to a notary like Jacopo. A lawyer promises to repay a banker 1000 lire when he wins his first case; after a time, the banker brings a false suit for 2000 lire, loses it, and collects his money. One of the most extraordinary stories contains only thirty-nine words. The point is simply that a banker gave money to the poor, and this unusual—and perhaps fantastic—event was enough to make a story.[82]

Together with the traveling minstrels came the wandering scholars and their Goliardic songs in Latin. Though few of these were of Italian origin, they spread throughout Italy.[83] In addition to the famous songs of wine, women, spring, and the wheel of fortune, some songs betrayed a black humor. The roast swan gracing the festive board sings for the diners a lament on his past beauty—a picture that may well have suited the macabre humor of Jacopone:

Olim latus colueram,
olim pulcher extiteram,
dum cignus ego fueram.
Miser, miser!
modo niger
et ustus fortiter!

Girat, regirat furcifer;
propinat me nunc dapifer,
me rogus urit fortiter;
Miser, miser!
modo niger
et ustus fortiter! . . .

Nunc in scutella iaceo,
et volitare nequeo,
dentes, fredentes video:
Miser, miser!
modo niger
et ustus fortiter!

Once I swam around the lake, once I existed as a beautiful thing, when I was still a swan. Wretched, wretched me, now so black and badly burned! The cook has turned me on the spit again and again, the fire has burned me deeply, and now the chef has laid me out. Wretched, etc. . . . Now I am lying on the platter and can fly no more; I see gnashing teeth around me. Wretched, etc.[84]

What the Goliardic poets discovered and taught Jacopone was the devastating effect of the short, rhymed line for the purpose of satire. The stately language of the church could also be used for jingles. Though he wrote in Italian, Jacopone's satires had the same bite.

The concupiscences of the world also involved dances and games, which appear to have had all the sophistication of musical chairs and such parlor treats. In Siena, the young bloods attacked with weapons of roses a sham castle defended by the ladies.[85] When the boys got together, the games became rough. There was the *pugna* or fist fight between teams of boys from different sections of the city. And football. If the *calcio fiorentino* of today is a true reproduction of the medieval game—and it may be[86]—then intersectional violence was released in a thoroughly uninhibited manner. So also with the battles with wooden swords and shields in Siena and the more genteel mock tourneys. In all areas of life the level of overt violence was very high. Law enforcement was certainly not left to a small group of professionals, and citizens of Perugia were required to keep gaff hooks for snaring fleeing muggers.[87] Against such a background of hair-triggered tempers the sudden changes of mood in Jacopone's poetry are more understandable.

But of all the games, the ones that most interested Jacopo were those involving money, the complicated and fascinating new toy of the urban classes.[88] Betting was a favorite diversion; Jacopone refers to the rolling of the dice in a game somewhat like the modern game of *morra*. Games of dice were often played in the inns, of which Todi had eleven as compared with six in San Gimignano, a pilgrim or tourist center even then. The commune felt the need to control such games, and several people between the years 1275 and 1280 were condemned for gambling.[89] Surprisingly enough, the game of chess, to which Jacopone referred in his poetry, provided the occasion for betting.

In turning to God, Jacopone turned away from all of this—the things of this world. But it is one thing to recognize intellectually the emptiness of ambition, money, power, sexual love, and pride, and quite another to free one's spirit of their domination. Thus the great religious teachers and mystics of Taoism, Buddhism, Islam, and Christianity unite in emphasizing the need for purification and the losing of one's self. For Jacopone it was a long and hard road.

III ∞ Jacopone the Penitent

T here are three states to the soul. In the first the soul takes cognizance of its sins and weeps with a compunction which drives it almost to desperation."[1] So wrote Jacopone many years later looking back over the long voyage of his life. After the death of his wife in 1268, he turned from the world to God and began to experience a profound and radical transformation. His former life filled him with violent horror and he was consumed with terror of the future:

> O vita fallace ed o' m'hai menato
> e come m'hai pagato - che t'aio servuto?
> Haime condotto ch'io sia sotterato
> e manecato - dai vermi a menuto;
> or ecco il tributo - che dài en tuo servire
> e non pò fallire - a gente ch'è nata.

> O false life, where have you led me and how have you paid me who has served you? You have led me to be buried and eaten by worms bit by bit. Here is the reward which you have given to your servants—and it cannot fail to people who are born. [*Lauda* XXIV, lines 169–175]

How, why, and when the power of God reached Jacopone are questions which those interested in the psychology of conversion would very much like answered. Unfortunately Jacopone himself did not provide any answers, for he simply accepted conversion as a fact. Consequently the several accounts of his conversion lead to speculation about its nature and causes. The story told in the *Franceschina* is both the earliest and the most complete:

> Feeling such a great transformation in himself, in his soul and in his heart, he was completely gathered unto himself. In his heart he began to cast his eyes about in a remarkable manner and with divine light and to

consider his past life, so much out of the way of God and of health. His previous life was blind and senseless and crazy and entirely unreasonable, and it was hurling him headlong into the horrible pits of eternal Hell.

So from that time forth, as he had lived in the world and its vanities, so he set out to live entirely according to Christ and virtue. And as he had been completely formed by pride, greed, and pleasure in himself and the world, so through the work of divine grace, he was totally transformed and gave himself to the virtue of holy humility and denial of himself, to holy poverty, and the love of God and of his neighbor. So he right away began to give away what he possessed to the poor for the love of God, took for his clothes a certain garb of a hermit, like a *bizocone,* and put aside all his substance, pride and arrogance. In the same way he put aside his notariat and all his secular occupations and gave himself entirely to the denial of his self and disdain of the world.[2]

This process probably took place over a considerable period of time. In later years, Jacopone referred to the long cloak "ch'anni diece enteri truovo - ch'i 'l portai gir bizocone [which for ten whole years I found and wore as a wandering penitent]," (*Lauda* LV, line 65). Thus the first stage of Jacopone's soul lasted ten years, from 1268 to 1278, and the period of his conversion may have been quite extended. Of course, it is not impossible that he was struck with sudden blinding light, as was Paul on the road to Damascus, but such dramatic and lightninglike transformations, though favored by revivalists throughout Christian history down to the present day, do not seem in fact to have occurred with any great frequency. Jacopone's nearest models were Franciscans, and in the case of Francis himself, there seems to have been a slow maturing of his vocation from the time that he was in prison and then fell sick to the time of his revelatory vision in the little chapel of St. Damian. Similarly Francis's first convert, Bernardo da Quintavalle, began his new life as a result of his one-night vigil with the saint and then under his benign influence grew gradually in grace.[3]

That Jacopone was launched on his way by the death of his wife seems most likely. This man in his thirties was set to crown the success of his material life with the founding of a family; in his year of married life he knew the joys of conjugality. So he could not help but be deeply shocked to see the house that he was building struck down by sudden death. It was built upon sand. Was this "accidental" death attributed by Jacopone to blind chance—the haphazard turning of the wheel of Fortune pictured by the Goliardic poets? Or rather was it a sign from God? In a world governed by the omnipresent, omniscient, and omnipotent God there is no place for "accident" owing to blind chance. Hence, did not Jacopone believe with Dante that Fortune was a mere servant of "Colui, lo cui saver tutto trascende [He whose wisdom transcends all]," (*Inferno,* VII, 73)? In view of Jacopone's later spiritual development and the fact that men in the thirteenth century widely accepted the idea of the direct intervention of divine providence in human affairs, it seems likely that right from the beginning Jacopone saw the death of his wife as retribution for his sins—a clear warning from God.

Did he at the same time feel that he was the cause of his beloved Vanna's death? That he was guilty? Surely he had asked her to go to the party and had forced her to conform to the fashionable conventions of his time and town. Then her secret resistance was poignantly revealed to him by her corpse. Another early biographer believed:

> It was not, however, the effect of the grief for the death of his wife, as the vulgar believed, but it was the effect of the deepest grief which he felt at that moment for the life which he had led up to that time—for the offense which he had committed against God, and for the wicked idea which he held of his wife as a worldly woman.[4]

There is much to be said for this view, as women in general do not play a very large role in the *laude*. Unlike the morbid Innocent III, Jacopone was not harried by horrible sexual fantasies. To him all the seven deadly sins were real and he does not single out for special attention:

La lussuria fetente, - ensolfato foco ardente,
trista lassa quella mente - che tal gente ci ha 'lbergata.

Fetid lasciviousness, burning in a sulphury fire, which depresses the minds of those who have harboured it. [*Lauda* XIII, lines 14–15]

Though there can be no final and definite answers to these questions on the origins and nature of Jacopone's conversion, there can be no doubt at all about its completeness.[5] In Jacopone's soul and in the poetry through which he expressed it, one element that stands out is his radical commitment to the hatred of his sins and to the love of God.

Per comperar amor tutto aggio dato,
lo mondo e mene, tutto per baratto;
se tutto fosse mio quel ch'è creato,
darìalo per amor senza onne patto;
e trovome d'amor quase engannato,
chè, tutto dato, non so do' so tratto;
per amor so desfatto, - pazo sì so tenuto;
ma, perchè so venduto, - de me non ho valore.

Credeame la gente revocare,
amici che me fuoro, d'esta via;
ma chi è dato più non se può dare,

nè servo far che fugga signoria;
prima la pietra porrìase amollare
ch'amore che me tiene en sua balìa;
tutta la voglia mia - d'amor si è enfocata,
unita, trasformata: - chi tollerà l'amore?

To buy love I have given everything, the world and myself—everything
in the bargain; if everything that has been created were mine, I would give
it for love without any contract. And I found myself almost crazed for love,
since having given all, I did not know what I was doing. I was undone by
love and have been taken for mad, but since I have sold myself, I have of
myself no value.

My friends thought they could call me back from this way, but who has
given himself cannot give again, nor can one who refuses lordship become
a servant. Stone will sooner soften than love release me from the bond in
which it holds me. All my will is so enflamed, united, and transformed in
love. Who can bear love? [*Lauda* XC, lines 27–42]

Like a good businessman, Jacopone has pictured the completeness of his
transformation in terms of contracts, bargains, value, and deeds of gift.
The seal of finality is legally affixed to his conversion. And like a Sicilian
poet, he is "enflamed," "crazed," "undone," the "vassal of an overlord."
But what a different love is his!

In order to express the depth of the contrast between his former life and
his new way, the poet summons physical images of brutal violence. His
sins, seeming to be friends, "hug him fast, enchain him . . . give him
secret and covert wounds"; they cruelly scorn and despise him; "my
power has vanished because the wound is open and festering too long"
(*Lauda* XXVII, lines 23–30). Such scenes of physical violence evoke the
street fights of Guelphs and Guibellines and the interminable skirmishes
with feudal enemies up and down the contado of Todi. Battle
situations—blows of blunt instruments, cuts and thrusts, fear at the
throat, and the furious lashing out—are known to Jacopone and become
the external experience through which he understands the conflict of
good and evil in his soul. He is embattled. Later in life he surveyed the
same scene analytically, and the fourth of his *Detti* contains a scholastic
treatment of the four battles of the soul, each laid out in neat categories.

In the midst of such a battle, there is no room for compromise, moderation, or reflection. Jacopone positively embraces immoderation; one of
his favorite words is "smesuranza." He cannot measure the distance
between good and evil, for the contrast between his evil and the greatness of Christ overwhelms him. Looking at himself in the mirror of Jesus'
life, he lashes out at halfway tepidity:

Guardando en quello specchio, - vidde mia temperanza:
era una lascivanza - sfrenata senza frino;

gli moti de la mente - non ressi en moderanza,
lo cor prese baldanza - voler le cose em pino;
copersese un mantino, - falsa discrezione
somerse la ragione - a chi fo data a servire. . . .

Signore, haime mostrata - nella tua claritate
la mia nichilitate - ch' è meno che niente;
da questo sguardo nasce - sforzata umilitate
legata da viltate, - voglia non voglia sente;
l'umilitata mente - non è per vil vilare,
ma en virtuoso amare - vilar per nobilire.

Non posso esser renato - s'io en me non so morto,
anichilato en tutto, - el esser conservare. . . .

Looking in that mirror I saw that my temperance was a lasciviousness completely unrestrained. I could not contain the motions of my mind in moderation; my heart was emboldened to have everything right away. False discretion covered itself with a mantle and submerged reason which it should have served.

Lord, you have shown me with your clarity my nothingness, which is less than nothing; from such a look perforce is born humility together with lowliness; I do not want to feel will. The humbled mind is not abased from cowardice, but for nobility and for loving virtue.

I cannot be reborn, if I am not dead in myself—annihilated in everything except my being. [*Lauda* XXXIX, lines 25–30, 51–58]

Jacopone has understood Jesus' teaching to Nicodemus (John 3:1–13). Strangely enough it is just his lack of moderation and his intemperance in language that has repulsed the more old-fashioned critics. Some have even denied that such verses can be called poetry. The vulgar, muddy realism and the depth of involvement are, according to Sapegno,[6] inimical to the spirit of poetry that requires balance, objectivity, and a spirit of contemplation. If such qualities are required, then surely Jacopone cannot appeal. However, in recent years our vision has been broadened by the existentialists who consider the total commitment of the artist an essential element in the creation of great art and by the symbolist and surrealist poets who have accustomed our ears to violent and realistic word pictures. As Quasimodo has said: "Our sensibility does not reject his dissonances."[7] Thus the limitations imposed by Crocean aesthetics have fallen away, and Jacopone comes through as a modern.

In his own day Jacopone's extremism led his contemporaries to think of him as mad. Looking at the external manifestations of his inner struggle, the townspeople were impressed with his unconventional behavior, which was carried to such extreme lengths as to appear truly demented. That such an emotional man as Jacopone should have acted out his interior tensions seems most likely, and in a sense the very composing of poetry to release his inner tensions is a sublimated form of such externalization. His acts, no less than his words, were highly memorable. So it is not hard to believe that the old men, and especially the old women, of Todi, as of many another Italian town, treasured and passed down the colorful tales about their most famous eccentric, until they were finally written down 150 years later. The resulting account in the *Franceschina* has the ring of truth about it:

> It was his practice to go into churches to say paternosters and ave marias and to cry over his sins. Sometimes he went out into the country vilifying himself like a crazy man and one entirely out of the way of reason, in the opinion of the world. He had left behind all his dealings with relatives and friends and was considered by every one to be dim-witted.
>
> His relatives thought of him with great shame and confusion, re-monstrating with him and insulting him as a madman, although at first they tried to force him to withdraw from that beginning life of perfection. Then, seeing that they could in no way change his opinion, they kept their peace—but with great annoyance.
>
> Thus one day there was a festa in the city of Todi, where was gathered a great part of the people. This blessed man in a fervor of spirit and on fire with disdain for the world, took off all his clothes, then taking a pack-saddle put it on his back, set a bit in his mouth, and went about on all fours just as though he were an ass. And saddled this way he went among those who were at the festa. Through this action by divine grace he spread such terror that all were moved with compunction of heart, considering how Ser Jacopone, so famous a procurator of the city of Todi, had taken on such lowliness. And all the people at that festa were confused and drawn from vanity in bitterness and sorrow of heart.[8]

Such a story is clearly in the center of Franciscan tradition. It was reported of Francis that he too was considered mad and that children chased him through the streets of Assisi, throwing stones at him as he went about begging for alms. Moreover, the theme of nakedness is a common one among Franciscans, the act of disrobing being symbolic of the abandonment of earthly possessions and the embracing of poverty. The picture of Francis taking off his clothes and in the presence of the bishop of Assisi, giving them to his father as a sign of the renunciation of his inheritance shows one of the most dramatic incidents in the early life of the founder—an incident vividly portrayed by Giotto and recounted in several of the early lives.[9] Francis's example was followed by others. Both he and Ruffino preached naked in Assisi, "gone mad out of an excess of penitence," causing "those present, children and grown-ups . . . to laugh and say: 'Now look, these friars have practiced so much penitence that they are now quite out of their wits.'"[10] Juniper, of whom so many extravagant eccentricities have been related, gave his habit to a poor man and returned to the friary naked. Just as Francis "offered himself naked to the arms of the Crucified One," so Jacopone wished to leave all his possessions and go naked to Christ:

> Cristo amoroso, ed eo voglio
> 'n croce nudo salire,
> e voglioce abbracciato,
> Segnore, teco morire;
> gaio siramme a patire
> morire teco abbracciato.

> Loving Christ, I wish to climb naked on the cross, and I wish to die, Lord, embraced by you; it would be a joy to me to experience death in your embrace. [*Lauda* XLII, lines 48–54]

The fact of nakedness and the human body itself seemed far from attractive to the men of the thirteenth century. Quite the contrary, both were shameful. Francis wrestled "naked with his naked adversary." Demons and damned souls were almost always pictured naked, as, for example, on the bronze doors of the Cathedral of San Zeno in Verona and on the portals of the Church of San Fortunato in Todi. Adam and Eve were shown naked in their shame being driven from the Garden of Eden, and the vice, Lechery, was usually represented as a shameful and repulsive naked woman.

It frequently happens that when men are converted and take up a new life, they change their names, and so did Jacopone. This name change was not made officially, for he would continue to sign himself Jacobus Benedicti de Tuderto, and chroniclers would refer to him as Jacobus Tudertinus, Jacobus de Benedictis, or Frater Jacobus de Tuderti. Rather he was given a new name by the common people—Jacopone, or as we might say "Big Jim." Though such a name may have stuck to him out of contempt, as some have thought, it is more likely that it grew up out of friendly familiarity. He was tall and his spiritual presence was outsize, even heroic. Yet people might have hesitated to call a dignified notary by such a nickname, whereas it would fit a wild penitent. Jacopone accepted it, as the later Methodists accepted a name that had its origin in public derision. He thought of himself as Jacopone, a plain man with a vernacular name as opposed to a proud man with a Latin name. In the time of his greatest distress, he was to cry out: "Que farai, fra Iacovone? se' venuto al paragone [What will you do, Fra Jacopone? You have come to your trial]," (*Lauda* LV, *incipit*).[11]

With the abandonment of his family name he also abandoned his family. The death of his wife without issue left him free from the responsibilities of supporting a family, and if this had not been the case, both he and the church would have been faced with the problem of sorting out the priorities. In the conflicting claims of family responsibility and the call of Jesus, church practice had long insisted on protecting the unity of families against the disruptive effect of a religious vocation, and men were generally not permitted to enter a religious life if this meant abandoning wife and children. Yet the church could not deny the call of Jesus. And Jesus was not a family man. Some aspects of Jesus' family relations did not enter the medieval consciousness: the incident in which Jesus refused to see his mother and brothers but turned to his disciples and those who do the will of God as his real family, was not interpreted as a rejection of his family; nor was the failure of Jesus' ministry in his home town, when he exclaimed, "No prophet is accepted in his own country," generally realized.[12] On the other hand, the absolute nature of the dedication of one's life to Jesus was most emphatically understood; neither riches, nor burying one's father, nor even bidding the family farewell were to stand in the way of taking up the cross.[13] The three Gospel passages that Francis chose to be his first rule made this abundantly clear: "[1] If thou wouldst be perfect, go and sell all that thou hast, and give to the poor, and thou shalt have treasure in Heaven; [2] take nothing with you on your journey; [3] he that will come after me let him deny himself."[14]

Though Jacopone was not yet a Franciscan, he had severed his connections both with his wealth and his family. The family was utterly antagonistic, as the following story from the *Franceschina*[15] illustrates:

> On another occasion, the brother of Ser Jacopone [named Ranaldo][16] put on a wedding reception; and having already gathered in his house many of his relations and others for this party and suspecting that Ser Jacopone would commit an impropriety and shame him at this party, as he was likely to do, sent word to him asking him to be more respectable than usual, not to play his tricks, to let him put on this reception in peace, and not to commit any folly. Ser Jacopone answered the messenger: "Tell my brother this, that as he intends to honor our relations with his wisdom, so I wish to honor them with my stupidity and folly." And so he did. For when the dancing and festivities were at their height, Ser Jacopone took off all his clothes, covered himself completely with honey, then stuck on a coating of feathers of different colors, and thus feathered went to his brother's house and joined the party to honor his relations. The people seeing this were in great bitterness, as much in embarrassment for the act as in compunction in their souls, seeing this man in so much humility and disdain.

It is to be noted that Jacopone was not invited to the party in the first place; hence, the family's rejection of their unconventional member was as complete as his rejection of their respectability.

Just how mad was Jacopone? Surely it is not necessary to invoke the modern categories of neuroses or psychoses to explain his behavior.

Inner tension he had in abundance, but he also had the ability to release it. The forms that the release took were not only socially harmless, so that there was no need for incarceration, but also sufficiently under control to take the recognized pattern of an accepted counterculture. Jacopone was as crazy as Juniper. Their extravagances had this in common: they almost always had a point, sometimes a moral lesson and sometimes the acting out of an accepted virtue. Juniper, hearing from a sick brother that he would like to eat a pig's foot, went and cut the foot off a live pig and brought it to the sick man. On another occasion, judging that too much time was spent preparing food and not enough praying, Juniper wildly cooked enough food for fifteen days, an inedible mess of whole chickens with their feathers on. When he appeared naked, he rejoiced in the taunts of the folk, acting out the virtue of humility. When a great crowd came out to hold him in reverence, Juniper joined a group of boys on a seesaw, thus illustrating his simplicity for the edification of the people. To make propaganda against those friars who were gathering worldly goods, he gave away everything he could lay his hands on—clothes, books, vestments, fancy altar clothes, etc.[17] Such extravagances, like those of Jacopone, were only superficially senseless, and underneath the obvious symbolism appeared the fanatical devotion of a radical Franciscan.

The opposition of families to the young men entering on a religious life is another prominent Franciscan theme. In the beginning, the rage of Francis's father and his attempt to dissuade his son through imprisonment set a pattern that continued in the movement. Perhaps one of the most touching stories is that of Salimbene, who together with his older brother, ran away from home at the age of fifteen to join the Minorites at Fano. The father, apparently a man of some importance, got a letter from the emperor to the minister general Elias, urging his sons to return home. Elias said that the decision was up to the son, and the father, having gone to Fano, pleaded in a deeply human manner with the wayward boy, picturing the grief of the mother over her loss. Salimbene answered him with a string of quotations from the Gospels, which no doubt seemed convincing to him and to his readers, but which may seem to us the spoutings of an adolescent prig, as we are inclined, unlike the men of the thirteenth century, to accord less authority to the Gospels than to the expression of personal experience. Finally the father lost his temper, threw himself on the ground, and cursed his sons in the thorough manner of the time. Later on he hired some pirates from Ancona to kidnap the boy, so that Salimbene removed from Fano to the interior at Iesi in order to avoid them.[18] Jacopone was, of course, a grown man, and so his conflict with his family was comparatively mild.

The passion that drove Jacopone away from his family and friends and into his new life was the fear of his own death, a motive that has moved

The damned in Hell; note the salamander. Detail of the portal of San Fortunato *(Photo by the author)*

The damned tortured by demons. Detail of the bronze doors of the
Basilica of San Zeno, Verona, twelfth century *(Photo by the author)*

men in all ages to turn to God. Today we are inclined to deprecate "shellhole Christianity," dismiss such a motive as unworthy, and banish from our consciousness the ugly fact of death. Jacopone, knowing that death was not only frequent but also highly visible, took an exactly opposite course. In the most famous of his penitential *laude*, he rubs our noses in all the physical aspects of death, in order to make the fact so real that it will lead to our conversion through fear.

> Quando t'alegri, omo de altura,
> va', pone mente a la sepultura.
>   E loco poni lo tuo contemplare,
> e pensa bene che tu de' tornare
> en quella forma, che tu vedi stare
> l'omo che iace ne la fossa scura.
>   "Or me responde tu, om sepelito,
> che cusì ratto de sto mondo e' scito!
> o' so i bei panni de que eri vestito,
> ch'ornato te veggio de molta bruttura?"
>   "O frate mio, non me rampognare,
> chè 'l fatto mio a te può iovare;
> poi che i parente me fiero spogliare,
> de vil cilicio me dier copretura."
>   "Or ov'è 'l capo, cusì pettenato?
> con cui t'aragnasti che 'l t'ha sì pelato?
> fo acqua bullita che t'ha sì calvato?
> non te c'è oporto più spicciatura."
>   "Questo mio capo ch'avi sì biondo,
> cadut'è la carne e la danza d'entorno;
> nol me pensava quand'era nel monno
> ca entanno a rota facea portatura."
>   "Or o' son gli occhi cusì depurati?
> fuor del lor loco sono gettati;
> credo che i vermi glie son manecati;
> del tuo regoglio non àver paura."
>   "Perduto m'ho gli occhi con che gia pecanno,
> guardando a la gente, con essi accennanno;
> oimè dolente, or so nel malanno,
> chè 'l corpo è vorato e l'alma en ardura."
>   "Or ov'è 'l naso ch'avevi per odorare?
> quegna enfertate el n'ha fatto cascare?
> non t'èi potuto dai vermi aiutare,
> molto è abbassata sta tua grossura."
>   "Questo mio naso, ch'avea per odore,
> caduto se n'è con molto fettore;
> nol me pensava quand'era en amore
> del mondo falso pien de vanura."
>   "Or ov'è la lengua tanto tagliente?

apre la bocca: non hai niente;
fone troncata o forsa fo el dente
che te n'ha fatta cotal rodetura?"

"Perdut 'ho la lengua con la qual parlava,
e molta discordia con essa ordenava;
nol me pensava quand'io mangiava
lo cibo e lo poto ultra misura."

"Or chiude le labra per li denti coprire;
par, chi te vede, che 'l vogli schirnire;
paura me mette pur del vedire,
caggionte i denti senza trattura."

"Co chiudo le labra che unqua non l'agio?
poco pensava de questo passagio;
oimè dolente, e come faragio
quand'io e l'alma starimo en ardura?"

"Or o' son glie braccia con tanta forteza
menacciando la gente, mostrando prodeza?
ràspate 'l capo, se t'è ageveleza
scrulla la danza e fa portadura!"

"La mia portadura se ne gia 'n sta fossa;
cadut' è la carne, remaste so gli ossa:
ed omne gloria de me s'è remossa
e d'omne miseria en me è empietura."

"Or lèvate en piedi, chè molto èi iaciuto;
acòciate l'arme e tolli lo scuto;
en tanta viltate me par ch'èi venuto,
non comportare più questa afrantura."

"Or co so adagiato de levarme em piede?
forsa chi 'l t'ode dir, mo lo se crede;
molto è pazo chi non provede
en la sua vita la sua finitura."

"Or chiama i parenti che te venga aiutare
e guarden dai vermi che te sto a devorare;
ma fuor più vivacce a venirte a spogliare,
partierse el podere e la tua ammantatura."

"No i posso chiamare, chè so encamato;
ma fàlli venire a veder mio mercato!
che me veggia giacer colui ch'è adagiato
a comparar terra e far gran chiusura.

"Or me contempla, o omo mondano,
mentre èi nel mondo, non esser pur vano;
pènsate, folle, che a mano a mano
tu serai messo en grande strettura."

When you rejoice, proud man, go and set your mind on the grave. And contemplate there and think deeply that you must turn into that form which you see in the man who is lying in the dark ditch.

"Now, answer me, buried man who left this world so quickly, where are the handsome clothes in which you were dressed, for I see you decked out with much ugliness?"

"O my brother, do not jeer at me, for my fate cannot gladden you, now that my relatives have undressed me and covered me with wretched rags."

"Now, where is your hair so neatly combed? With whom have you been fighting that he has so skinned you? Was it boiling water that made you so bald? [This refers to the practice of boiling cadavers of crusaders, etc., in order to be able to send the remains home for burial.] You don't need a part any more."

"The skin on this head of mine and the locks around it, which were so blond, have fallen away. I did not think of this when I was in the world and strutted about with a fine coiffure."

"Now, where are the eyes which were so clear? They have been cast from their sockets; I think the worms have eaten them; they were not afraid of your pride."

"I have lost my eyes with which I sinned in looking at people and conniving with them. Unhappy me, now I am in trouble, for my body is eaten and my soul is burning."

"Now, where is your nose that you had to smell with? What hellishness made it fall off? You couldn't help yourself against the worms; your pride is much reduced."

"This nose of mine, which I had to smell with, fell off with a great stink; I did not think of this when I was in love with the false world full of vanity."

"Now, where is your tongue which was so sharp? Open your mouth; you don't have any. Was it cut off or was it perhaps your teeth which chewed it off?"

"I have lost my tongue with which I spoke and spread much discord; I did not think of that when I ate and drank without measure."

"Now, close your mouth to cover your teeth; it seems to one who is looking at you that you are grinning at him; I am afraid to see your teeth fall out without being pulled."

"How can I close my lips when I don't have them any more? I thought little of this fate. Unhappy me, now what shall I do when my soul and I are burning?"

"Now, where are your arms with which you showed your prowess in threatening people violently? Scratch your head if you can. Shake your locks and strut!"

"My noble bearing lies in this ditch; the flesh has fallen away and the bones remain. All glory has been taken from me and I am full of every misery."

"Now, get on your feet, for you have lain down too long. Put on your arms and take your shield. It seems to me that you have fallen so low that you shouldn't put up with this degradation any more."

"How can I get on my feet? Perhaps whoever hears you will believe you now. A man who does not provide for his end during his life is very mad."

"Now, call on your relatives to come and help you and protect you from the worms which are eating you up. They were quick enough to despoil you of your clothes and partition your property."

"I cannot call out because I am gagged, but make them come and look at my estate. Let them see him who was keen at buying land and making enclosures. Now, look at me, o worldly man; while you are in the world, don't be vain any more. Think, fool, that in time you will be put in the narrowest ditch." [*Lauda* XXV]

The savage realism of this intense dialogue portrays the explosiveness of Jacopone's feeling. He hammers away with the incessant repeating of "now" to drive home the immediacy of his fear, and follows it up with the brutal questions "where are . . . ?" The latter are reminiscent of the refrain "where are the snows of yesteryear?"; but what a difference between the nostalgic sentimentality of Villon and the direct grilling of Jacopone! Again, the grinning skull is for Jacopone stark commonplace reality—far from the elegiac reflections of Hamlet contemplating the skull of poor Yorick. Short, hard pictures of horror are piled on each other, tumbling out in a relentless staccato. He is spare of his words; each must carry its full weight, as they should in a notarial document. The functions of that body of which everyone is intensely aware in his intimate daily activities are marshaled forth to make us equally aware of what shall be lost in death. He would have us see a skull every morning when we get up and face ourselves in the mirror to shave and comb our hair. It is only when he has exhausted the strain of the immediate that Jacopone turns to the futility of war, of amassing property, and of caring for one's family at the expense of one's soul.

Which of the speakers is Jacopone? Is he the merciless attorney for the prosecution who fills his questions with callous disdain and coarse raillery, who only once shows fear, and never pity? Or is he the dead wretch, pleading in vain for a grain of sympathy and repeating with doleful remorse the story of what he should have done with his life? In fact, Jacopone is both. He is the moralist, for the moralist condemns in others the failings that in his heart he knows are also his. (Failings that he does not have are not in his experience and are consequently ignored.) He is also the dead man, for Jacopone knows in every crease of his body that he will die.

In a moment of greater calm, Jacopone wrote what amounts to a paraphrase of the "Quando t'alegri." The poem appears among many other penitential *laude* in the Urbino collection and opens with "Peccatore, or que farai - quando verra la morte? [Sinner, now what will you do when death shall come?]." It develops into a severe and august statement of the reality of death.[19]

Such a vivid sense of the presence of death was by no means unusual. The writings of Bernard of Clairvaux, innumerable sermons, and the sermons in stone on the great cathedrals—all proclaimed the message of guilt and fear. One of the popular tracts of the times was the *De Con-*

temptu Mundi of Innocent III. Written in the 1190s when Innocent, still a
cardinal, was out of favor at the court of Celestine III, an enemy Orsini,
the work has frequently been underestimated by historians more interested in Innocent's splendid public career than in his tortured soul.[20] In
the thirteenth century, his vision of the horrors of death had a wide
appeal, and Brunetto Latini was to translate it in the 1280s into Italian so
that it would be more readily available to the laity. Like Jacopone,
Innocent delights in driving home his points with stentorian repetition
and brutal realism:

> Now I will consider with tears from what man is made, what makes man,
> and what man must do. Certainly formed of earth, conceived in sin, born in
> pain, he does depraved things which are not allowed, ugly things which
> are not fit, vain things which are not needed. He will become the kindling
> for fire, the food of worms, a mass of dung.
>
> I say it openly and I will say it openly: man is made of dust, mud and
> ashes—and of something still more vile, the dirtiest of human seed. He was
> conceived in the pricking of the flesh, the heat of lust, the stink of lascivi-
> ousness, and which is the worst, the stain of sin. Born to work, pain, fear,
> and what is more wretched, death. . . . he will become the food of fire
> which will eternally burn and burn so that it cannot be extinguished, the
> food of worms which eternally bore and eat—an immortal mass of dung
> which eternally stinks and which is ugly and terrifying.[21]

Jacopone's involvement with death in this first stage of his spiritual
journey was further shown by a story in the *Franceschina* that seems to
illustrate the "Quando t'alegri." The structure of much of the
Franceschina account is that of associating incidents in his life with
specific poems, so that it has been suggested that the incidents were
invented as glosses on the poems.[22] However, it could just as well be the
other way around, i.e., that the poems were placed next to the remembered eccentricities of Jacopone in order to make the latter more vivid.
Here is the story:

> A citizen of Todi once had bought some chickens in the market, and
> seeing Jacopone going through the piazza, called him over and said: "Will
> you do me the favor of taking these chickens to my house?" He answered
> that he would gladly do it. . . . But the citizen, fearing that Jacopone was
> going to play a trick on him, as well he might, said: "Don't do this in your
> way, but take them sensibly to my house." Jacopone said: "Don't worry;
> leave it to me and I'll take them to your house with the best sense I have."
> And he went up the street to San Fortunato, where he knew the citizen had
> his tomb, and lifting up the stone, he put the chickens in.
>
> When he got home, this citizen asked his wife if Ser Jacopone had
> brought home a pair of chickens which he had bought in the market. She
> said no. The citizen said: "Now he has played a trick on me as I thought he

might. I thought he would do something crazy." His wife said: "Now you fixed it all right. You know his ways and yet you got mixed up with him. . . ."

He left the house right away and went to find Ser Jacopone, to whom he said: "You did it your way all right, Ser Jacopone. . . ." Ser Jacopone said: "I certainly took them to your house." The citizen answered: "Watch out what you say, for I have been home and haven't found them and my wife says she doesn't know anything about them."

Then Ser Jacopone said: "Come and I'll show you that I'm telling the truth and that I have taken them to your home." And leading him to San Fortunato, he lifted the stone which was on the tomb and showed him his chickens, saying: "My very dear friend, this is your home. So don't get angry with me any more, for I have done exactly what you asked me to do. . . ."[23]

The scene is pictured in the popular hagiography of Jacopone, and it is just the sort of practical joke that must have delighted Jacopone's contemporaries and been remembered by the friars for its homely moral. It is a form that has long had great appeal to the Italian sense of humor, which delights in poking fun at the deepest fears and most avid desires. Salimbene loves to tell such stories in his chronicle. Later Boccaccio was to raise the genre to high art in the Calandrino cycle of the *Decameron*, and Poggio in the fifteenth century tells dozens of them in the *Facezie*. Even today, Carlo Levi reports the same kind of jokes in *Christ Stopped at Eboli*.[24]

The theme of the horrors of death was to have a great vogue in the waning of the Middle Ages, especially after the catastrophic visitations of the Black Death. The Gothic portals of the Church of San Fortunato were decorated with the figures of many naked, tortured sinners, and the theme was to reach its apogee in the grand and morbid ballads of Villon. In Jacopone's own day, the "Quando t'alegri" was among the most famous of his poems, as it was spread from one end of Italy to the other by the *disciplinati*.

Jacopone's relationship to the movement of the *disciplinati* has been much studied. Certainly both were driven to the same extremes of violent penitence. More important, it was the *disciplinati* who completely transformed the *lauda* and made it a vehicle of popular revivalism.

The origins of the *lauda* are lost in the origins of Italian literature itself. No one knows how far back into the Dark Ages it was that laymen began to gather in private houses for the singing of *laude*. Named after the monastic office of Lauds, the *lauda* as a form of worship was encouraged by the reformed Benedictine monasteries of the eleventh and twelfth centuries, as was the practice of self-flagellation.[25] The hymns, sung in Latin, consisted of brief excerpts from the Gospels or the Psalms, selected to memorialize the high festivals of the Christian year, and they were

later paraphrased into the volgare so that common people could participate with more understanding. Among the earliest of independent compositions in Italian is a *planctus* or complaint of the Virgin set in a
primitive passion play, which has been found at the Abbey of Montecassino and dated in the late twelfth century.

A new force was given to this form of worship by the Franciscan
movement with its emphasis of going out to the people. Francis's *Canticle
to the Sun*, also called the *Laudes Creaturarum*, is, of course, a landmark in
the development of the form as well as a masterpiece at the very dawn of
Italian literature.[26] It was undoubtedly sung in public processions,
though it did not immediately gain the almost universal popularity and
reverence that it enjoys today. Also the Franciscans spread the practice of
penitence through self-flagellation, and Anthony of Padua led crowds of
hysterical flagellants through the streets of his city in 1230. (In fact the
Franciscans still practice self-flagellation in the more remote houses of
southern Italy.)

The first climax of revivalism took place in 1233—the year of the
Alleluia, dramatically described by Salimbene as a

> time of calm and peace during which the arms of war were put aside, a time
> of rejoicing and happiness, of joy, exaltation, praise and jubilation.
> Litanies and holy laude were sung by nobles and people, citizens and
> country folk, young men and girls, old people and children. In all the cities
> of Italy there was this devotion, and in my own city of Parma I saw that every
> parish wanted to have processions in the streets led by its standard bearer,
> and on the standard was the picture of the martyrdom of its saint. . . .[27]

Numbers of Franciscan preachers excited the passions of the people,
but perhaps the most popular leader was a certain Benedetto della Valle
Spoletana, who was a simple man not connected with any order but
friendly to the Franciscans. He had a long black beard, wore a hair shirt
and over it a black cloak that reached to his feet, with a broad red cross
emblazoned on it front and back. He traveled all over central Italy,
followed about by crowds of children, and was nicknamed "the Horn,"
for Benedetto attracted the people by blowing on it. Salimbene continues:

> He began his praises in this fashion, shouting in the vulgar tongue:
> "Praised and blessed and glorified be the Father."
> And the children repeated it out loud.
> Then he said the same words, adding "be the Son."
> And the children took it up chanting in chorus.
> For the third time he repeated the words, shouting, and added: "be the
> Holy Spirit."
> And then: "Alleluia! Alleluia! Alleluia!"
> And blew the trumpet.[28]

The second crisis of revivalism occurred in 1260–1261 and must have been witnessed by Jacopone when he was still an unregenerate notary. It started in Perugia, sparked by the visions of Rainerio Fasani, an old hermit who in his youth had been reached by the preaching of Francis. According to the legend of his life set down by the *disciplinati* of Bologna in the early years of the next century, Rainerio had "for eighteen years and more" been practicing flagellation, when one night as he was performing this discipline, he saw the image of the Virgin in his cell burst into tears. Continuing his devotions, he saw that he was visited by St. Bevignay, accompanied by St. Jerome, St. Florentius, St. Caesarius, and St. Ciriacus. They all urged him to go to the Church of St. Florentius, which he forthwith did and continued his flagellation naked on the floor in front of the altar and in the presence of the saints. The sexton saw him alone, for he could not see the saints, asked him how he got in, and then went away to secure the locks on the doors. Rainerio looked up to the image of the Virgin and found it crying again. On each side stood two young men. St. Bevignay explained that the Virgin was indeed present with St. Michael and St. Gabriel on each side of her. She spoke to Rainerio telling him to publish before all the people that they should join him in the penance of flagellation. Urged on by St. Bevignay, Rainerio went to the Bishop of Perugia, who not only blessed his work but also did in fact declare a period of penitence. All this happened on May 4, 1260, when the town officials declared a public stoppage of work for fifteen days and joined the penitents. Large numbers of men and boys, naked except for their private parts, went through the streets of Perugia flagellating themselves and crying out their repentance. The women and girls were urged to perform the same rites at home.[29]

This event might have been merely an isolated incident of mass religiosity, had not the form of expression caught on elsewhere. By October of 1260 and throughout the winter and spring of 1261, the movement spread with contagious rapidity. Several factors joined to make this development possible and in the process contributed to the nature of the manifestation itself.

Foremost was the expectation that the world was to end in 1260, that the Apocalypse was at hand, and that Christ was to come again to judge the quick and the dead. This expectation was based on the prophesies of the Calabrian Abbot, Joachim of Fiore, which had been very much kept alive in Franciscan circles despite the fact that the Franciscan Gerard of Borgo San Donnino had been condemned for the Joachimist heresy in 1256.[30] As Salimbene, himself a convinced Joachimist at this time, wrote:

> And in the same year should have begun the doctrine of Abbot Joachim, who divided the history of the world into three periods. . . . In the first period through the power of mystery, the Father worked with the pa-

triarchs and the sons of the prophets, firmly maintaining that the operations of the Trinity are indivisible. In the second period the Son worked
with the apostles and the followers of the apostles. The Son says in the
Gospel of John 5: "My Father works up to now and I also work." In the third
period, the Holy Spirit will work with the monks. . . . And they say that
this period was to have its beginning during this flagellation, which
appeared in the year 1260. . . . when those who flagellated themselves
went crying words which were divine and not human.[31]

The addition of the Joachimist element gave the movement a strong
tinge of social revolution.[32] On the one hand, the passing of the age of the
apostles and their followers indicated that the entire structure of the
secular church was outmoded in the new era of peace and love to be
ushered in by the regular orders. On the other, those secular rulers most
hated by the friars and the people were identified with the Anti-Christ
whose appearance was to herald that of the returning Christ. Before his
death in 1250, Frederick was frequently cast in this role; then his lieuten-
ant, the bloodthirsty Ezzelino da Romano, was another candidate. As
Salimbene wrote: "I have this firm conviction: just as the Son of God
wished to have a particular friend, who was like Him, that is the blessed
Francis; so did the Devil. And he chose Ezzelino."[33] Gerard of Borgo San
Donnino was equally convinced that King Alfonso III of Castile was the
Anti-Christ. Whoever was chosen for the role, pope or prince, saw
directed against himself the full power of a subversive movement.

Of imposing proportions. A Paduan annalist reported that men and
boys "lined up two by two in a procession through the piazzas of the city,
each carrying a penitential scourge, striking themselves on their shoul-
ders with groans and cries until the blood came . . . imploring pardon for
their sins from God and the Virgin. Not only during the day, but also at
night carrying lighted candles, hundreds, thousands, and even ten
thousand penitents milled around the churches in the depths of the
coldest winter, and prostrated themselves before the altars. . . ."[34] The
fervor had spread up and down the valleys of Umbria and then over the
Appenines to the Romagna at Bologna and Modena, where both bishops
and podestà joined the processions. Imola, Reggio, Parma, Padua, and
Tortona had their demonstrations, and during the winter the rage spread
westward through Genoa and Provence as far as Dijon, and eastward
through Mantua, Acquilea, and Cividale into Austria and the Ger-
manies. Some secular rulers suppressed the movement—which they had
not done in 1233. In the kingdom of Naples, Manfred, as befitted the
natural son of Frederick, prevented all penitents from entering. The lord
of Cremona, "who loved the good things of this life better than the
salvation of souls,"[35] threatened all penitents with the gallows and kept
them out. So also the king of Poland stopped the movement at his
frontiers.

In their processions the flagellants sang *laude*, believing the old Latin proverb: "Qui bene cantat, bis orat [Who sings well, prays twice]." "They cried out to God so that the fields and mountains re-echoed."[36] And this fact indicates the third element in the movement; the flagellants and Joachimists were joined by the *laudesi*, or singers of *laude*.

By the early years of the thirteenth century, substantial groups of *laudesi* existed in both Bologna and Florence. As they grew, their organization became more pronounced, and the year of the Alleluia brought such vigor to the Florentine *laudesi* that they founded the Order of the Servants of Mary. One of the earliest *laude* that has survived dates from 1254 in Siena. Hardly more than biblical paraphrases and containing only two themes, worship of the Virgin and repentance, the early *laude* were stiff and awkward renderings in half-formed dialects with repetitious and monotonous rhymes, suitable for private meditation. They were the work of unknown and uncultured worshipers.

When the great revival of 1260 struck, these quiet *laude* quickly developed, taking on the rhymes and liveliness of popular ballads. Suddenly transformed into the wild marching songs of great crowds, "these poor hymns in the volgare, distilled out of tears and blood, like the pious who carried them about singing in unison, seemed to fuse all the souls together in the unison of the voices. . . . The other more ancient *laude*, flourishing in the mouths of the faithful during quiet devotions . . . could not have the impetuosity of the hymns sung in the processions of 1260."[37] Even after the excitement died down, it left groups of earnest hymn singers scattered up and down the land.

At Cortona, the hymnbook of the *laudesi*, or *disciplinati* as they were coming to be called, survived, and it includes the only *laude* written by a known author. He was a certain Garzo, a notary like Jacopone and probably the great-grandfather of Petrarch. Clearly more cultured than most authors of *laude*, Garzo shows the influence of Guittone d'Arezzo and had the command of a simple ballad style. One of his most powerful *laude* treats, like Jacopone, with the theme of death:

> Chi vol lo mondo desprezzare
> sempre la morte dea pensare.
>
> La morte è fera e dura e forte,
> rompe mura e spezza porte:
> ella è si commune sorte
> che verun ne pò campare.

Whoever wishes to disdain the world should always think of death. Death is fierce and hard and strong; it breaks walls and splinters doors. It is such a common fate that no one can escape it.[38]

Death was massively present on September 4, 1260, the date of the great battle of Montaperti. One contemporary chronicler thought that the battle contributed to the spread of the movement, for it involved both large armies and heavy casualties by thirteenth-century standards and was one of the most massive encounters of that time.[39] So much slaughter may well have made Tuscans and Umbrians think that this was indeed Armageddon.

The total movement of 1260–1261 had the effect of splashing across all of north and central Italian society new forces that had heretofore vegetated in unrecognized corners: the flagellant devotion of a few monks and hermits, the Joachimist millenarianism of the radical Franciscans, and the penitential hymns of the *laudesi*. How did it all seem to Jacopone? He can only be imagined in his unregenerate state, looking down with disdain on the half-naked marching men from the windows of his stone palazzo. However, as Giovanni Papini has suggested,[40] it may well have been that he was moved by the simple fervor of the masses. In 1270, just about the time that Garzo was writing his *laude*, the case was different, for Jacopone was himself a penitent—or as he said, a *bizocone*. (No one knows precisely what the word means, but it is usually translated as "penitent" and may be derived from the German word, *Bezenger* or "witness.")[41]

It is not realistic to be more specific in defining the three movements of the flagellants, the Joachimists, and the *laudesi* since all three were in a state of germination in the 1260s and 1270s. Only later did they develop definite separate characteristics.[42] The flagellants who sparked the demonstrations of 1260 developed into organized groups and continued their special form of penance under the direction of monks or secular clergy. Joachimism remained a general cultural trend especially strong among the Franciscan spirituals. The *disciplinati* growing out of the earlier groups of *laudesi* became organized into associations like that of Bologna, the constitution of which was set down in 1286. This and other constitutions, such as that of 1303 in Todi, reveal a precise set of devotions under the supervision of friars and secular clergy. Worshipers met twice a week in a private home for devotions opening and closing with the singing of *laude* and containing other prayers and sometimes flagellation; often the group would continue their devotions by proceeding to a church which they would enter singing *laude*. Members were expected to say prayers at the canonical hours and to avoid taverns, dancing, gambling, luxury, usury, and belonging to a political party. Discipline was maintained by the imposition of fines. Another organization of laymen was the famous Third Order of St. Francis. While this group dated back as far as the lifetime of the saint, it can hardly be thought of as an "order," since its rules and customs were so informal: merely to say the simplest of prayers at the canonical hours, to try to live a Christlike life, and to submit to the spiritual guidance of a friar. It was not until 1289 that the Third Order was given a more definite organization by the Franciscan pope, Nicholas IV.

For many years Jacopone was thought to have been closely associated with the *disciplinati,* that he was in effect their poet and the composer of the *laude* which they used in their daily devotions. Then it was discovered that in the surviving hymnbooks of the *disciplinati,* there are more than 200 *laude,* of which very few are by Jacopone. The "Quando t'allegri" and the "Donna del paradiso" were among the most popular among the *disciplinati,* and their popularity is attested to by the fact that the simple worshipers inserted different stanzas of their own in the original text. The contrast between the often wordy, repetitious, and pedestrian nature of the insertions and the spare vigor of Jacopone's poetry is striking.[43] Similarly, if one compares the work of Garzo with that of Jacopone, the gulf that separates them is equally striking. All but a few of Jacopone's poems are simply not suited for hymn singing by uneducated groups, though some were set to music.[44] They are too much a personal expression, too complicated in their thought, too compressed in their expression, and too subtle in their interior spiritual light. It is inconceivable that peasants and artisans would want to sing them as hymns, no matter how much they might respond to his vigorous dialect. The recent discovery of the close connection between Jacopone and the Umbrian *laudesi,* made by Bettarini in *Il laudario urbinate,* indicates the presence of a more sophisticated and spiritually advanced group, a true "school" of Jacopone. In sum, Jacopone took the *lauda* and made it into an art form. As Angelo Monteverdi has written: "And finally, when the time came, the *lauda* found its poet, Jacopone da Todi. He kept the popular tone and accepted its simple and coarse form; but he knew how to pour into it, with a robust art, the fullness of his soul—drunk with divine love, pervaded by the hatred of . . . human miseries and vanity, conscious of the value of his loves and hates, and expertly learned in the secrets of the mystic life."[45]

Jacopone's vision of the last judgment, so close in theme to the fear of death, contains a prophecy of horror with the power of the "Dies Irae." It opens:

Or se parrà chi averà fidanza!
la tribulanza ch'è profetizata,
da onne lato veggio tonare.

La luna è scura, el sole obtenebrato,
le stelle de lo ciel vegio cadere;
l'antiquo serpente pare scapolato. . . .

Tutto el mondo veggio conquassato
e precipitando va en ruina;

como l'omo che è enfrenatecato,
al qual non può om dar medicina,
li medici sì l'hanno desperato. . . .

Now we will see who has faith! I hear the tribulation which has been
prophesied thundering on every side.
The moon is dark, the sun in shadow; I see the stars fall from the sky; the
ancient serpent is loosed. . . .
I see all the world smashed and hurled into ruin, like a man who is mad,
for whom there is no medicine and the doctors have given up hope. . . .
[*Lauda* L, lines 1–6, 32–36]

The scene is one that was believed imminent in 1260; periodically in later
years, waves of insane fear gripped the common people. Until recently
we were inclined to dismiss such apocalyptic terrors as fantastic; but now
that the atomic bomb has lent scientific respectability to the concept of
the apocalypse and succeeding generations of young people have become convinced that their lives will be short and violent, we are less
ready to denigrate the terrors of people of other ages, just because they
were conceptualized differently.

The inevitability of death and judgment led Jacopone to press forward
and embrace them, like the souls who fall like autumn leaves to the
shores of Acheron and crowd on the skiff of Charon, eager to experience
their inevitable and eternal damnation (*Inferno*, III, 103–117). In *Lauda* XI,
he begs: "Signore, damme la morte - nante ch'io più te offenda! [Lord,
give me death before I offend you more!]" He knows that he is unwilling
to change his evil ways and says it is better that he be killed right away.
He is depressed to the point of contemplating suicide; he is not worth the
pity of either God or man, for his repentance has come too late.

Exploring the means of death, Jacopone turns to sickness, a particularly nasty way to die in that culture. As Innocent III had pointed out,
medicines were practically useless and doctors, helpless. "Human nature," he wrote, "is corrupted more and more from day to day, so that
many illnesses which were harmless in the past are now mortal."[46]
Sickness, being so often fatal, was thus more fearful. In *Lauda* XLVIII,
Jacopone asks: "O Signor, per cortesia, - mandame la malsanìa! [O God,
please send me sickness!]" There follows a horrifying list of illnesses
with the disgusting symptoms graphically drawn. However, as in Boccaccio's description of the plague, where the physical facts are topped by
their social and moral consequences (*Decameron*, preface),[47] so
Jacopone's emotional tension increases when he considers his relationships with other men:

A me venga cechitate, - muteza e sorditate
la miseria e povertate - ed onne tempo en trapperìa.

Tanto sia el fetor fetente, - che non sia nul om vivente
che non fuga da me dolente, - posto en tanta enfermarìa.

Let blindness, dumbness, deafness, misery, and poverty come to me and
may they all last. May the stink be so foul that there would be no living man
who did not flee from me, doleful in such infirmity. [*Lauda* XLVIII, lines
18–21]

Like Lear he calls down on himself all the adversities of violent nature:
frost, hail, storms, lightnings, thunders, and darkness. Finally he asks
for death and a grave in the stomach of a voracious wolf, so that his relics
will be excrement, concluding:

Signor mio, non è vendetta - tutta la pena c'ho detta,
chè me creasti en tua diletta - e io t'ho morto a villania.

My Lord, all those ills I ask are no vengeance, since you have made me in
your likeness and I have killed you with wickedness. [Lines 36–37]

Such a conclusion drives home the concept that the horror of death pales
in comparison with the horror of treason to God. A similar thought is
behind *Lauda* XII, which begins:

Sì como la morte face - a lo corpo umanato,
molto peio sì fa a l'anema - la gran morte del peccato.

Just as death destroys the human body, the great death of sin does much
worse to the soul.

And again Jacopone rehearses all the ills of the body as symbols of the ills
of the soul.

Closely related to the attitude toward death is that toward old age. In
youth-oriented societies old age seems to be driven from the consciousness, just because it represents the approach of death, a fact to be
shunned even more. As might be expected, Jacopone takes the diametri-
cally opposite point of view as he introduces us in *Lauda* XXII to an
intimate, friendly conversation between two old men. He begins "Audite una entenzone [Hear a dialogue]," but his "entenzone" has only the
form of a courtly *tenson*, being a travesty on the sweet discussions of
young lovers. One old man is ragged, the other, well-dressed; the first,
addressing his old friend as "compar mio," tells how his son steals his
hard-earned goods, dresses him in rags, and terrifies him with tongue
lashings. The sympathetic friend tells of his saintly daughter-in-law who
takes such good care of him and so blesses God. This reply causes the first
to complain of his daughter-in-law who has the voice of a horse, which

can be heard by all the neighborhood in the early morning, insulting him with burning words that split his mind. The friend replies that he had thought he was badly off until he heard this tale and roundly curses the malicious tongues of women. Thus encouraged, the first tells of what a gay blade he had been in his youth, of how his reputation has been ruined by the prostitute daughter of an innkeeper, and finally of how he is now beset with all the disgusting physical weaknesses of old age. Jacopone's list of the latter rivals that of Innocent III, who wrote that few reach old age but that those who do are sad wrecks.[48] One is tempted to think that Jacopone was indulging in black humor, so realistic is the scene and so gothically exaggerated the ills of the poor "compar." It is, of course, impossible to determine what people in the thirteenth century found funny, but we can be sure that Innocent at least was not joking. Nor in the end is Jacopone, for the wretched old man rejects the sympathy of his friend, claiming that his sins more than justify his misfortunes. Jacopone then ends the poem with a grand condemnation of the world and a humble prayer for God's mercy.

At one point, Jacopone does not even believe in God's mercy. He descends to the depths of pessimism; like the members of Alcoholics Anonymous, he hits the bottom. His vehicle for expressing this depth is to picture a trial, a situation that as a man of law he knew well. He is the prisoner in the dock and calls out to the judge:

"O Cristo pietoso, - perdona el mio peccato
ch'a quella son menato, - che non posso più mucciare."

"O merciful Christ, pardon my sin, for I am so deep in it that I cannot flee." [*Lauda* XXI, lines 1–2]

Then the Enemy, i.e., the Devil, comes on the scene in the role of prosecuting attorney, and Christ, the august and remote judge, tells him to proceed:

"La prova, se ella è vera, - entenderolla a distritto
chè onne bono omo spera - ch'io sia verace e dritto;
se hai il tuo fatto scritto - or ne di' ciò che te pare."

"I shall listen impartially to your proofs, to determine if they are true, since every good man hopes that I be truthful and honest; if you have his case written up, tell me how it seems to you." [Lines 16–18]

The Enemy starts with Jacopone's main sin, which is usury and cheating the poor, and goes on to describe his fashionable life of parties and dancing. He calls in as witness Jacopone's guardian angel, who simply remarks that the Enemy speaks the truth and that the sinner always disdained him.

Then Jacopone confronts his judge alone, as all men must when they face death:

"De cio che m'è provato - nulla scusanza n'agio,
pregote, Dio beato, - che m'aiuti al passagio;
che m'ha si empaurato - menacciato del viagio,
si è scuro suo visagio - che me fa angustiare."

"I have no excuse for what has been proven against me. I pray you, blessed God, to help me at the passage, for the voyage has threatened and terrified me so much. The way is dark and makes me tremble." [Lines 50–53]

But Christ is immovable:

"Longo tempo t'ho aspettato - che te dovessi pentire;
con ragion sei condannato - che te dèi da me partire;
del mio viso sei privato - che mai nol porrai vedire,
fate gli aversere venire - che 'l degian acompagnare."

"O Signor, co me departo - de la tua visione!
co so adunati ratto - che me menino in pregione!
poi che da te me parto, - damme la benedizione,
famme consolazione - en questo mio trapassare!"

"Ed io sì te maledico, - d'ogne ben si' tu privato!
vanne, peccator inico, - che tanto m'hai desprezato!
se me fusse stato amico, - non sarìe così menato;
a lo 'nferno se' dannato - eternalmente ad estare."

"For a long time I have waited for you to repent. You have been justly condemned and you must leave me. You are deprived of my presence; you must never see me. Have the enemies come who must take you away."
"O Lord, how can I leave your presence? How quickly they have come to lead me to prison! Now that I am leaving you, give me your blessing, console me in this my passage!"
"So I curse you! You are deprived of all good! Go, wicked sinner, who has so disdained me! If you had been my friend, you would not have been so led off. You are damned to hell, to stay there forever!" [Lines 54–65]

At the end, the Enemy calls his thousands of demons and dragons, who drive Jacopone with spears, haul him in chains, and screeching a triumphant song, cast him into the fire.

Jacopone shows how real his fate seems to him by picturing it as a drama involving four personae. In only one other *lauda* was he to burst from the dialogue form into a true dramatic presentation, and that was when he created what many have thought to be his greatest masterpiece, the "Donna del paradiso," *Lauda* XCIII. Such a power of pessimism is not to be found elsewhere in the thirteenth century. Even Innocent III, who is just as thorough in cataloguing the evils of the world, sees some slight evidence of a higher life and remains throughout an exalted preacher revealing the sins of *other* people. Even Dante, who peoples hell with his friends and enemies, is only passing through on a much longer journey and only occasionally doubts his own salvation. Jacopone is himself in hell, utterly without hope.

Such is the pessimism of Leopardi, who sees at the end of the road only the loss of the soul in complete oblivion. It is a pessimism with which we are entirely familiar today, for Sartre in *Huit clos* portrays hell as the eternal niggling of predetermined sinners entangled in ceaseless recriminations. Some have argued that Jacopone did not experience such total pessimism, that on the contrary the way of salvation was always open to him.[49] Such a view falls into the common error of thinking of Jacopone as a monolithic unity, that he was either a "mad penitent" or a "mystical poet" or a "poetic mystic" or a "satirist" or any one sort of human being.[50] In fact, he was all of these, for he has given us a history of the voyage of his soul. Such descriptions are of stations on the way. At this station he was on the bottom.

The way up from the bottom is through penitence. In *Lauda* IV, "O alta penitenza," he speaks of his intense hatred of himself—his "mirabile odio" and "falso amor proprio." Such a hatred of self can only be understood in relation to perfection. Jesus had said: "Be ye therefore perfect, even as your Father which is in heaven is perfect" (Matthew 5:48). Francis's admonition is no less clear: "But that all the friars may know that they are bound to observe the perfection of the holy Gospel, I would have it written, both at the beginning and end of the Rule, that the friars must obey the holy Gospel of our Lord Jesus Christ."[51] Such counsels of perfection are disturbing to those who have faith in the power of individual human beings for self-fulfillment on their own; the goal is too high and so is rejected as just another Christian impossibility. Perfection is, however, Jacopone's goal:

> O vita di Iesù Cristo, - specchio de veritate,
> o mia deformitate - en quella luce vedere!
> Pareame essere chevelle, - chevelle me tenea,
> l'opinion ch'avea - faceame esser iocondo;
> guardando en quello specchio, - la luce che n'uscia
> mostro la vita mia - che giacea nel profondo;
> venneme pianto abondo - fra l'essere e 'l vedere. . . .

> O life of Jesus Christ, mirror of truth; O, to see my deformity in that light!
> I seemed to be somebody, I thought I was somebody, the opinion I had of
> myself made me happy. Looking in that mirror, the light that came from it
> showed me my life, that I was lying in the depths. Seeing the contrast, there

came on me a flood of tears. How great was the distance between my being
and what I saw. . . . [*Lauda* XXXIX, lines 1–8]

This is the source of the violent polarity in Jacopone's soul, a contrast
so complete that his personality seems almost split. It is the first step up
from the bottom, as he described it later in his *Trattato:*

> Whoever wishes to arrive at the recognition of truth by the short and
> straight way, and perfectly to possess peace in his soul, must totally
> separate himself from the love of all creatures, and especially of himself,
> and totally submerge himself in God, keeping back nothing for him-
> self. . . .[52]

For Jacopone this was a heroic struggle, which he conceptualized as the
conflict of body and soul, a conflict very familiar to the Christian civilization of his time through the Pauline teaching. Calling on his experience
in the courts of law and the general dialectical cast of mind in his time, he
presents the conflict in the form of a dialogue between the body and the
soul:

> O corpo enfracedato, - io so l'alma dolente;
> lièvate amantenente - chè sei meco dannato.
> L'agnolo sta a trombare - voce de gran paura;
> opo n'è appresentare - senza nulla demura. . . .

> O rotten body, I am your sorrowing soul; get up immediately for you are
> damned with me. The angel is blowing his horn—a voice of great fear—
> now we must present ourselves without delay. . . . [*Lauda* XV, lines 1–4]

The body hangs back, terrified of the demons of hell, but the soul urges it
on, since it is joined by love in every sinew, humor, and vein to the body.
The body, overcome with sickness, calls on the famous doctors of the
human race to be cured—in vain. Finally in this state of unresolved
dialectical contrast, both body and soul arrive before the throne of Jesus
Christ.

On another occasion, Jacopone goes into further detail in a *tenson*
describing the conflict. He begins like a singer in the piazza:

> Audite un 'ntenzione - ch'è 'nfra l'anima e 'l corpo,
> battaglia dura troppo - fin a lo consumare.

> Hear a *tenson* that takes place between the soul and the body; the battle
> lasts so long that it has entirely consumed me. [*Lauda* III, lines 1–2]

The soul brings forward for use on the body the implements of penance:
the scourge of the flagellants, the hair shirt of Donna Vanna, and the hard

bed of the friar. At each penance, the body complains, but the soul urges it on: matins instead of lying in bed, begged crusts instead of cooked food, and water instead of wine. Each complaint and each answer fill a quatrain apiece in a rhythmical counterpoint. Just at the memory of a woman, the body must undergo stronger penance. Jacopone finishes off the tract curtly, like a precise notary, so as not to bore the reader.

It has been noted that the ballad form itself, in which this *tenson* is cast, carries into the very marrow of the poetry the dualism of the thought.[53] The *reprise* with which the poem opens is in effect an invitation to the dance, and each quatrain that follows ends with a line rhyming with the *reprise*, which is, of course, repeated. Going further into the structure of the poem, one finds that each verse of the quatrains has an interior rhyme that not only contains a complete thought but also signals a dance movement to one side or the other. So one bobs back and forth to a kind of schizophrenic tune.

Such a close and precise merging of the thought with the verse form is a sign of the highest art—and highly innovative, for who but a bold artist would have adapted a common dance of the streets to the expression of his inner conflict. As Underhill has rightly emphasized, Jacopone was thoroughly conscious of the dilemma in his soul.[54] *Lauda* XXXVIII, done in the same ballad form, explores with reasoned simplicity the dichotomies of love of God and hatred of self, hope for salvation and despair at his condition, boldness and fear in the face of death, and sadness in the presence of Christ. Jacopone struggled for the "megio virtuoso," the golden mean; and fails to achieve it. Others cannot help him:

> Se io mostro al prossimo - la mia condizione,
> scandalizo e turbolo - de mala opinione;
> s'io vo coperto, vendoglme - e turba mia magione;
> questa vessazione - non la posso mucciare.

> If I show my condition to my neighbor, I shock and disturb him into a bad opinion of me. If I am secretive, I sell myself to him and disturb my soul. I cannot bear this vexation. [Lines 27–30]

Even his life of penitence is full of contrasts; fasting, wearing rags, contemplation, silence, and poverty each meet with resistance on his part. He finds it no joking matter that he cannot achieve moderation. Just as in *Lauda* III, to which this poem is a sophisticated companion, Jacopone cuts short the recital with the notarial comment: "abbrevio miei detta - 'n questo loco finare [I abbreviate my sayings and end up here]." In both cases the implication is that he could go on forever describing the endless conflicts within himself.

When Jacopone comes to examine the specific sins that he is trying to overcome, he sees them in the stereotypes of his time, and his writing becomes formal and abstract, losing the passionate drive of his introspective lyricism. Popular preaching, didactic tracts, allegorical poems, conventional art forms, and confessional practice had concretized the seven cardinal sins into a formal system as rigid as the categories of Freud. Generally, the list specified by Gregory the Great seven centuries before was followed: Pride, Anger, Envy, Greed, Sloth, Gluttony, and Lust. So Jacopone ticks them all off in *Lauda* XIII, "L'anema ch'è viziosa." It is quite obvious that Jacopone understood that pride was at the root of all the others, because as he looked back over his past life, it was the "omo de altura" that stood out. In a sociological sense his past life followed the patterns and aspirations of the nobility, since the bourgeoisie in an agricultural town like Todi aped the manners of the nobility. Now the chief sin of the nobility was pride; whereas that of the bourgeoisie was greed—a sin they were just beginning to elevate to the eminence that Adam Smith was later to celebrate.[55] In a psychological and spiritual sense Jacopone saw clearly that the very consciousness of self was the chief barrier between the individual and God. However, when he describes the sin of pride in *Lauda* XIV, "La superbia de l'altura," he does so in a scholastic manner; the resulting poem has a flatness that contrasts strongly with the magnificence of the "Quando t'alegri."[56]

Similarly Jacopone's treatment of the greed of heirs in *Lauda* XIX, "Figli, nepoti, e frati," is cold and lifeless. The thought is the same as that of Machiavelli, but the expression has none of the bitter force of the latter's dictum: "Men forget more easily the death of their father than the loss of their patrimony."[57]

As to women, Jacopone knows only too well their attractiveness, and in the manner of the misogynistic moralists of his age, he condemns them precisely because they are attractive to him. They are compared to the basilisk, the legendary serpent that hypnotizes its victim with glance and breath before killing and consuming him.

> O femene, guardate - a le mortal ferute;
> nelle vostre vedute - 'l basilisco mostrate.

> O women, look at the deadly wounds; in your looks you play the basilisk.
> [*Lauda* VIII, *incipit*]

They are the servants of the devil, because Jacopone does not see women as people but only as objects related to his own sexual desire. Hence, women's efforts to beautify themselves, their hair, their complexions, their skins—or as Jacopone calls it their "leather"—are horrible to him in so far as they are successful. If women justify their cosmetic activities on the grounds that they must please their husbands, Jacopone answers that this is not the way, for it only makes husbands fearful and jealous. Even the physical weakness of women is thrown at them, since it leads them to use their tongues to "throw words which pierce and wound hearts." One of the most memorable sayings attributed to Jacopone is: "I would notice just as much seeing the beautiful face of a woman as the head of an ass."[58]

How seriously are we to take such comments? Not very, partly because the tirade against women is confined to this one poem and partly because it follows accepted, indeed hackneyed, forms. Considering this one poem, it is notable that Jacopone neither explodes with the emotional force of his introspective outbursts nor does he present the brutal, realistic pictures which he uses, for example, to project his fear of death. In comparison with other misogynists, his horror of women is skin-deep. By contrast, the writings of the patristic period and later penitential sermons abound in attacks on women.[59] Innocent III displays a perverted abhorrence of menstrual blood, citing the ancient Hebrew practices for the purification of women and retailing the current superstitions that "by contact with it, grain does not ripen, bushes dry up, grasses die, trees lose their fruit; and if dogs eat it, they become mad." To Innocent childbirth is "most ugly to see, uglier to hear of," and babies—even when they are normal, and there are many monsters born—are "crying, weak, vacillating, little different from brute animals—indeed in many respects much less than animals."[60] What a distance is shown here from the idealization of both women and children in quattrocento art!

Innocent's tract gave rise to a widespread literature of the early thirteenth century illustrating the sins of women in the volgare. Moralists such as Girardo Patecchio da Cremona paid special attention to the foibles of women in his *Splanamento de li proverbi di Salomone*, Solomon being considered especially expert in this field; the anonymous *Proverbia quae dicuntur super natura feminarum* is entirely devoted to a violent libel against women, again drawing heavily on the wisdom of Solomon. Even at the end of the century, the pedestrian and relatively tolerant moralist, Bonvesin de la Riva, reflects Innocent's horror of the details of feminine anatomy.[61] In short, Jacopone was merely following an accepted formula.

In this first stage of his spiritual development, Jacopone fell easily into the role of minatory preacher. Like most converts he was holier than the pope and set about castigating in others the sins that he was trying to overcome in himself. Even though this attitude was also the standard fare of popular preaching, it entered into the mainstream of Jacopone's psyche, and he poured into it the conviction of personal experience. Not only do most of the stories of his eccentric activities, and especially the incident of the chickens, reflect his didactic urge, but he also composed several *laude* in this vein. Perhaps the most dramatic is *Lauda* VI, in

which he uses the oft-repeated cry of "Beware!" at the beginning and end
of short, rhymed tercets:

> Guarda che non caggi, amico,
> guarda!
> Or te guarda dal Nemico, - che se mostra esser amico;
> no gli credere a l'iniquo, - guarda!
> Guarda 'l viso dal veduto, - ca 'l coragio n'è feruto;
> ch'a gran briga n'è guaruto, - guarda!
> Non udir le vanetate, - che te traga a su' amistate;
> più che visco apicciarate, - guarda!
> Pon a lo tuo gusto un frino, - ca 'l soperchio gli è venino;
> a lussuria è sentino, - guarda!
> Guàrdate da l'odorato, - lo qual ène sciordenato;
> ca 'l Signor lo t'ha vetato, - guarda!
> Guàrdate dal toccamento, - lo qual a Dio è spiacemento,
> al tuo corpo è strugimento, - guarda!
> Guàrdate da li parente - che non te piglien la mente;
> ca te faran star dolente, - guarda!
> Guàrdate da molti amice, - che frequentan co formice;
> en Dio te seccan le radice, - guarda!
> Guàrdate dai mal pensire, - che la mente fon ferire,
> la tua alma enmalsanire, - guarda!

Beware that you don't fall, friend, beware! Beware of the Enemy who
pretends to be a friend; don't believe in the evil one, beware!

Keep your eyes from seeing things since they will wound your courage,
which will be cured only with great difficulty, beware!

Don't listen to vanities which will trap you into their false friendliness
and you will be stuck more fast than a bird caught in mistletoe paste,
beware!

Put a bridle on your taste, since its domination is poison; it is the sink of
lust, beware!

Beware of your sense of smell, which leads to immoderation, since the
Lord has forbidden it for you, beware!

Beware of your sense of touch, which is displeasing to God and a
destruction of your body, beware!

Beware of your relatives; keep them from overcoming your mind and
making you depressed, beware!

Beware of many friends, who crowd around you like ants and dry up the
roots of your growth in God, beware!

Beware of evil thoughts, which will wound your mind and sicken your
soul, beware! [*Lauda* VI, entire]

The constant repetition of the rhymes at such short intervals lends
added force to the one word "beware" and is reminiscent of the Latin

technique of the Goliardic poets. For example, the drinking song, "In taberna quando sumus," ends up with a long rollicking list of rhymed Rabelaisianisms: "Bibit hera, bibit herus, / Bibit miles, bibit clerus. . . . etc."[62] Jacopone was fully aware that he was stealing the rhymes of the taverns for the purposes of the street preacher. It suited his realistic bent and his style. Into the familiar theme of the five senses, which were such a trial to him, he pours the passion of his exhortation in such a condensed form that he tortures the syntax to squeeze the thoughts into the lines. The stanza on the family harks back to his troubles with his brother, and that on many friends seems to have a contemporary message—a warning to those alienated souls who seeking company in their misery, join humanist encounter groups to find only a transitory balm. This poem is a good example to explain why Jacopone's work has been thought difficult, since almost every line requires a gloss in order to be understandable in modern Italian. Yet in his own time he could be easily understood, and the very condensation of his thought gave it a racy urgency.

Two other *laude* develop the same didactic theme. The first, *Lauda* IX, "O frate mio, briga de tornare [O my brother, hasten to repent]," develops into a friendly dialogue, the one brother urging a turning from the world, and the other, clinging to the impediments to the development of his soul. The second, *Lauda* XVIII, "Omo, tu se' engannato [Man, you are deceived]," is an address to a man blinded by the desire to build up an estate, ending with the reminder that "you can't take it with you."

The first stage of the journey of Jacopone's soul was drawing to a close. He was beginning to be drawn up from the depths of despair and to see the hope that was to come to him in the second stage. In an objective and analytical *lauda*, he describes the five ways in which God appears to man:

> En cinque modi appareme - lo Signor en esta vita;
> altissima salita - chi nel quinto è entrato.
> Lo primo modo chiamolo - stato timoroso,
> lo secondo pareme - amor medecaroso. . . .
> Nel primo modo appareme - nell'alma Dio Signore;
> da morte suscitandola - per lo suo gran valore
> fuga la demonia - che me tenean 'n errore,
> contrizion de cuore - l'amor ci ha visitato.
>
> Poi vien como medico - ne l'alma suscitata,
> confortala e aiutala, - chè sta sì vulnerata;
> le sacramenta ponece - che l'hanno resanata,
> chè l'ha cusì curata - lo medico ammirato.

The Lord appears to me in five ways in this life; who has entered into the fifth has climbed the highest peak. I call the first, the timorous stage; the second seems to me to be the medicine of love. . . . The Lord appears in my soul in the first way; he revives it from death and through his great power makes the demons flee that have held me in error; love fills my heart with contrition. Then he comes as a doctor to the revived soul, comforts and helps it, since it is so wounded, offers it the sacraments which have healed it. Thus the beloved doctor has cured it. [*Lauda* XLV, lines 1–4, 7–14]

Such an abstract analysis, which has little poetic passion, might indeed appear to be the mere mouthing of accepted descriptions of the growth of the spiritual life. This interpretation is especially likely when it is realized that Jacopone's ideas follow a typical Franciscan pattern. In the beginning Francis "began to despise himself and to hold in some contempt the things he had admired and loved before. But not fully or truly, for he was not yet freed from the cords of vanity nor had he shaken off from his neck the yoke of evil servitude. . . . Praying, he always prayed with a torrent of tears, that the Lord would deliver him from the hands of those who were persecuting his soul, and that he would fulfill his pious wishes in his lovingkindness; in fasting and weeping he begged for the clemency of the Savior, and distrusting his own efforts, he cast his whole care on the Lord." Then Francis progressed to the second stage: "And though he was in the pit and in darkness, he was nevertheless filled with a certain exquisite joy of which till then he had had no experience; and catching fire therefrom, he left the pit. . . ."[63]

Francis's experience was confirmed in Jacopone's day by the saintly Franciscan, Giovanni de la Verna, who is the only man definitely known to be a friend of Jacopone's. Giovanni wrote:

> The first stage through which the soul passes begins in tears, in grief over one's sins, in compassion for one's neighbor [thus the didactic urge], in the compassion of Christ, and in the bewailing of one's sin. The second exists in the fervor and ardor for the love of God with all one's strength; and this purges all the roaring of the soul, which took place and continues to be heard; and it is full of turmoil and of labor.[64]

That Jacopone actually followed the route that Francis had traveled and on which Giovanni was embarked together with him, is indicated by two considerations; at least one of these will be convincing. The first is that the voyage of the soul to God is in all times and places much as they all describe it. A universal experience was expressed in thirteenth-century intellectual categories and orthodox Catholic symbolism, and those who have shared the experience even fitfully in different ages and different faiths have no difficulty in recognizing its validity. Such a consideration is convincing to few, for as Jesus said, "straight is the gate, and narrow is the way, which leadeth unto life, and few there be that find it" (Matthew

7:14). The many are inclined to think of the grace of God either as a form of self-hypnosis or a special magical gift bestowed upon the fortunate few but not upon them, rather than a course of action without prerequisites, like piano lessons only harder. The second consideration will be convincing to the many as well as to the few. This point is that Jacopone captured in genuine poetry the moment of transition between the first and second stage. In *Lauda* XX he begins in the depths of the gloom to which he and we have become so accustomed:

> O me lasso, dolente - ca lo tempo passato
> male l'ho usato - en ver' lo Creatore.

> O weary, grieving me, for I have spent my past life so badly towards the Creator. [*Incipit*]

He rehearses all the habits of his past life from which he is trying to free himself. Then he sees the light at the end of the tunnel:

> La vita non me basta - a farne penetenza
> chè la morte m'adasta - a darne la sentenza;
> se tu, Vergine casta, - non acatte indulgenza,
> l'anema mia en perdenza - girà senza tenore.

> Regina encoronata, - mamma del dolce figlio,
> tu se' nostra advocata; - veramente assimiglio
> per le nostre peccata - che non giamo en esilio;
> manda lo tuo consiglio, - donna de gran valore.

> Life is not long enough for me to do penance, for death is at hand to give his sentence—if you, chaste Virgin, do not obtain indulgence so that my soul will not fall helpless into perdition.
> Crowned Queen, mother of the loving son, you are our advocate; you are truly the one to help us so that we do not go into exile for our sins. Send your counsel, lady of great worth. [Lines 27–34]

Jacopone turns to the mother image and finds in it a way to approach the more august figures of Christ and God. It is more human and closer to him from memories of early childhood. Such a way was closed to Protestants after the reformation, which reduced the Virgin to her historical size. Some have bemoaned the loss of this archetype,[65] but some Protestants have been able to find another way—identification with other worshipers, like the all-too-human Peter and Paul, on their way to identification with Jesus. But in the thirteenth century of Jacopone, the Virgin still reigned, and when he turned to her, he struck a living spring of hope:

O Regina cortese, - io so a voi venuto
ch'al mio cor feruto - deiate medecare.

Io so a voi venuto - com'omo desperato
da omne altro aiuto; - la vostro m'è lassato;
se ne fusse privato, - farieme consumare.

O gracious Queen, I have come to you that you might heal my wounded
heart. I have come to you as a man who has despaired of all other help; only
yours is left to me; if I were deprived of this, I would be burned. [*Lauda* I,
lines 1–5]

He casts the Virgin in the role of a doctor, a role that was outlined in *Lauda*
XLV, and appeals to the same love that she felt for her son. She answers,
and the fact of her answering is in itself an indication that there is hope
and that the second stage is arriving. The Virgin gives him his medicine
and tells how it will cure him—again the symbol of the body is used to
portray the progress of the soul:

E piglia decozione - lo temor de lo 'nferno;
pens'en quella prescione - non escon en sempiterno;
la piaga girà rompenno - fallarate arvontare.

Denante al preite mio - questo venen arvonta,
chè l'officio è sio, - Dio lo peccato sconta;
ca se 'l Nemico s'aponta, - non aia que mostrare.

And take this decoction, the fear of hell; think of that prison from which
you will never escape; the ulcer will break and make you vomit.
Throw up this poison in front of my priest, for it is his office to discount
sin before God; and if the Enemy opposes, he will have nothing to bring
against you. [Lines 27–32]

Notice that the priest as the intermediary performing the sacraments is
accepted as a matter of course by Jacopone; he was not to deviate from
this orthodoxy during the whole of his long journey.

Yet a far more important intermediary is Christ himself. Even in the
thrall of his worst depression, he turns lovingly to Christ. In *Lauda* XXVII,
he begs for help: "Amor diletto, - Cristo beato / de me desolato - agge
pietanza [Beloved love, blessed Christ, have pity on my desolation],"
(*Incipit*). He longs for the abundance of Christ within himself to root out
his propensities for evil, and even indicates that there is some hope.
Similarly, in *Lauda* XLII, he prays for guidance: " 'Nsegnatime Iesù
Cristo [Teach me, Jesus Christ]," (*Incipit*). This poem develops into a
direct dialogue between Jacopone's soul and Christ; Jacopone is striving

for union with Christ—even unto the death on the cross[66]—and remains in the position of a humble and inadequate penitent. And there is not much hope, for Christ is demanding, giving his teaching like a firm and still somewhat remote master.

Christ appears to Jacopone again as a teacher in *Lauda* XL, another dialogue. Here, however, the dialogue takes place between a questioning angel and Christ and serves to explore the miracle of incarnation as Christ explains the reasons why he came into the world of men. He came as a mediator between God and man, to bring peace between them so that man will be consoled in his subjection to God. The angel, being a realist, points out how thoroughly impractical Christ's venture is, but he persists. He is the "school of life" and in his school Jacopone can find hope.

Hope dimly appears as Jacopone perceives in Christ the element of love, an element that was to grow in strength and majesty until it completely absorbed the soul of the poet. At this stage the love is there in Christ, but Jacopone does not yet really believe that it can extend to him. In *Lauda* XXVI, Christ speaks:

> Omo, de te me lamento - che me vai pur fuggendo
> ed io te voglio salvare.
> Omo, per te salvare - e per menare a la via,
> carne sì volse piglare - de la Vergine Maria. . . .
> Como om ch'ama lo figlio - quel è mal enviato,
> menacciagli e da consiglio - che da mal sia mendato,
> de lo 'nferno t'ho menacciato - e gloria t'ho empromessa
> se a me te voi tornare.
> . . .e co stai sì endurato - ch'a tanto amor non t'encline?
> frate, or pone ormai fine - a questa tua sconoscenza,
> chè tanto m'hai fatto penare!

O man, I grieve over you that you still flee from me, though I want to serve you. Man, to save you and to lead you to the way, I wished to put on flesh from the Virgin Mary. . . .

As a man who loves his son who has fallen on an evil path, threatens him and counsels him that he amend his evil ways; so I have threatened you with hell and promised you glory if you wish to turn to me.

. . . How is it that you are so obdurate that you do not give in to so much love? Brother, finally put an end right now to this indifference of yours which has given me so much pain! [Lines 1–4, 15–18, 28–30]

Christ ends his exhortation with the statement that he condemns Jacopone against his will, since he loves him so much, but condemn him he does. The medicine of the second stage is just beginning to work, and the cure seems to Jacopone to be still far off.

In this poem it is noticeable that Jacopone refers to himself as "brother." Such a term could have merely a generic meaning, for Jacopone frequently uses the word as an ordinary friendly salutation. It could also mean that he was a friar. In 1278, he joined the Franciscan order, probably at San Fortunato in Todi.

Jacopone would have naturally turned to San Fortunato, because the church was only a few blocks from his home and the Franciscans were by far the most active Christians in Todi. The movement had been brought there in the first flush of its vigor by Ruggiero, who had been provincial of the Marches in 1220 and later served in the same capacity in the Duchy of Spoleto, including Todi, until his death in 1236. The year before, he had founded the first friary at Todi, which like most early Franciscan establishments must have been an extremely humble place. As at Paris, London, and elsewhere, it was outside the walls in a small chapel called Sant' Arcangelo. In the same year, two communities of nuns of the Second Order were gathered: Santa Maria Maddalena and Monte Santo. Both of these were also outside the walls and no doubt also very humble, for none of them have survived.

But such a stage of apostolic poverty was not to last. Aided by the various bishops and popes, the Franciscans rapidly grew, moved into town, and pushed aside the now decadent Benedictines. In 1254, the community of Sant' Arcangelo traded houses with the rich Vallombrosian abbey of San Fortunato in the heart of the thriving town. The friars moved into the eleventh-century church, which was later replaced with the present Gothic structure, and were granted the very considerable revenues attached to it. The few remaining monks inherited the apostolic poverty of Sant' Arcangelo. Despite the fact that the whole transaction had been ratified by Alexander IV, friction and legal action developed because the Franciscans were loath to grant the monks even the crumbs from the table. Papal favor not only encouraged the material wealth of the house but also made it virtually independent of the bishop and even of papal legates. The friars had the right to appeal directly to the curia in the event of any contention.[67]

Though Jacopone found that turning to the Franciscans was a natural move, he was certainly disturbed by their wealth and power. A later story illustrates the satirical mood in which he approached the order. When he presented himself, the brothers are said to have told him: "If you wish to live with us, you must become a donkey; so even as a donkey, you may dwell among donkeys." Jacopone went away and came back wearing a pack saddle, telling them: "Brothers, see I have become a donkey. So admit the donkey to live among donkeys."[68]

The more sober account found in the *Franceschina* reflects the same contrast between the sensible and even worldly friars and the individualistic Jacopone:

Having thought to follow a more secure way, he was inspired to enter into the order of the Brothers Minor, as separated from and disdainful of the world and attached to the way and life of Christ and the apostles. Before the brothers would invest him with the habit, they tested him in various ways, thinking that he might be mad. . . . Eventually convinced, they gave him the habit and the name of Brother Jacopone. The latter, though he was a learned man, never wished to have any other station than that of a simple and humble layman, and in this state he persevered until the end of his life.[69]

Jacopone wanted to be a certain kind of friar.

IV ∞ *The Perfect Brother*

Jacopone set out to become a perfect brother, and he succeeded. After his death, he was called by the Spanish Franciscan Alvarez de Pelayo "frater Jacobus Benedicti Tuderti, frater minor perfectus."[1] By that time the term "perfect" had come to identify a member of the spiritual party within the order, but in 1278 the lines of conflict were just beginning to be drawn between the spirituals with their insistence on hewing to the letter of the Rule of 1223 and the Testament of Francis, and the conventuals pressing to relax the Rule to conform to the needs of the church and the human limitations of ordinary men. Like the other spirituals, Jacopone threw himself into the rigors of the Franciscan life with the same intense devotion that he expressed in his poetry.

> When he was clothed with the habit of St. Francis, not only did he make himself known as a strict observer of all the Rule with the most perfect obedience to his superiors and even to all the brothers, but he also became enamoured of holy poverty, wishing to clothe himself only in the most wretched and torn habits in the friary and never wearing sandals on his feet. Later, as though he had never done any penance up to that time, he went about with great fervor to maltreat and mortify his body with frequent fasts of bread and water mixed with wormwood, to do all the meanest jobs in the friary, to flagellate himself every day severely until the blood came, and to pass the whole night in fervent prayer. . . .[2]

With such an extreme interpretation of the Franciscan life, it must have been difficult for Jacopone to adjust to the requirements of conventual living. The freedom of the *bizocone* was gone forever, and he could no longer take refuge in the status of madman to whom everything was allowed. Such freedom had long been looked upon with concern by the church, ever fearful of disorderliness and heresy, and in 1298 Boniface VIII, most conscious of hierarchical discipline, prohibited the *bizocone* from wearing a special habit and ruled that they must associate themselves with some religious order. In the broad historical perspective, it can be seen that the Franciscan movement fulfilled the goal of channelizing many of the aspirations of the most divergent individualists into the accepted forms of the established church.[3] Jacopone became a member of the establishment—a friar.

But not a priest. Like most of the early followers of Francis, he remained a layman, unwilling in his humility to accept the status and responsibilities of the priesthood. Even Francis permitted himself only the rank of deacon, and no minister general of the order was a priest until the election of Alberto da Pisa in 1239. But by the time of Jacopone's entrance into the order, the priestly and learned element had taken over virtually complete control and filled all the higher offices.[4] Thus, Jacopone's adherence to the lay status represented in itself his determination to recapture the simplicity and fervor of the heroic days of the *poverello*.

Clearly, living the Franciscan life did not immediately change Jacopone's spiritual state, for he brought into the order all the guilt and fear with which his soul was tortured. He had a lot more crying to do before ridding himself of the hang-ups of his early life, and as he grew older, the attractions of food grew in importance as an expression of the demands of the body. A particularly graphic story in the *Franceschina* illustrates both the extreme penance of Jacopone and the difficulties of the brothers in living with him:

> Once this blessed man was tempted with gluttony, that is, to eat a *corada* [the pluck of a lamb]. He wished as a true fighter against vices to keep to the way of moderation, that is, to satisfy both the body and the soul. And so he got a *corada* and hung it up on a nail in the cell where he slept. In the morning when it was time to eat, he went up and looked at the *corada* for a spell, put a bit of it on his face, and then went about his business, that is, to go to the refectory with the other brothers to eat bread and drink water according to his habit. So persevering he did the same every day . . . until it began to be full of vermin and stink, and Fra Jacopone visited it with much more consolation than at first. Hence not only was the cell full of that horrible and intolerable stink, but also, by God, the whole dormitory and all the place around. . . . So the brothers began to smell that terrible stink . . . but did not know where it came from. . . . A few of the brothers began to think that this stink was more around Fra Jacopone's cell than elsewhere, and so they began to suspect that Fra Jacopone had done another one of his usual fantastic tricks, since the brothers considered him unbalanced because of his contempt of himself. . . . Finally the brothers opened the cell and found that *corada*, all rotten and full of worms and giving off such a stink that they couldn't go in, but Fra Jacopone smelled it like a specially pleasant aroma. Then the brothers took hold of Fra Jacopone very roughly and for penance put him in the latrine . . . saying: "If you like the stink so much . . . you can have as much as you want." Then Fra Jacopone acted

with as much joy as though he were a well-famished gourmet placed in front of a table laden with the most appetizing delicacies, and stood in there jubilantly singing at the top of his voice that beautiful lauda which begins: "O iubilo del core, - che fai cantar d'amore! O joy of the heart, which makes me sing of love!"[5]

This story was thought so horrible by Underhill that she did not translate it,[6] but it shows Jacopone acting out, as did Francis, the drives of his inner life. Despite his Gothic exaggeration, Jacopone was closer to Francis than the learned scholastics versed in the intricacies of abstract philosophy, for both thought in terms of symbols and parables and not in terms of rules and deductive logic.[7]

The new status of friar imposed on Jacopone new problems, for though Jacopone accepted wholeheartedly the Franciscan precept "sint minores [may they be lowly]" and followed to the letter the injunction to mix on a basis of equality with the dregs of society, he was still a somebody, a friar. It must have been hard for him to accept any status that might set him apart and above the most humble man. In a broader sense any one who embarks on a religious path faces the temptation to think of himself as somehow better than his fellows. Jacopone expressed his struggle with the problem in *Lauda* XLVII, a dialogue between him and the Devil, in which the latter weaves a complicated set of arguments to entrap the poet, continually shifting his ground like an expert dialectician. The opening boldly sets forth the conflict:

> Or udite la battaglia - che me fa el falso Nemico,
> e serave utilitate - se ascoltàti quel ch'io dico.
> Lo Nemico sì mi mette - sutilissima battaglia,
> con quel venco sì m'aferra, - sì sa metter sua travaglia.
> Lo Nemico sì mi dice: - "Frate, frate, tu se' santo;
> grande fame e nomenanza - del tuo nome è en omne canto.
> Tanti beni Dio t'ha fatti - per novello e per antico,
> non gli t'averia mai fatti - se nogl fossi caro amico.
> Per ragione te demostro - che te pòi molto alegrare,
> l'arra n'hai del paradiso - non te pòi mai dubitare."
> "O Nemico engannatore, - como c'entri per falsìa!
> fusti fatto glorioso - en quella gran compagnia.
> Molti beni Dio te fece - se gli avessi conservate;
> appetito sciordenato - su del ciel t'ha trabocate.
> Tu diavol senza carne, - ed io demone encarnato,
> c'agio offes'el mio Signore, - non so el numer del peccato.

Now listen to the battle which the false Enemy made against me and it will be useful to you to listen to what I say. The Enemy brought against me such a most subtle attack. With what astuteness he seized me! So well does he know his business.

The Enemy said thus: "Brother, brother, you are a saint; you have great
fame and acclaim; your name is praised with song on all sides. God has
given you so many blessings both early and late; he would never have done
this if he were not your dear friend. Thus I prove to you by reason that you
can be very happy; you have your place in heaven; you can never doubt it."

"O deluding Enemy, how much falseness is in your argument! You were
made glorious in that great company of angels. God gave you many blessings, if you had known how to keep them, but your boundless appetite cast
you down from heaven. You are a devil without flesh and I, a devil
incarnate, for I have offended my Lord and do not know the number of my
sins." [Lines 1–16]

The Enemy is not put off at all by such a vigorous counterattack on the
part of Jacopone, but comes back at him again and again. Each time he
changes his ground, and each time Jacopone takes the exact opposite
ground. A perfectly logical counterpoint develops. First the Enemy
agrees with Jacopone by saying that surely he will be damned because he
has sinned many times while Satan himself only sinned once; Jacopone
answers that he has faith in God, whose goodness has led him to love
Him and whose justice will save him. Then the Enemy becomes God's
advocate and urges Jacopone to free himself from the needs of his body;
Jacopone answers that he must take care of his body in order better to
serve God. Continuing as God's advocate, the Enemy reproaches him for
not caring for the poor; the answer: if Jacopone were totally immersed in
this work, he would lose his life of contemplation. So be a contemplative,
go into the desert and be silent, urges the Enemy; but Jacopone counters
that it is wrong to be silent when one should speak out for the glory of
God. Taking him up on this, the Enemy says that his preaching is
vainglorious, but Jacopone insists that his secret prayer must become a
spoken prayer for the edification of others. In sum, it can be seen that the
poet has explored the dark side of each of his behavioral patterns and
then brought the bright side to bear on it.

This is indeed one of Jacopone's difficult poems, for each antagonist's
ground changes with startling rapidity. Each cues the other into a switch.
Such a logical complexity results that it becomes increasingly difficult to
realize which antagonist is speaking, and the thought twists about as it
does in the divine poems of John Donne. Certainly Jacopone's legal mind
shows through as he analyzes the problems of a religious man, and the
dialectical structure of the poem follows the intellectual patterns of his
time.

In the end the Enemy admits he is beaten:

"Frate, frate, haime vento; - non te saccio più que dire;
veramente tu se' santo, - sì te sai da me coprire! . . ."
"Se en tuo ditto me fidasse, - più sirìa che pazo e stolto
chè da onne veritate - sì se delongato molto. . . ."

"Brother, brother, you have defeated me; I know no more what to say to you; truly you are a saint for you know how to defend yourself so well against me! . . ."

"If I had any faith in your words, I would be more than mad and stupid, since you are so far from all truth. . . ." [Lines 89–90, 98–99]

This admission of defeat is, of course, the greatest lie of all, for the Enemy is never beaten, especially by mere reason. Jacopone ends like a warrior with his shield in place: "Or te guarda, anima mia! [Watch out, my soul!]"

In looking about him at the lives of his fellow religious, Jacopone began to see the limitations of the asceticism that had been such a strong element in the first stage of his spiritual growth. External practices were in themselves not enough. He joined the spirituals in pointing out that merely being poor, chaste, and obedient missed the whole point of the spiritual life and that it was imperative to seek after perfection in the inner life by following the spirit of the Gospels and the Rule. Jacopone states the case dramatically in a dialogue with a dead nun, whom he addresses: "Che fai, anema predata? [What are you doing, harried soul?]," (*Lauda* XVI, *incipit*). She answers that she has been damned, leading him to despair of his own salvation, "pensando la perfezione de la vita tua ch'è stata [thinking of the perfection of your past life]." She rehearses her life, saying that she was a virgin, never looking at a man, that she was silent for thirty years, though other nuns spoke (one can imagine the pursed lips), that she fasted and wore ragged clothes for fifty years.

"Sostenetti povertate, - freddi, caldi, e nuditate;
non avi l'umilitate, - però da Dio fui reprovata. . . .
    Quando udìa chiamar la santa, - lo mio cor superbia enalta;
or so menata a la malta - con la gente desperata."

"I underwent poverty, cold, heat, and nudity, but I did not have humility and so I was punished by God. . . . When I heard myself called the saint, my proud heart was lifted up, and so I was led off to prison with the hopeless folk." [Lines 20–21, 24–25]

From the Montanists of the third century to the environmentalists of today, it is hard to imagine a person more superior than the outraged ascetic. Jacopone takes the lesson to heart and despairs again for his fate, but the nun tells him not to give up hope. He must never attribute to his own honor what belongs to God. This is the universal message of humility for all the ages.

In the Franciscan atmosphere around Jacopone the virtue of humility was expressed through voluntary and complete poverty. Even if Todi had not been, as it was, both the site of several Franciscan houses and close to the very center of Franciscan traditions, Jacopone, the reformed notary who had given away all his earthly wealth, would have been attracted to the order by the ideal of apostolic poverty. This teaching was the central innovation of the whole movement, one of the few of Francis's teachings on which he was never willing to compromise the counsels of perfection. The mystical marriage of the saint to Lady Poverty, described in one of the earliest Franciscan writings and pictured by Giotto in the Lower Church of Assisi,[8] reflected a truly prophetic vision: the acquisitive spirit was the greatest danger to the Christian life. In Francis's lifetime the acquisitive society was just being born, but, as every one knows, it was to grow in the ever more wealthy communes and in the rising bourgeoisie to engulf the life of the modern world. Francis set his face firmly against the entire property-holding mentality.

Drawing upon his naïve understanding of the poverty of the apostles pictured in the Gospels, Francis urged that the brothers were not "to appropriate to themselves" anything whatsoever, and the provision was included in the Rule of 1223 and confirmed in the Testament.[9] However, Francis was a poor maker of rules and rather taught by the parables of his actions. Here the message was illustrated again and again: in his abandonment of all his inheritance, in his going naked to symbolize his complete poverty, in his horror at even touching money, in his moving with his followers out of an abandoned barn when a peasant and his animal came to take it over, in his provision that the poor little chapel of the Portiuncula, which he had rebuilt and where he had spent so many years in prayer, should remain the property of the Benedictines, in his horror at the friars having a house of study in Bologna and his reluctantly accepting the situation when Cardinal Ugolino, the protector of the order, said he owned it, in his moving out of a cell when a brother had inadvertently called it Francis's cell.[10] Brother Giles, one of Francis's close associates, said that the saint did not like ants because they stored up food for the future, but liked birds who did not hoard and were as free as the air.[11] However, Francis approved of the work habits of ants, and so counseled the friars to work at odd jobs to support themselves, and failing that, to beg. Disregarding the dietary rules of other orders, they were to eat what was put in front of them. The essential point was that whatever was necessary for the basic needs of maintaining life was to come from haphazard and occasional sources; a friar living on a secure income was a contradiction in terms. The same life was enthusiastically espoused by women. When Clare founded the Second Order in the chapel of St. Damian at Assisi, the little community came close to real starvation, not being allowed to beg. Though she was in ill health for the last thirty years of her life, Clare never accepted any special treatment.

Francis allowed his order only one piece of property, the site of the cells near the summit of Mt. Alverna; no doubt he accepted the gift of this property because it was a wilderness for which no one else had any use. When death approached, the saint, fearing that his order would be led to compromise with the ways of the world, urged in his *Testament* that the friars, wherever they lived or stayed, were to remain "wayfarers and pilgrims."[12]

As a Franciscan historian sadly remarked: "In the progressive weakening of his ideal, poverty was the first and principal victim."[13] The process of erosion had begun already during the lifetime of the saint, for the great crowds who flocked into the order required organization and some more regular means of support. Francis knew that he was not cut out for this job, and so at the general chapter of 1221, he turned over the affairs of the order to a minister general—first Peter Catani, who soon died, and then Elias of Cortona. Saying: "Henceforth, I am dead to you,"[14] he lived out his life with the humble companions of the early days, largely cut off from the administration of the order.

Though there is no sure evidence that Francis was in any way forced to condone the relaxation of the order or that he had anything but respect for that great organizer, Elias of Cortona,[15] the fact remains that this relaxation did take place with extraordinary rapidity and has been primarily associated with the generalship of Elias, the Judas of Franciscan history. Elias's faults—and he had many—made him a convenient scapegoat, but in sober fact he merely represented more important forces at work. Describing the nascent conflict in the order, a recent historian wrote: "For one group, the requirements of the apostolate were so important that it was felt that they should condition the observance of poverty; for the other, the observance of a certain standard of poverty was the overriding necessity, which, it was thought, should determine the forms of the apostolate."[16] In such a conflict, it was obvious that the papacy would support the first group, and it was natural that the friars should turn to the pope for guidance, especially in 1230 when the throne was occupied by Gregory IX, the same Cardinal Ugolino who had been protector of the order since almost the beginning and a close associate of the saint. His bull, "Quo Elongati," and the bulls of Innocent IV, "Ordinum Vestrum" of 1245 and "Quanto Studiosus" of 1247, effectively regularized in canon law the procedures by which the Franciscans were becoming rich from the gifts of pious admirers..

Even the two greatest ministers general that the order ever had, Giovanni da Parma and Bonaventure, from 1248 to 1274, were unable to stem the tide of wealth. Bonaventure, in defending the order against its external enemies and guiding his fellow friars, produced the classic statement on Franciscan poverty, forbidding "proprietas," the ownership of property, but allowing "usufructus," the enjoyment of a moderate income from property. But he repeatedly found that he could not curb the drive of a minority of friars to manage property and to live comfortably. The latter became the core of the conventual party. In 1272, shortly before his death, "he grieved so bitterly over the general laxity of this time," reported Pierre de Jean Olivi, "that at Paris in the full chapter, at which I was present, he said that since he had become general, he had perpetually longed to be ground to powder, that the order might be brought back into the purity and intention of the blessed Francis and his companions."[17]

The Bonaventuran interpretation of Franciscan poverty was elevated to the status of accepted doctrine by Nicolas III's bull, "Exiit qui Seminat" of 1279. The pope, who had been cardinal protector of the order for nearly twenty years and was thus well acquainted with the issues, appointed a commission of experts to draw up the bull; the latter included such disparate personalities as, among others, Jacopone's fellow townsman, Benedetto Gaetani, to whose keen legal mind were attributed some of the subtleties of the work, Cardinal Bentivenga d'Acquasparta, an associate of Jacopone at San Fortunato, the former minister general Geronimo d'Ascoli, and Olivi, the patron saint of the spirituals.

During all this period, the spiritual party was in gestation; a considerable number of humble friars had kept alive the ideal of poverty and were living out their lives in the remote hermitages of Umbria, Tuscany, and the Marches. Some of the early companions of Francis survived well into the second half of the century. There was, above all, Leo, who until 1271 led a life of utter simplicity in the small friary at Greccio and was frequently visited by those who wished to hear firsthand accounts of the saint, evoked in a flood of adoration out of the mists of memory. There was Ruffino, who also lived till 1271, at the Portiuncula in Assisi. There was Giles, "homo idiota et simplex,"[18] perhaps even illiterate, who lived at Cibbotola near Chiusi and whose sayings were taken down by loving companions. There was Angelo who was with Clare on her deathbed in 1253, when she wrested from the reluctant Innocent IV the promise that the absolute poverty of her Damianites would be preserved.

Such simple men passed on their concept of Francis to a second generation of holy men. Corrado d'Offida collected the early stories in his hermitage near Iesi until his death in 1306,[19] and his stories were an inspiration to Angelo Clareno and Fra Liberato, the leaders of the spiritual party. The retired minister general, Giovanni da Parma, lived peacefully at Mt. Alverna until 1279 and was one of those who set Ubertino da Casale on the road to being the principal preacher and polemicist of the spirituals. Also at Mt. Alverna was Giovanni de la Verna, the friend of Jacopone who died in 1322.

How close Jacopone was to all these men is impossible to determine in the absence of firm historical evidence. However, there can be no doubt that the stories which they told of the poverty and simplicity of Francis circulated widely in the homeland of the saint, for they formed the basis of the rich vein of Franciscan lore set down in the next century—the *Legend of St. Francis by the Three Companions*, the *Mirror of Perfection*, and the incomparable *Fioretti*.[20]

By the time Jacopone was becoming prominent in the order, the lines of battle between the spirituals and the conventuals had become much more clearly defined than in the days of Elias. As with many a war, it is easier from a distance to understand the reasons for the conflict than the passions and brutality connected with it. It was Olivi who first defined the program of the spirituals. After serving on the papal commission for "Exiit qui Seminat," Olivi went back to his native Provence and turned out a flood of scholastic writings—Ubertino said his works filled seventeen volumes of the size of Peter Lombard's *Sentences*.[21] While accepting the provisions of this bull, Olivi insisted on the concept of the "usus pauper," i.e., that the friars should enjoy income only sufficient to cover the bare necessities of existence. And he was very specific about what such necessities involved and what they excluded. Olivi came to Florence as *lector* at the *studium* in 1287 and became a formative influence over Ubertino. The latter shared his stand completely and after Olivi's return to Provence, continued to preach the spiritual doctrine, first in Florence, where he was probably heard by Dante, and later in Perugia. When he finally came to set his thoughts down in the *Arbor Vitae* of 1305, it was in the spirit of a rigid sectarian.[22]

In the meantime, the conventuals had been continuing to erode the doctrine of poverty. Martin IV's bull, "Exultantes in Domino" of 1283, permitted the order to manage properties, which they technically did not own, through proctors who had complete power of attorney under the direct supervision of the friars. It "destroyed the whole idea of Franciscan poverty."[23] The most forthright expression of wealth was the building of many new churches. Already the great church at Assisi, a creation of Elias, could be seen by the spirituals only as a monstrous distortion of the Franciscan ideal. Between 1289 and 1305, a wave of building, based on the boom conditions of the economy, struck the order, and great churches, which are still the pride of their respective cities, were begun at Pisa, Parma, Florence, Mantua, Siena, and even Todi. Another expression of wealth was the founding of libraries, stocked with expensive books in centers of learning like Paris, Padua, Bologna, Florence, Siena, and Assisi. The personal habits of a few friars served to project blatantly the image of wealth and reflected the fact that they were fully sharing in the general rise of the standard of living. They rode on horseback like nobles; they wore flowing gowns of fine wool with fashionably wide cowls. Some managed to secure individual incomes despite the Rule, and some went about begging, accompanied by young boys delegated to handle the money—a hypocritical mockery of Francis's injunction not to touch the filthy stuff. Chapters general repeatedly relaxed the Rule, and enforcement was lax.

Merely by looking about him in Todi, Jacopone could see on every hand the decadence of the Franciscan ideal of poverty. The brothers had merely stepped into the shoes of the Benedictines. His own house of San Fortunato was one of the largest property holders in the town and defended its rights against both commune and bishop with dogged persistence. With papal backing it successfully resisted all attempts to levy taxation on its lands. The nuns of the Todian monastery of St. Francis received a special dispensation from Alexander IV in 1258 to accept pious donations of property; they needed the gifts, for theirs was a new foundation dating from only 1251. The case was different with the sisters of Monte Santo, who as early as 1236 had taken over the ancient Benedictine Abbey of San Leucio on the very acropolis of Todi, the present-day Rocca. San Leucio's holdings were enormous. An inventory of the properties passing over to the sisters, ordered by Gregory IX and carried out between 1244 and 1251, shows 59 tracts of land, 36 townhouses in the best quarter, and a mill. Aided by the popes, the sisters were able to prevent the commune from taxing the mill. They even overcharged for their services, and a sharp and extended litigation took place with the commune over the milling fees—a conflict that was resolved, in their favor, only after Alexander IV threatened in 1259 to put the commune under an interdict. The records of Todi during the last half of the century are replete with contracts and litigation concerning Franciscan property. So much for Francis's injunction never to go to law in matters of property.

Under the laws of the commune, the gifts that Franciscans received from thieves and usurers in return for absolution were limited to the value of one hundred ounces of gold. Whether or not the friars forced the penitents to restore the stolen money is not known, but it is known that the order had to pass regulations insisting that they do so.[24] There are so many records left of Franciscan dealings in property that one gains the impression they were concerned with little else—a false impression, since records relating to property holding are more likely to survive. Nonetheless, it is abundantly clear that with some notable exceptions, the bourgeoisie merely took their acquisitive instincts with them when they entered the order. This development is what all the complicated arguments on Franciscan poverty were all about.

One would expect that Jacopone would have wielded his pen mightily on the side of the spirituals in the controversy over poverty, and so he would have done if he had still been in the penitential period of his spiritual development. At that time he was severe in his condemnation of greed, thinking of life as an eternal conflict between vice and virtue (*Laude* XIII, XIV, and XLIII). But he had changed. Now he accepted poverty joyfully with the same grateful adoration that Francis expressed toward nature in the *Canticle of the Sun*. In *Lauda* LIX, he salutes "Povertade enamorata, - grand'è la tua signoria [Beloved poverty, great is your dominion]." Poverty speaks and claims as her own all the lands and peoples of the earth, listing them in a tumbling succession unto "de là del mar gente infiniti - che non saccio là 've stia [the infinite peoples so far across the sea that I don't know where they are]." She continues in rollicking rhymes to lay claim to all the wealth of creation:

> Le terre ho dato a lavoranno, - a li vassali a coltivanno,
> gli frutti donon en anno en anno, - tant'è la mia cortesia.
> Terra, erbe con lor colori, - arbori e frutti con sapori,
> bestie miei servitori, - tutte en mia belfolcarìa.
> Acque, fiumi, lachi e mare, - pescetegli en lor notare,
> aere, venti, ucel volare, - tutti me fonno giollarìa.
> Luna, sole, cielo e stelle - fra miei tesori non son covelle
> de sopra cielo sì ston quelle - che tengon la mia melodia.

> I have given the land out to be worked, for the vassals to cultivate; I give the fruits from year to year, so great is my generosity. Lands, grains with all their different colors, trees with their tasty fruits, the beasts, my servants—all are in my charge. Brooks, streams, lakes and seas, little fishes in their swimming, breezes, winds, and flying birds—all sing my praises. Moon, sun, sky, and stars are not the least of my treasures, and beyond the sky are those who dance to my tune. [Lines 16–23]

How can Jacopone have come to such a conclusion—the great paradox that wealth and poverty, the two extremes, are one in the joy of God? His final couplet gives the answer:

> Poi el mio voler a Dio è dato, - possessor so d'onne stato,
> en lor amor so trasformato, - ennamorata cortesia.

> For my will has been given to God; I am the possessor of every state; I have been transformed in their love—everloving kindness. [Lines 26–27]

He has come to the same conclusion that Paul did, when he wrote to his beloved Philippians: "I know . . . how . . . both to abound and to suffer need. I can do all things through Christ which strengtheneth me" (Philippians 4:12–13). It is highly unlikely, however, that Jacopone gained this revelation directly from Paul; for as we shall see, his vision grew out of his own spiritual experience, each stage of which he has documented.

Jacopone's second hymn to poverty, *Lauda* LX, carries out the same theme in greater detail and with philosophical overtones. It begins with a declaration of the utter peace to be found in poverty—the peace that Jesus proclaimed in the Sermon on the Mount, when he counseled to take no thought for food or drink or clothes, "for your heavenly Father knoweth that ye have need of all these things" (Matthew 6:24–34).

> O amor de povertate, - regno de tranquillitate!
> Povertate, via secura, - non ha lite nè rancura,
> de latron non ha paura - nè da nulla tempestate.

> O love of poverty, reign of peace! Poverty, the sure way, has neither conflict nor hate, fears no robber nor any storm. [Lines 1–3]

Poverty doesn't need wills or judges or notaries—items with which Jacopone had been well acquainted in his youth. Again like Jesus, Jacopone asserts that one is possessed by what one desires. Progressing to the third heaven, described by Paul, Pseudo-Dionysius, and Bonaventure, he sees that all human desires are reduced to nothingness—the love of knowledge, the fame of holiness, and even the hopes and fears for the future life have become superfluous and irrelevant. The whole human personality is engulfed in the love of God.

> Vive amore senza affetto - e saper senza entelletto,
> lo voler de Dio eletto - a far la sua voluntate.
> Viver io e non io, - e l'esser mio non esser mio,
> questo è un tal traversìo, - che non so diffinitate.
> Povertate è nulla avere - e nulla cosa poi volere;
> ed omne cosa possedere - en spirito de libertate.

> Love lives without desire, knowledge without intellect; the will chooses to do the will of God. I live and yet not I; my being is not my being; so great is this paradox that I can't define it. Poverty is to have nothing and not to wish to have anything and yet to possess everything in the spirit of liberty. [Lines 56–61]

Such a position on the issue of poverty could be of little use to the earnest reformers who were trying to bring the order back to the strict observance of Francis's teachings and were consequently involved in a quasi-Marxist social conflict. The mystic vision placed Jacopone above the conflict. Thus in the matter of poverty, though certainly not in other respects, the dictum of a recent writer is correct: "Jacopone da Todi . . . played a more secondary role in the story of the Zealots."[25] Despite the fact that Jacopone in his grasp of the state of nothingness echoes the Pauline experience, "I live; yet not I, but Christ liveth in me" (Galatians 2:20), he has been accused of taking a heretical stand in this poem. A modern Franciscan writer wishes that the poem were not authentic, as he finds it "incriminating"; and charges Jacopone with quietism, nihilism, and pantheism.[26] The poem is, of course, authentic, and though the good Franciscan's charges may be true in the abstract, the church of Jacopone's time was not so much concerned with dogmatic purity as it was with the actions resulting from thought.[27] And Jacopone was never accused of heresy.

The second element defining the position of the spirituals was their attitude toward learning. From the very beginning, attitudes toward learning were closely related to those toward poverty, and here Jacopone's position was equally individual—but even more radical than that of the spirituals. The example of Francis was neither consistent nor clear, for learning was related in an insoluble manner to both poverty and preaching. On the one hand, learning required books and leisure, which were necessarily expensive and so militated against the strict doctrine of poverty; on the other, effective preaching required learning.

Francis himself was no intellectual. Yet he was not only a great preacher but introduced into the world a new type of preaching—the simple exposition of the Gospel message brought home to everyone by homely examples. "Although the evangelist Francis preached to the unlearned people through visible and simple things, in as much as he knew that virtue is more necessary than words, nevertheless among spiritual men and men of greater capacity he spoke enlivening and profound words. He would suggest in a few words what was beyond expression, and using fervent gestures and nods, he would transport his hearers wholly to heavenly things. He did not make use of the keys of philosophical distinctions; he did not put order to his sermons, for he did not compose them ahead of time."[28] Like the Quaker George Fox he spoke extempore out of the fullness of his spiritual life, and on one occasion when he found he had nothing to say, he remained silent. The impact of his message was such that enormous crowds came to hear him, and Franciscan and Dominican preachers throughout the thirteenth century enjoyed enthusiastic popularity, partly because no other groups, and notably the parish priests, were trained to give popular sermons. The original permission to preach, granted by Innocent III, limited the Franciscans to penitential preaching; being laymen untrained in theology, they were not to preach on doctrine.

Such preaching did not require great learning. Francis even gave away the only New Testament that the friars had in order to answer to a poor woman's request for food, saying that her need was greater than theirs. The Franciscans invented the breviary as a short and inexpensive way to have the word of God on hand under all circumstances. But Francis insisted, with droll satire, that no brother should own a breviary and refused his permission for the acquisition of a beautiful and expensive book. Later on the spirituals made much of this aspect of Francis's teaching: "Francis wished his brethren not to desire knowledge and books. . . . as if he would say: 'Books and science should not be esteemed, but rather virtuous labors, since knowledge puffeth up, but charity edifyeth.'"[29]

On the other hand, Francis had a deep respect for doctors of theology and specifically called Anthony his "bishop." Now, Anthony's preaching, while no less popular than that of Francis, was both learned and doctrinal. Francis realized that such preaching was necessary both for the conversion of infidels and the refutation of heretics, and so the learned men in the order could justly claim Francis's blessing.

Thus developed one of the great paradoxes of Franciscan history: the order founded by a simple mystic became studded with the shining names of some of the greatest intellectuals of the age from Bonaventure and Robert Grosseteste to Roger Bacon and Duns Scotus. All the minister generals of the order, from Haymo of Haversham (1241) to Giovanni da Mirrovalle (1304) with only one exception, came from academic circles. Even Giovanni da Parma, the idol of the spirituals, was a *lector* in theology.

As with the doctrine of Franciscan poverty, Bonaventure formalized the resolution of the conflict. When he entered the order in about 1240, it was already wealthy and learned, and he was a student at Paris. He accepted it as it was, since he was neither an ascetic nor a simple unlearned man. It might be said that the whole of his intellectual life was a defense of the traditional mystical philosophy of the church against the Aristotelian and Averroist innovations of his time. Thus succeeding ages have been impressed with the mystical aspects of his thought, while men of his own time wondered at his intellect. With a sort of wistfulness, he recognized that grace came to such a simpleton as Giles or to "any woman" as much or more than to him; "yet he could not follow. He could reach it only by the long and winding paths of learning."[30] Francis had already distinguished between useful and useless learning, and Bonaventure by his life's work defined useful learning as that which led to the recognition of God's grace.

And promoted it. Somewhat disingenuously, he interpreted the Rule to support his position. Francis's injunction to live by manual work was pushed into the background, for Bonaventure wished the friars to have good books, moderate comfort, and leisure to devote to learning. He required gifted friars to study theology as a preparation for preaching and expected that their efforts would be rewarded with promotion. And they were.

By and large, the spirituals accepted the Bonaventuran position, since their leaders were all either learned men or preachers. Olivi was formed in the Paris schools, and such of his writings as have survived are so crammed with scholastic subtleties that modern writers have attributed his influence to his charismatic personality rather than to his thought processes.[31] While respecting learning, Olivi accepted Augustine's statement: "God may well be loved but not thought." Ubertino, as might be expected, was more radical. He had not found any spiritual inspiration in Paris—quite the opposite—and shared Joachim of Fiore's opinion: "The truth which remains hidden to the wise is revealed to babes; dialectics closes that which is open, obscures what is clear; it is the mother of useless talk, of rivalries and blasphemy. Learning does not edify and it may destroy."[32] Ubertino's objections to learning are socially oriented: "Almost all the dissention that exists in the provinces of many orders arises because of the ambition to be promoted to study, that they might become *lectors* and prelates and dominate others."[33] Yet he fell under the influence of Olivi, became a great preacher, and like Olivi was led to make a distinction between his learning and vain learning. Angelo Clareno straddled the issue in the same way. In his praise of Giovanni da Parma, he wrote: "He tried to bring into obedience all those brothers who . . . gave their spirits to curiosity and the love of science, since it is not in the collecting and composing of words, but in the workings of faith that the love and knowledge of God is proved. . . . Did not God, he said, stupefy the wisdom of the world by the stupidity of the cross?"[34] Yet even Angelo learned Greek during his underground life in Greece and gained some fame as a translator of the Greek fathers. None of these leaders could afford a resolutely antiintellectual stand because they were all intellectuals.[35]

But Jacopone was not an intellectual. Like Francis, his spirit moved from image to image by association. He had a "free, arbitrary and personal syntax. . . . Thought flows through broken lines, with brusque repetition, sudden returns, jumps forward, following the undisciplined movements of his feeling, or breaking away from the chains of logic to proceed with rapidity."[36] The only way that Jacopone could be claimed as an intellectual would be to consider him as inheriting a poetic tradition, but even here he wrote not to please, like the Sicilians, and developed his own style in contrast to the elegant formalism of the latter. So Jacopone's condemnation of learning is not piecemeal or provisional; it is the total rejection of a way of life thoroughly foreign to him:

> Tale qual è, tal è; - non c'è religione.
> Mal vedemmo Parisi - c'hane destrutto Ascisi;
> con la lor lettorìa - messo l'ò en mala via.
> Chi sente lettorìa - vada en forestarìa;
> gli altri en refettorio - a le foglie coll'olio.
> Esvoglierà el lettore - servito emperatore;
> enfermerà el cocinere - e nol vorrà om vedere.
> Adunansi a capitoli - a far li molti articoli;
> el primo dicitore - è 'l primo rompetore.
> Vedete el grand'amore - che l'un a l'altro ha en core! . . .

So it is; there is no more religion. We see Paris as bad; it has destroyed
Assisi; it has set it on the bad way with its learning.

Whoever follows learning goes abroad; the rest stay in the refectory to eat
greens with oil. If the *lector* loses his appetite, he is served like an emperor;
if the cook falls sick, no one goes to see him. They gather in the chapter to
make many regulations; the first to propose them is the first to break them.
See the great love they have for each other in their hearts! . . . [*Lauda* XXXI,
lines 1–10]

Jacopone had uncovered a rich vein of social satire and to a few modern
critics,[37] this has seemed to be his chief claim to fame. Certainly the poem
has all the vigor of the later writings of Ubertino, and it is interesting to
speculate whether he had heard of Ubertino's preaching during the early
1290s in Florence and later in Perugia.

Faced with the certainty of the last judgment, Jacopone felt strongly the
need for reform. In *Lauda* L,[38] he finds that the pope, cardinals, their
advisors, and the entire clergy are caught in the darkness of the apocalyptic holocaust. Those who escape the almost universal sin of greed are
caught by the pride of learning:

Se alcuno ne campa d'esta enfronta,
metteglie lo dado del sapere:
enfia la scienza en alto monta,
vilipende gli altri e sè tenere;
a l'altra gente le peccata conta,
li suoi porta drieto a non vedere,
voglion dir molto e niente fare.

If any one wishes to escape from this disaster [the last judgment], he puts
on the yoke of learning, blows up science to a high mountain, disdains
others and praises himself, counts the sins of others and hides his own
behind himself so that they cannot be seen, wishes to say much and do
nothing. [*Lauda* L, lines 46–52]

Jacopone feels that the supports of society and of reason are entirely
inadequate for his salvation and cries out in despair: "O sire Dio, chi
porrà scampare? [O lord God, who can escape?]" From his own experience, he knows that learning is simply irrelevant to growth in the spiritual life.

An incident occurred in Todi that led Jacopone to express himself with
grisly persistence on the ideas of both poverty and learning. A certain
Ranaldo di Bartolo Massei had risen to prominence and incorporated in
his life everything Jacopone detested. Described by a later Franciscan
historian as "a most learned theologian of his times and a great father of
our order,"[39] Ranaldo was a *lector* and probably maintained a school at

Todi. In 1287, he rose to further prominence as rector of the Ospedale della Carità, a position that the now-aged Cardinal Bentivenga d'Acquasparta had held as a sinecure for twenty-nine years. The hospital was, as we have seen,[40] by far the most important eleemosynary institution in Todi. Established in 1249, it was the pride of Todi; Florence was not to have its like until 1316, Venice, until 1380. In conformity with the Rule of the Franciscans, the wealthy establishment remained the property of the commune and was only administered by the order, though in 1296, the friars, flouting the Rule, tried unsuccessfully to wrest the ownership from the commune. It was clear that Ranaldo had risen to the summit of respectability in Todi and could look back on a life of learning and public service. Some time after 1287, Ranaldo died. Here is the *lauda* that Jacopone addressed to him:

> Frate Ranaldo, dove se' andato? - de quodlibet si hai disputato?
> Or me lo di', frate Ranaldo, - chè del tuo scotto non so saldo;
> se èi en gloria o en caldo - non lo m'ha Dio revelato.
> Honne bona conscienza - che 'l morir te fo en pazienza;
> confessasti tua fallenza - absoluto dal prelato.
> Or ecco ià la questione: - se avesti contrizione,
> quella ch'è vera onzione - che destegne lo peccato.
> Or se ionto a la scola - ove la verità sola
> iudica omne parola - e demostra omne pensato.
> Or se ionto a Collestatte - do' se mostra li toi fatte;
> le carte con fore tratte - del mal e ben c'hai oprato.
> Chè non giova far sofismi - a quelli forti siloismi,
> nè per corso nè per risme - che lo vero non sia apalato.
> Conventato se 'en Parese - a molto onor e grande spese;
> or èi ionto a quelle prese - che stai en terra attumulato.
> Aggio paura che l'onore - non te tragesse de core
> a tenerte lo menore - fratecello desprezato.
> Dubito de la recolta - che dal debito non sia sciolta,
> se non pagasti ben la colta - che 'l Signor t'ha comandato.

Brother Ranaldo, where have you gone? Have you held disputations about quodlibets? Now tell me, Brother Ranaldo, for I don't know if you have paid your debt; God has not revealed to me whether you are in glory or are burning. I know for sure that you died patiently, confessed your sins, and were absolved by the priest.

Now, here's the question: did you have contrition which is the true unction which takes away sin? Now, you have come to the school where truth alone judges every word and reveals every thought. Now, you have come to Collestatte [the castle of death], where you show your deeds; the account is drawn up of the good and evil which you have done.

For it avails naught to make sophisms and those strong syllogisms, either in prose or in verse, in order that the truth may be hidden. You got your doctorate at Paris, with great honor and great expense; now you are cramped in a ditch, for you are buried in the earth. I fear that honor has drawn from your heart the desire to be a despised humble brother. I doubt that the harvest of your works has absolved your debt, if you have not well paid the tribute commanded by God. [*Lauda* XVII, entire]

The bitter satirist hurled his comeuppance at the proud prelate. Jacopone not only despises the learning of Paris but also believes that Ranaldo is frying. No more could earthly fame save Brunetto Latini from being found by Dante on the hot sands of the seventh circle (*Inferno,* XV). But Jacopone does not have the compassion of Dante, who was a protohumanist. He gloats over Ranaldo's destruction. To later generations accepting the humanist belief that earthly fame (*onore*) is at least as important as the problematical fate of the soul in the future life, Jacopone's attack appears outrageous. It overlooks the common fairness and respect due to the dead. But it must be remembered that Jacopone lived in an age that was capable of instituting full judicial investigations of dead popes, as in the case of Boniface VIII. To him and to most of his contemporaries the requirements of salvation vastly outweighed the decencies of human relations.

In the last years of his life at the time of the fullest development of his spiritual powers, Jacopone came to a more balanced, though no less radical, view of learning. The *lauda* on the divine madness of the love of God contains a philosophy that is not to be found in Paris: "en Parige non se vidde - ancor sì gran filosofia." It concludes:

Ma chi va cercando onore, - non è degno del suo amore,
chè Iesù fra doi latrone - en mezzo la croce staìa.
Ma chi cerca per vegogna, - ben me par che cetto iogna;
ià non vada più a Bologna - a 'mparar altra mastria.

But whoever goes seeking honor is not worthy of his love, for Jesus hung on the cross between two robbers. But whoever seeks through humility to gain his ends needs no longer go to Bologna to learn other mastery. [*Lauda* LXXXIV, lines 12–15]

Just as the spirituals shared an enthusiastic dedication to poverty and a certain diffidence toward learning, they were equally distinguished by a fervent belief in the imminent end of the world in the Apocalypse as prophesied by Joachim of Fiore. As we have seen, Jacopone's *Lauda* L on the theme of the *Dies Irae* was full of such apocalyptic symbols,[47] and his Franciscanism had a decided Joachimist tinge.

In effect the Franciscans had become the carriers of Joachimist traditions, since the order founded by Joachim, the Florensians, took but a minor role in the spreading of his doctrines and served mainly as a repository for Joachimist writings.[42] By the late 1240s a strong Joachimist party had arisen among the Franciscans and had produced several pseudo-Joachimist prophecies.[43] It is hard to understand why the church allowed such a subversive doctrine to survive; Joachim's apocalyptic writings were not even examined when his trinitarian ideas were condemned at the Lateran Council of 1215. The explanation lies in the fact that the subversive possibilities of the doctrine were not understood until the work of the Franciscan Gerard of Borgo San Donnino in 1254. To the latter not only was Francis the herald of the third state of the world in which the entire rule of the secular clergy would be replaced by a reign of love under the guidance of friars and monks, but also Francis and his writings were virtually equated with Jesus and the Gospels. Such a conception of the "eternal evangel" came very close to the doctrine of continuous revelation later developed by the Quakers and was an outright anarchist point of view.

The authorities took note. Gerard was condemned. Giovanni da Parma, minister general of the order, was also a convinced Joachimist and felt that he had to resign, so great was the outcry against the order. His successor, Bonaventure, who was elected at his suggestion, felt compelled to condemn him, though he was not punished but allowed to retire to Mt. Alverna. Even such a Joachimist as Salimbene repudiated Gerard, as did the later spirituals; he had gone too far.

It might have been expected that when the millenary hopes of the flagellant movement in 1260–1261 went down to defeat, Joachimism would have perished in the subsequent disillusionment. Though some, like Salimbene, were disillusioned, the doctrine raised hopes that were both too strong and too resilient to be abandoned. A mistake had been made: it was only that the date of the arrival of the last stage of the world had been miscalculated. Joachim himself had warned against setting too precise a date for the final victory of the returned Redeemer over the Anti-Christ, and the spirituals were similarly cautious.

The doctrine was essentially an evolutionary one, firmly based on the historical thought of the period, which held: "History is the progressive assimilation of society to the mystical body of Christ. The human race progressively receives a fuller revelation of the meaning of time and historical existence and progressively becomes more perfect."[44] Even Bonaventure, the condemner of Giovanni da Parma, accepted such an evolutionary view of history, though he was not convinced that in the third and final state of the world, the role of the church was to be supplanted. He was a "Joachimist *malgré lui.*"[45]

Giovanni da Parma passed on his Joachimism directly to Ubertino when the latter visited him at Mt. Alverna in 1285. As Ubertino later wrote, both Giovanni and Bonaventure accepted the idea that Francis was the Sixth Angel of the Apocalypse heralding the last age; and so, of course, did Ubertino. He preached that the followers of Francis were to be perfect brothers in the observance of the Rule to the letter and that the church, in so far as it opposed them, was an agent of the Anti-Christ. This latter-day Joachimism departed from the teachings of Joachim in one important respect: Ubertino was strongly Christocentric, whereas Joachim had looked to the power of the Holy Spirit, the third member of the Trinity, to usher in the third state of history. A corollary of this concept was that the life of Francis was exactly conformed to the life of Jesus, symbolized especially by the identity between the experience of the stigmata and that of the Passion. Introducing his *Arbor Vitae* of 1305, Ubertino wrote: "I was importuned by many that I should expound certain passages of Scripture; others sought that I should compose sermons; others that I should make a commentary on the Apocalypse; and others more instantly prayed that I should describe the life and heartfelt Passion of Christ Jesus." He looked to "Christ as the beginning, end, and center of all his labor."[46]

Olivi fully shared his Christocentrism and reinforced his Joachimism when they met in Florence in 1287. As might be expected from a scholastic, Olivi gave a precise definition of Joachimism in his *Postilla in Apocalypsim*, written in 1297 or 1298: "Just as in the sixth age [of the first state], rejecting carnal Judaism and the outworn beliefs of earlier centuries, Christ, the new man, came with a new law and life and cross; so in the sixth age [of the second state], rejecting the carnal church and the outworn beliefs of earlier centuries, he [Francis] renewed the law, life, and cross of Christ. For this reason Francis appeared at the very beginning of the sixth age, marked by the wounds of Christ and completely crucified and conformed to Christ."[47] Probably Olivi did not realize the revolutionary significance of his statement, and had he lived, would certainly have been horrified at the wide acceptance of his millenary ideas among the heretical Beghards and Fraticelli of the next century.

Such a doctrine of the imminent arrival of utopia gave both heretics and spirituals great courage. Like the early Christians and the early Marxists, they could face their tribulations in the firm conviction that they were only transitory. In the approaching end, they would be justified and blessed.

None needed such courage more than Angelo Clareno and Fra Liberato. These friars had begun their lives as Pietro da Fossombrone and Pietro da Macerata, later changing their names to facilitate their underground activity—in the manner of Lenin and Trotsky. Leaders of a revolt in the Marches, which had broken out in 1275 at the mere rumor that the Council of Lyons was going to force the Franciscans to abandon the rule of poverty, they and their followers were imprisoned as long as eleven years in the isolated hermitages of that mountainous region. Chained to the walls of underground cells, they were kept in complete isolation, the friars who fed them being prohibited from speaking with them. A certain Tommaso da Tolentino objected to the cruelty of their punishment, was in turn imprisoned, died, and was refused burial. It is hard to understand why these spirituals were harried with such vigor by the Franciscan authorities, when the saintly Corrado d'Offida, a "perfect brother" of Iesi who sympathized with their stand, was deeply respected by both spirituals and conventuals. Perhaps it was because Angelo and Liberato mixed with the peasantry, preached subversive social doctrines, and led the upper classes to fear a *jacquerie*. In the Marches, the peasants faced the nobility without the buffer of a town middle class between them, like the *cafoni* and *galantuomini* of the modern Mezzogiorno. The Marches in fact lay outside the territory of communal civilization, for there, none of the towns except Ancona, were nearly as big as Todi. There the feudal nobility controlled town life and had wrested virtually complete independence from the pontifical authorities.[48]

Clareno even in this early period may have been evolving the view of history that was reflected in his *Historia septem tribulationum*, actually written down in the 1320s. His history, the major source of all our knowledge about the spirituals, is based on Joachimist assumptions: the seven tribulations of the Franciscan order about which he wrote mark the seven divisions of the sixth age—the very last working out of providence before the final conflict.

Clareno and Liberato were freed by the new minister general, Raymond Godefroid, who visited the Marches in 1290. After investigation, Godefroid exclaimed: "Would that we and the whole order were guilty of such a crime!"[49] His powers were in fact so limited that he dared not allow the spirituals to remain in the Marches for fear that they would again be persecuted; so he acceded to their request that they be sent on a mission to Armenia. The mission was an outstanding success, recognized not only by Ubertino but also by the Chapter General of Paris in 1292.

It is not likely that Jacopone knew Clareno and Liberato before their return to Italy in 1294, nor is it certain that he knew of the thought of Ubertino and Olivi, which achieved written expression only later. But nothing can be more certain than that Joachimist ideas were current in the early 1290s. For example, in Venice the Franciscan Giacomino da Verona wrote at this time an apocalyptic poem in two parts—the first on the heavenly city of Jerusalem and the second on the hellish Babylon.[50]

Jacopone, in his two *laude* on Francis, shows that he not only fully shared the Joachimist position but also no doubt contributed to the spread of apocalyptic ideas among the friars. In *Lauda* LXII, he addresses Francis as the embodiment of Christ: "O Francesco, da Dio amato, - Christo en te s'ène mostrato [O Francis, beloved of God, Christ showed

himself in you]." Such an invocation parallels the beliefs of Olivi and
Ubertino, and Jacopone like them never devotes much attention to the
Holy Spirit in this poem or in any others, as Joachim would have done.[51]
The poem continues by defining the first two stages of history, those
initiated by Adam and by Jesus. Using military terminology most appropriate to the raging conflict between the spirituals and the conventuals,
Jacopone states that God chose Francis to be the *gonfalonier* or standard-
bearer of his cavalry. Then a dialogue develops between Francis and the
Devil in which the saint musters his forces, the spiritual party, against
the great Enemy: the rule of poverty, the evangelical vigor of the friars,
the creation of the Second Order to marshall women for the fight, and the
creation of the Third Order for married laymen and women. The army of
the righteous welcomes all the people of the world in the fight against
evil, and finally the Devil is forced to make his last stand:

> "Non volgio più suffrire, - per anticristo voglio gire;
> e vogliolo far venire, - chè tanto è profetizato."

> "I will suffer no more, I will turn to the Anti-Christ; I will make him
> come, for he has been so much prophesied."

Francis answers:

> "Con lui te darò el tratto, - el mondo t'artorrò affatto,
> enfra li tuoi troverò patto - che i vestirò del mio vergato."
> "La profezia non me talenta, - a la fin sì me sgomenta,
> che te de' armaner la venta, - allor siraio enabissato."
> La battaglia dura e forte, - molti siròn feriti a morte,
> chi vincerà averà le scorte - de d'onne ben sirà ditato.

> "With him I will give you the final blow and wrench the world com-
> pletely from you; I will make peace with your followers and clothe them
> with my habit."
> "Prophesy does me no good; in the end I am discomfited, for you must
> have the victory and I shall be cast into the abyss."
> The battle will be long and hard, and many shall be wounded unto death;
> the victor will gain the spoils and be blessed with every reward. [Lines
> 74–81]

The second of Jacopone's Franciscan poems, *Lauda* LXI, elaborates on
the Joachimist identification of the poor man of Assisi with Jesus, opening with the lines:

> O Francesco povero, - patriarca novello,
> porti novo vexello - de la croce signato.

O poor Francis, new patriarch, you carry within yourself the new vessel and are signed by the cross. [*Incipit*]

The salutation of "patriarch" is reminiscent of the fact that some of the Franciscan pseudo-Joachimist prophesies were attributed to David. Others were attributed to Merlin and the Erythraean Sibyl—thus the line in the *Dies Irae*, "teste David cum Sibylla [according to the testimony of David and the Sibyl]." Jacopone goes on to describe the seven "figures" of the cross in the life of Francis, possibly referring to the Joachimist *Liber figurarum*, a version of the prophesies allegorically illustrated for popular consumption.[52] The use of the magical number seven may be a reference to the seven tribulations of the sixth age, or it may be that Jacopone is following the model of Bonaventure, who saw the six ways to God symbolized by the six wings of the Seraph in Francis's vision at the time of receiving the stigmata.[53] Like Bonaventure and the spirituals, the poet places central importance on the experience of the stigmata, following both the traditional account in the early lives and the spiritual work "Considerations on the Stigmata," which was probably in existence at this time and was later included in editions of the *Fioretti*.[54]

However, then the poem develops into a more individual interpretation of the message of Francis, for Jacopone sees in the experience of the stigmata the identification of Francis with the crucified Christ in the "highest divine love" that is beyond human understanding, but not human experience. He ends with a personal prayer full of the intense mysticism that engulfed his later days:

O anima mia secca - che non puoi lacrimare,
currece a bever l'esca, - questo fonte potare,
loco te enebriare; - e non te ne partire,
làssatece morire - al fonte ennamorato.

O my dried-up soul which cannot cry, run to drink at the spring, to drink at the fountain, to get drunk in that place and never leave it again. Let me die in that beloved fountain. [Lines 91–94]

From 1278 to 1294 Jacopone was slowly growing in the Franciscan life. For much of the time he probably was at the Church of San Fortunato, where he came in contact with Matteo d'Acquasparta, a fellow townsman and friar at the same house. Matteo probably spent but little time at Todi because as a master theologian trained in Paris and *lector* at the papal court since 1281, his career took him out into the larger world. But he must have come back to Todi to found the friary at Acquasparta in 1290. Despite his learning, Matteo may well have been acceptable to Jacopone, for when he became minister general of the order from 1287 to 1289, he

St. Francis receives the stigmata. Detail of the portal of San Fortunato
(Photo by the author)

tried to follow a conciliatory policy in relation to the spirituals, came to an agreement with Olivi, and was responsible for Olivi's appointment as *lector* in Florence. Matteo's brother, Cardinal Bentivenga, spent the last years of his life from 1287 to 1289 partly at Todi, and his will, granting a princely collection of books to San Fortunato, was, as we have seen, witnessed by Jacopone. So Jacopone had at hand a fine library. Not only were the great Latin fathers handsomely represented but also a wide selection of scholastic works by such writers as Anselm, Bernard, Richard of St. Victor, Bonaventure, and Aquinas. It is especially worthy of note that a Latin translation of the Pseudo-Dionysius and the *Commentary on the Apocalypse* of Joachim were available to Jacopone.[55]

Since Jacopone was also attracted to the hermitical life of a contemplative, he probably did not spend all his time in the middle of Todi at San Fortunato, but retired to the house of Sant'Angelo at Pantanelli. This house stood in a lonely spot on the malarial flats of the Tiber near its junction with the Paglia, about five miles below Orvieto in the lands of the counts of Baschi. There, according to a strong local tradition, Jacopone spent several years.[56] Perhaps it was from here that he addressed his letter to Giovanni de la Verna; the letter consists of a poetic introduction and conclusion in Italian, framing a Latin text. In it he consoles Giovanni, who had fallen ill of a quartan fever, with the thought that the illnesses of the body, so long as they do not threaten the soul, are the normal trials of human existence and merely serve to fortify the soul through suffering.

> Vale, fra Ioanne, vale! - non te 'ncresca pater male.
>
> Fra la 'ncudene e 'l martello - sì se fa lo bel vasello:
> lo vasello dè' star caldo, - che lo corpo venga en saldo.
> Si a freddo se batesse, - non falla che non rompesse;
> si è rotto, perde l'uso - e è gettato 'n fra lo scuso.
>
> Farewell, Brother Giovanni, farewell! Don't be sad in suffering evil: between the hammer and the anvil is made the beautiful vessel; the vessel must be hot to have a sound body. If the iron is beaten cold, it cannot help but break; if it is broken, it is of no use and is thrown away with the rubbish. [*Lauda* LXIII, lines 3–7][57]

Jacopone was following the same life of meditation as was Giovanni and was equally conscious of the "five stages of the soul" described by Giovanni.[58] He shared Giovanni's mystical raptures, which were later reported in the *Fioretti*. It is impossible to determine, in the absence of historical evidence, whether Jacopone had similar relationships with the other mystics of his time in central Italy, especially Angela da Foligno, Pier Pettignano of Siena, Corrado d'Offida, and Pietro da Morrone;

however, it does not seem likely, as such contemplatives led solitary lives and probably traveled about very little.

Jacopone also spent some time at the papal curia, perhaps during the years 1290 and 1291, which Nicolas IV spent mostly in nearby Orvieto, drawn there by his interest in the building of the great cathedral.[59] One of Jacopone's *Detti* refers to an experience at court:

> A man should esteem himself in his own eyes deeply vile and abject . . . When I was at the curia, it was said to me: "Is it not boring for you to talk with such people? I am surprised that you can put up with it." I answered: "On the contrary, I am surprised that they put up with me and do not drive me out like a devil."[60]

His later writing shows some knowledge of the curia, but it seems hardly conceivable that he could have spent much time there. What could he have done? Unlike Matteo d'Acquasparta, who may have been his patron at court, he was not a learned man and so could not be a *lector*; unlike his other great fellow townsman, Benedetto Gaetani, he was not a canon lawyer and so could not join the crowds of proctors handling the legal business of innumerable ecclesiastical foundations. And surely he could never be a diplomat like Benedetto and rise to the cardinalate in the diplomatic service. Unlike Ubertino, who became a chaplain in 1307 for Cardinal Napoleone Orsini, he was not a priest. And he most likely would not have joined the fifty-odd scribes who engrossed the papal bulls.[61] What indeed could a poet do at the court of Nicolas IV? Especially one who shared Giovanni da Parma's disdain for the high clergy. When offered a cardinalate, the latter replied to the pope: "I don't care for your dignities; and this is spoken of every saint whose glories are sung: 'He did not seek honors of earthly dignity and arrived at the kingdom of heaven.' And as for giving you counsel, I tell you that I will give it, and wise counsel too, if any one will listen to me. But in the Roman court in these days, there is no talk but of war, and jokes, but not of the salvation of souls."[62]

When Jacopone came to have something to do with the papal court, it was a time of particularly acute violence. Nicolas IV had found it inconvenient to spend much time in Rome because of the continual fighting between the Orsini and Savelli on the one hand and the Colonna on the other. Prudently the pope threaded his way between the two parties from his safer residence at Orvieto, Viterbo, or Rieti. He died on April 4, 1292. The conclave met in Rome and immediately became deadlocked between the two parties, the Orsini being represented by cardinals Matteo Rosso, Napoleone, and Latino Malabranca and the Colonna by Jacopo and Pietro. In the continual fluctuation of alliances common at the time, Benedetto Gaetani sided mostly with the Colonna, but a two-thirds majority was unobtainable. As in 1268, the Roman nobility, on whom the election of the pope in fact depended, were unequal to the task, and a prolonged interregnum ensued. The conclave moved to Perugia for safety and the deadlock continued for more than two years. The catalyst for its resolution was the visit in the spring of 1294 of King Charles II of Naples, who came to seek papal support for his efforts to reconquer Sicily. As he had the support of the Orsini, he was opposed by the Colonna as a matter of course. Finally Latino Malabranca proposed the name of Pietro da Morrone, an aged hermit of the Abruzzi with whom he had been in contact for many years and who as prior of the monastery at Morrone was the head of a new order, the Morronists or Celestines, a hermitical variant of protean Benedictinism. Since both parties were tired of the struggle and no other solution was in sight, the deadlock was resolved on July 5 with lightning rapidity, Benedetto Gaetani casting the fifth and deciding vote for Pietro. All that the cardinals had in mind was to find an old and do-nothing pope to act as caretaker until the balance of parties might change. Each hoped to use the new pope in his own way.[63]

Charles II was the first to reach Pietro. The splendid monarch, accompanied by his court and several high prelates, climbed the hill above Sulmona to announce his election to the hermit in his hovel—a scene of brilliant pictorial contrast so attractive to the medieval mind and aptly described by an eyewitness, Jacopo Stefaneschi.[64] The old man at first did not understand the message, then tried to hide, and finally was led to give his fatal consent, what Jacopone called his "voglio." The king stage-managed the accession of Pietro with consummate skill. He led the pope-elect, grasping the bridle of his donkey, from Sulmona to Aquila. Here the octogenarian might well feel secure, as he had many friends in that city and had had built there the lovely church of Santa Maria di Collemaggio, which is still one of the gems of the region. No less important, the cardinals would feel safe in coming to Aquila, because it was a border town and it appeared that by going there Charles intended to bring Pietro to Rome, instead of taking him, as he later did, virtually a captive to Naples. Though at first hesitant, the cardinals eventually all came to the coronation, the wary Benedetto Gaetani being the last to arrive. On August 22, 1294, with his horse held on one side by his liege lord, the king of Naples, and on the other by the king of Hungary, Pietro proceeded to his own church to receive the tiara and take the name of Celestine V.

The hearts of the faithful beat high. It was one of those rare moments when the egalitarian possibility inherent in the medieval church became an accomplished fact: the son of a peasant had risen through saintliness to the highest throne in Christendom. The cheering of the people continued so loud and long that the hermit pope was repeatedly called to the window of the royal fortress to give his apostolic blessing. More particularly, the hopes of the spirituals rose to new heights. They had probably known Pietro for a long time; the new pope, Corrado d'Offida, Angelo Clareno, and Fra Liberato—all had spent years in quiet meditation in ascetical hermitages lost in the high Appenines. As Clareno wrote: "Then the accession of Brother Pietro da Morrone to the pontificate was pleasing to the minister general [Raymond Godefroid] and all the more prominent brothers in whom it was believed that Christ and his spirit firmly lived—and especially to brothers Corrado d'Offida, Pietro da Monticulo, Jacopone da Todi, Tommaso da Trivio, Corrado da Spoleto, and others who aspired to the pure observance of the Rule."[65]

But Clareno was wrong. All of the spirituals *except* Jacopone were elated. Jacopone saw more clearly. He addressed *Lauda* LIV to the new pope:

> Que farai, Pier da Morrone? - èi venuto al paragone.
> Vederimo el lavorato - che en cella hai contemplato;
> se 'l mondo de te è 'ngannato, - sèguita maledizione.
> La tua fama alt'è salita, - en molte parte n'è gita;
> se te sozzi a la finita, - agl buon sirai confusione.
> Como segno a sagitta, - tutto 'l mondo a te affitta;
> se non tien bilanza ritta, - a Dio ne va appellazione.

> What will you do, Pietro da Morrone? You have come to your trial.
> We will see by your works what you have contemplated in your cell; if the world is misled by you, damnation will follow. Your fame has risen on high and run far and wide; if in the end you dirty yourself, you will bring confusion to the good. Like an arrow to the target, all the world aims at you; if you do not hold to a just balance, the wrath of God will be called down on you. [Lines 1–7][66]

This was a truly prophetic vision. Jacopone saw the man, the soul writhing at the time of its greatest trial. Here he is in notable contrast to Dante, who thought of Celestine as "colui che fece per viltate il gran rifiuto" (*Inferno*, III, 59–60). Imprisoned in his Guibelline abstractions, Dante could see Celestine only as a political pawn, one who through cowardice resigned high office and paved the way for Dante's great enemy, Boniface VIII. So Celestine has been fixed in the eternal marble of Dante's poem as a coward; great tragic poet though he was, Dante did not understand the tragedy of Celestine. But Jacopone did—only too well. Just as he consoled his friend, Giovanni de la Verna, in his sickness with the picture of that trial as a forging of the soul, so he followed with love the poor old hermit into the metallurgical furnace of a much greater trial:

> Se se' auro, ferro or rame - proveràte en esto esame;
> quegn' hai filo, lana o stame - mostreràte en est'azone.

Questa corte è una fucina - che 'l buon auro se ci afina;
s'ello tiene altra ramina, - torna en cenere e carbone.
　　Se l' officio te deletta, - nulla malsanìa più è 'nfetta;
e ben è vita maledetta - perder Dio per tal boccone.
　　Grande ho aùto en te cordoglio - co te uscìo de bocca: "Voglio";
chè t'hai posto iogo en coglio - che t'è tua dannazione.

If you are gold, iron, or copper, it will be refined in this trial; you will show the thread of your life in this alchemy. This court is a furnace in which good gold is refined; if another metal is mixed in, it will turn to dust and ashes.

If you take delight in your office, there is no more infectious disease, and it is surely a cursed life to lose God for such a mouthful. I had great pity for you when the words "I will" came from your mouth, for you have put on yourself a yoke which will be your damnation. [Lines 8–15]

Jacopone knew what Celestine was in for; he knew at first hand the consummate greed of Benedetto Gaetani and the merciless jockeying for power of the Orsini and the Colonna:

L'ordene cardenalato - posto è en basso stato;
chiaschedun suo parentato - d'arricar ha entenzione.
　　Guàrdate dagl prebendate - chè sempre i trovera' afamate;
e tant'è la lor siccitate, - che non ne va per potagione.
　　Guàrdate dagl barattere - che 'l ner per bianco fon vedere;
se non te sai ben schirmire - canterai mala canzone.

The cardinalate has fallen to a low state; each one wants to enrich his relatives. Watch out for the prebendaries whom you will always find famished, and such is their thirst that no drink will ever quench it. Watch out for the swindlers who make black seem white; if you don't know how to parry their thrusts, you will sing a bad song. [Lines 24–29]

Celestine did sing a bad song, a song so bad that it very nearly dragged Jacopone to his destruction. Despite his reservations, Jacopone was caught up in the hopes of the spirituals, and here Clareno was right.

　　Clareno and Fra Liberato had returned from the East to their home in the Marches, hoping to gain from the minister general some protection for themselves and their followers. "We came to Italy," wrote Clareno, "and passing through our province while sick, we could in no way gain access to the provincial vicar, Brother Munaldo, . . . nor could we be presented to the minister general. We got an answer from him [the provincial vicar] that he would rather receive and harbor in his province many fornicating brothers than us two."[67] With the election of Celestine V, Clareno and Liberato reached the minister general, who advised them and the above-mentioned leaders of the spiritual party to appeal directly to the pope. They—and perhaps Jacopone was in the group[68]—caught up with Celestine at Vieste in the Gargano, whither the old man had been taken by Charles in a long circuitous progress that was to end in Naples in November.

Celestine listened to the complaints of the spirituals and in his kindly simplicity, reached a decision that was to ruin them. He decreed the schism of the Franciscan order, setting up the spirituals as a new order—the "poor hermits of Celestine" under Liberato as minister general and with Napoleone Orsini as cardinal protector. Though the spirituals were now free to follow the Rule in its perfection, they had earned their freedom at the expense of the implacable hostility of the majority of the Franciscans. Nor could they return to the fold without expecting the most bitter persecution. Later it was said of Liberato: "O Brother Liberato, Brother Liberato, I swear to you by Him who created me, that never was meat sold to poor men at so high a price as I could sell you; the brothers would drink your blood if they could."[69] If things went wrong, the spirituals were trapped and Jacopone was trapped with them.

Things did go wrong. Celestine became a helpless tool in the hands of Charles; in September he appointed twelve cardinals, all but one Frenchmen or Neapolitans, thus giving Charles a clear majority in the college. The sympathetic Dominican hagiographer, Jacopo da Voragine, wrote sadly: "He gave dignities, prelacies, offices against all custom, at any one's suggestion, and at the dictates of his own untutored simplicity."[70] Realizing that he did not in the least understand the business of the papacy, he tried to turn it all over to a committee of cardinals; Matteo Rosso Orsini turned him down. He slept on a wooden pallet in a cell of the Castel Nuovo in Naples, lived on bread and water, as he always had, and advised the cardinals to do the same, as they always had not. In desperation Celestine tried to resign, but the Neapolitan people rioted to save their own holy man who, it was believed, could hang his cowl on a sunbeam. On December 13, he finally resigned, technically of his own free will, but actually harried out of office by those crowds of politicians eager to use him. Even out of office, his office pursued him. He escaped from his successor, Boniface VIII, and spent months wandering in the Appenines sheltered by his own hermits and his own people. Eventually the fugitive was captured by the agents of the king as he tried to escape across the Adriatic. On his way back to Rome, the holy man cured a lame child and made whole again the withered hand of a man—sure signs of his spiritual power. Since any political opponent could use Celestine to start a rebellion—and Boniface VIII did not lack for political opponents—the new pope imprisoned him in the fortress of Fumone, where he died on May 19, 1296. Later the enemies of Boniface invented colorful stories: Celestine hermits exhibited an iron spike which they said Boniface's jailer had driven into his skull; others said that Boniface had rigged a speaking tube to Celestine's cell in Naples and imitating the voice of God, had intoned into it "resign, resign!" Such practical jokes were played on mystics not only in those days, but also today.[71] The stories made good propaganda and though not factually true, effectively symbolized the truth: the old saint (Celestine was canonized in 1313) was hounded to his death by the politicians, chief among whom was Benedetto Gaetani. It was the tragedy that Jacopone foresaw.[72]

It has been said of Celestine that he left "two instruments to avenge his memory . . . a new religious order . . . and a poet, Jacopone da Todi."[73] A third must be mentioned, and this is the idea of an "angel pope." Such a concept had appeared as early as 1274 in the writings of Roger Bacon, but it had attained little currency until Celestine embodied it. In the first years of the next century, Ubertino and other spirituals of Joachimist tendencies fervently looked forward to the creation of another such pope to lead the righteous in the last days against the Anti-Christ.[74]

To them Boniface VIII was a precursor of the Anti-Christ. The contrast between him and his saintly predecessor can hardly have been greater, and as conflict waxed around the irascible Boniface, extreme partisans thought in black-and-white terms—devil and angel. The balanced judgment of a great historian expresses the shock of the change: "It was no less dangerous for the circumstances of the church to have as pope a man of political genius, but devoid of every qualification as a saint, than a saint devoid of the talents of a ruler."[75]

Even the election of Boniface was controversial. Charles had overplayed his hand in his domination of Celestine, and the cardinals were in unseemly haste to elect his successor and get out of Naples. No one had ever resigned the papacy before, and the question arose as to whether or not such a procedure was possible. It was reported on good authority that the crown was first offered to Matteo Rosso Orsini, who refused it out of doubt as to the legality of the procedure. Then it was offered to Benedetto Gaetani, who accepted. He had no such compunctions. Jacopo Colonna later said that there was much murmuring at the conclave, but both he and his nephew Pietro voted for Gaetani.

Boniface acted with decisive speed. On December 27, only fourteen days after the resignation of Celestine, he abrogated almost all the acts of the latter, listing them with legal precision just to make sure. The appointments to the cardinalate and to a few other high offices were the only provisions of Celestine left in force. Included in this sweeping decree was, of course, the act creating the "poor hermits of Celestine."

The shock to the spirituals must have been intense. Angelo and Liberato did not wait to hear more, but fled to the island of Trixonia in the Gulf of Corinth. Jacopone, Corrado d'Offida, and other spirituals stayed in Italy, but they had nowhere to turn.

At first there did not seem to be much danger, for Boniface was no more concerned with the dissensions among the Franciscans than Leo X was with the monks' squabbles of Luther's time. That he was friendly to the order in general was known from his work on the bull "Exiit qui seminat." Furthermore, he had been sent as papal legate in 1290 to Paris to defend the privileges of the friars against the attacks of the French secular clergy. Here he showed that cantankerous vigor that was to characterize his reign: "We wish that the privilege remain in all its force. I would like to see here all the masters of Paris, who in their fatuousness have thought that they could interpret in their own manner a papal privilege. Do they think that the court of Rome gave it without reflection? . . . I affirm to you that the Roman court would prefer to dissolve the University of Paris rather than abrogate this privilege."[76] Note that what inspired Gaetani was not so much concern for the friars as outrage against those who opposed the Holy See. He had a high idea of papal power.

And it was to this sentiment that the conventual friars appealed. When a deputation came to him in April, 1295, to complain against the spirituals, Boniface answered them: "Leave them alone, for they do better than you!" But the conventuals replied: "Lord holy father, they are heretics and schismatics and preach through all the land that you are not pope, that there is no authority in the church, and other such things."[77] The charge was substantially correct—in view of what Ubertino and Clareno later wrote and especially in view of the condemnation of such ideas by Olivi in his letter to Corrado d'Offida of September 14, 1295.

With his customary brusqueness, Boniface moved in on them. On April 8, he decreed that the "poor hermits of Celestine" were to return to the control of the Franciscans. This action was to throw them to the lions. On October 29, he summarily dismissed Raymond Godefroid from the minister generalship. The Provençal had two strikes against him: first, he was friendly to the spirituals, and second, he was close to King Philip the Fair of France, with whom Boniface was already developing the enmity that was to last for the rest of his life. Then he appointed as minister general Giovanni da Mirrovalle, a splendid selection from both the papal and conventual point of view. On the one hand, Giovanni was well known to Boniface, unquestionably loyal to the papacy, and a firm defender of the conventual point of view—he was among those who had condemned Olivi's writings in 1282—and on the other hand, he was a man of pure life, unlike those relaxed conventuals who were no credit to the order. According to Clareno, he was a "humble, merciful man."[78] Those spirituals who did not enter into active rebellion against Boniface could hope for lenient treatment, and Corrado d'Offida, who was later hailed before the minister general, was let off with an admonition.

Unfortunately Jacopone was not in this category, for he was drawn into active rebellion. It is not known where he was in 1295 and 1296, but he may have taken refuge among the Celestine hermits at Palestrina.[79] In any case, he was drawn into the Colonna party—a party brought into being by the ruthless acquisitiveness of Boniface.

If a high idea of papal power was the main theme of Boniface's pontificate, his promotion of his family was a strong second. He made his two nephews, Pietro and Francesco, cardinals in December, 1295, and set about erecting a veritable Gaetani principality in central Italy. He secured for his elder brother, Roffredo, by marriage and diplomacy the counties of Caserta and Fondi, he obtained by highly questionable means the Aldobrandeschine lands in the territory of Orvieto,[80] and he purchased huge tracts in the Campagna Marittima, mainly from the Annibaldi, to add to the ancestral estates at Anagni. It has been calculated that Boniface spent as much as 500,000 florins, or the equivalent of two years' entire income of the curia, in his rapid acquisition of land. This policy expressed greed on the heroic scale of a capitalist tycoon. Nor was he nice in distinguishing what he did as Benedetto Gaetani and what he did as Boniface VIII. For example, he got himself chosen podestà for two years in Todi, insisting for some obscure reason that he held the position as Benedetto Gaetani. In all the wild charges and countercharges about his life and morals that were later brought against him, no one ever denied that he was grasping. When his enemies accused him of using papal funds to buy his family lands, his nephew Francesco admitted ruefully that "it was so."[81]

Such a policy threatened all the nobility of the Campagna, but none more so than the Colonna. In self-defense, they turned to the enemies of Boniface, and Cardinal Jacopo almost certainly entered into treasonable relations with both the French and the Aragonese courts in 1296. The Colonna also became protectors of the spirituals, for in that century no great distinction was made between political and religious opposition to the pope. Friendship with the spirituals was in any case easy for Cardinal Jacopo, for he had been a great admirer of Giovanni da Parma, was a man of simple and even ascetic life, and in his extreme old age became the protector of Clareno.

Territorially speaking, the Colonna were in an exposed position, for Stefano Colonna, count of the Romagna, held Ninfa, which had now become an enclave amid the lands acquired by the Gaetani. Boniface needed Ninfa and bought its lands from the Annibaldi for 140,000 florins. A papal convoy bringing 200,000 florins from Count Roffredo to Boniface was captured outside the walls of Ninfa by Stefano on May 3, 1297.

Why did Jacopone get mixed up with such a lot? Certainly he knew of the activities of the Colonna, including perhaps their relations with the French and the Aragonese; the Colonna were not that different from the Gaetani, even if Cardinal Jacopo was somewhat more respectable than

Boniface. As a spiritual leader, Jacopone also probably knew of the letter in which Olivi had previously explained to Corrado d'Offida the necessity of accepting Boniface as the legitimate pope, though most likely he did not know of Olivi's tract on the resignation of Celestine, written sometime in 1296 or 1297 and expounding the argument more fully.[82] Thus he went into rebellion with his eyes open. His motives must be reconstructed through speculation. He deeply shared the aspirations of the spirituals and was equally deeply antagonized by all that he must have known of the grasping character of the pope. It was easy for him to think of Boniface as Benedetto Gaetani, for even the latter could do so; and it must have been hard for him to think of Gaetani as a true spiritual leader. Several *laude,* probably written at this time, show his concern for public affairs and the survival of that earlier pattern of his—the tendency to see life as a conflict between good and evil, a continual battle.

The fight is the apocalyptic one between Christ and Anti-Christ in the day of judgment, as prophesied in the Joachimist *Lauda* L. To Jacopone Boniface is the embodiment of Anti-Christ; in *Lauda* LI the religious orders cry out:

> "Vendica nostra eniuria, - alto, iusto Signore;
> la curia romana, - c'ha fatto esto fallore,
> corriamoci a furore, - tutta sia dissipata.
> "Fansi chiamar ecclesia - le membra d'Anticrisso!
> aguardace, Signore, - non comportar più quisso;
> purgala questa ecclesia - e quel che ci è mal visso
> sia en tal loco misso - che purge i soi peccata."

> "Avenge our wrong, O high, just Lord; the Roman curia has done this sin; let us run with fury that all be driven out. The limb of Anti-Christ has called itself the church. Watch out, Lord, don't put up with this any more! Cleanse this church of those who have lived evilly in it; may they be sent to that place where they may purge their sins." [Lines 56–62]

It is, of course, in hell that, in later years after the noise of battle had died down, Dante placed the simoniacal Boniface, with his legs being roasted in the fires of the third ditch of Malebolge (*Inferno,* XIX, 52–57). Boniface is said to have thought that simony was impossible for a pope, since he reasoned quite correctly that if the papacy did not receive payments for church offices, a large share of its income would be lost. There is a big difference, however, between Dante's attack and Jacopone's. The former was writing about a long dead pope, whose past sins were being posthumously sifted by a papal commission; while the latter, a rebel churchman, was assailing his reigning monarch.

Jacopone hammered away at the two prime sins of Boniface—his illegitimate election and his greed. In *Lauda* LIII, the church laments its condition:

> Piange la Ecclesia, piange e dolura,
> sente fortura di pessimo stato. . . .
> "So circundata da figli bastardi,
> en omne mia pugna se mostran codardi,
> li mei legitimi spade nè dardi
> lo lor coragio non era mutato.
> "Li mei legitimi era en concorda,
> veggio i bastardi pien di discorda,
> la gente enfedele me chiama la lorda
> per lo reo exemplo ch'i'ho seminato."

> The church laments, laments and cries and feels pain at its most evil state.
> . . .
> "I am surrounded by bastard sons; in all my battles they show them-
> selves cowards; the courage of my true sons is not daunted by swords and
> arrows. My true sons were at peace; I see the bastards full of discord; the
> faithless folk call me 'the whore' for the wicked example which I have
> given." [Lines 1–2, 11–18][83]

Such was the war propaganda of 1297. It was a call to arms.

Boniface had planned his campaign well. He "placed a sword between brothers."[84] Of the four sons of Oddo Colonna, Cardinal Jacopo, the eldest, had managed the family estates to the exclusion of the interests of the other brothers; so Boniface supported the claims of the latter, with the result that one of them, Landolfo, was a leader of the papal forces. The Colonna cardinals came to treat with Boniface in Rome on May 6. Though they restored the stolen money, they found that Boniface would be satisfied with nothing less than the crushing of their house. Retiring to Longhezza, their fortress outside the walls, they made up the Longhezza Manifesto during the night of May 9–10.

This was a simple and direct document. "We do not believe you to be the legitimate pope and we denounce you to the sacred college of the lord cardinals."[85] Twelve reasons were adduced to support their position, four of which had already been countered by Olivi. In the end they called for a General Council to resolve the question. The manifesto was signed by a number of lay lords and prelates—and by Jacopone da Todi and two other Franciscans, Deodato Rocci da Montepenestrino and Benedetto da Perugia. At dawn copies were spread around Rome and one was even laid on the high altar of St. Peter's. By noon the Colonna had their answer. Through the mouths of the seventeen other cardinals, Boniface replied in effect that if the procedure of his election were illegitimate, why did the Colonna vote for him and then take two years to discover their mistake? It was an unanswerable argument, but the time had come for fighting, even though bulls and manifestoes bounced back and forth for the next six weeks in full-blown propaganda warfare.

At first the Colonna had good reason to hope. They were in contact with the ubiquitous French minister, Pierre Flotte, and could expect that Philip the Fair would come to their aid. The Parisian doctors, who had little love for Boniface after their humiliation by him in 1290, expanded the Longhezza Manifesto into a full-length scholastic tract, *Rationes ex quibus probatur quod Bonifacius legitime ingredi non potuit Celestino vivente.*[86] The Colonna might even hope, as a later tract implied,[87] that Philip might take this opportunity to absorb some of the church lands in France in the manner later made famous by Henry VIII. Boniface, however, was more than equal to such combat. He parried the French threat and sent his fellow townsman, Matteo d'Acquasparta, as cardinal legate into Tuscany to preach the crusade—against Christians, as a contemporary wryly remarked. The Guelph communes responded. Eventually the Colonna were driven to hole up in their main fortress at Palestrina.

There for a year and a half, Jacopone was cooped up "en disciplina [in deprivation]" (*Lauda* LV, line 2). From there, in the midst of rough soldiers like Stefano and Sciarra Colonna (that same Sciarra who helped drag the old pope from his throne in 1303), he launched his most vitriolic attack on Boniface:

> O papa Bonifazio, - molt'hai iocato al mondo;
> pensome che giocondo - non te porrai partire.
>   El mondo non ha usato - lassar li suoi serventi
> che a la sceverita - se partano gaudenti;
> non farà legge nova - de fartene esente,
> che non te dia i presente - che dona al suo servire.
>   Bene me lo pensava - che fusse satollato
> d'esto malvascio ioco - ch'al mondo hai conversato;
> ma, poi che tu salisti - en officio papato,
> non s'aconfè a lo stato - essere en tal desire.

> O pope Boniface, you have laughed a lot in the world; I don't think that you can leave it laughing.
>   The world does not usually leave its servants to depart from it rejoicing at the separation; it won't make a new law just to except you, but will give you the presents which it makes to its servants. I had certainly thought that you were sated with this yoke that you took on in the world; but when you rose to the papal office, you didn't take on the holy state, having such worldly desires. [*Lauda* LVIII, lines 1–10]

As we can see, Jacopone hurls at the pope the same fear of death that he himself first felt on entering into the spiritual life and deprives him of any

The monument to Jacopone erected at Todi in 1906 on the
six hundredth anniversary of his death *(Photo by the author)*

Contemporary portrait statue of Boniface VIII, executed for the Duomo
of Florence by Arnolfo di Cambio, now in the Museum of the Opera del
Duomo *(Photo by the author)*

hope that his papal office will save his soul. Then he marshals the only too well authenticated evidence of Boniface's greed, the very origin of the Colonna quarrel:

Vizio enveterato - convèrtese en natura:
de congregar le cose - grande hai avuta cura;
or non ce basta el licito - a la tua fama dura,
messo t'èi a robbatura - como ascaran rapire.
Pare che la vergogna - derieto aggi gettata,
l'alma e lo corpo hai posto - ad levar tua casata;
omo ch'en rena mobile - fa grande edificata,
subito è ruinata - e non gli può fallire.

You have absorbed inveterate vice into your own nature; you have taken great trouble to amass things; your harsh greed has not been satisfied within the law, for you have turned to robbery and stolen like a bandit. It seems that you have put shame behind you; you have gambled your body and soul in raising your house. The man who builds a great house on shifting sands is suddenly ruined—and that cannot fail. [Lines 11–18]

These charges were drawn directly from the Colonna manifestoes, and Boniface certainly embezzled the goods of the church for his own family. Jacopone goes on to detail the misdeeds of the pope: he extorted an enormous sum of money from one Sancho Gundisalvi, an archdeacon of Palencia, before allowing him to enter into the archbishopric of Seville (Lines 23–26); he put a sword between the Colonna brothers in order to capture their castle (Lines 27–30). Then appealing to the beliefs of his time in evil omens, Jacopone recalls that when Gaetani was saying his first mass in 1291, a great darkness and a storm descended on the church, and that when he was crowned pope, the stairs of the Lateran Palace collapsed killing forty men— "a miracle by which God showed how much he liked you" (Lines 35–42). These, it seems, were events that actually occurred. The pope was also guilty of blasphemy, for in Holy Week he held high festivities in Rome at the knighting of his nephew Roffredo—"dancing and singing which scandalized all the pilgrims" (Lines 67–74). Furthermore, Boniface trafficked with astrologers to try to prolong his own life (Lines 75-78). Jacopone winds up by charging him with heresy:[88]

Non trovo chi recordi - nullo papa passato
ch'en tanta vanagloria - esso sia delettato;
par che 'l timor de Dio - derieto aggi gettato,
segno è de desperato - o de falso sentire.

I cannot find one who can remember any past pope who delighted so much in vainglory; it seems that you have put behind you the fear of God—a sign of a desperado or of heresy. [Lines 79–82]

The charge of heresy backfired. With this poem, Jacopone blew whatever chance he may have had for being officially canonized. Still to this day a controversial document, it has been condemned as a "horrible poem" and Jacopone considered a heretic—at this moment of his life anyway.[89] On the other hand, the power of the poem has led anthologists to give it a prominent place in their selections,[90] and one man of letters who appreciated revolutionary rhetoric wrote: "Though Jacopone in his *laude* attains unquestioned moments of the highest lyrical and most profound theological expression, yet in his satires he builds more dynamically, without reserve and with a greater feeling for naked truth. Thus the satires answer to a more authentic vocation in that they are an intimate part of Jacopone's nature."[91] Without denigrating Jacopone's undoubted power as a satirist, one may well question that the "greater feeling for naked truth" lies in the mind of the reader rather than in that of the poet.

But Jacopone was not a heretic, though certainly a rebel. His attack on Boniface is no more extreme than that of Ubertino, and the latter confounded heretical Apostles in disputations that took place in 1307. Furthermore, there is evidence that the spirituals in Clareno's group and elsewhere in central Italy vigorously rejected contact or confusion with such heretics as the brothers of the free spirit.[92]

Palestrina fell in September, 1298,—not by treachery as Dante alleged in his hatred of Boniface[93] but because of the exhaustion of the Colonna. The latter were indeed deluded in what they might expect from the implacable Boniface, but they surrendered unconditionally and ended up in hiding or in exile. Palestrina was, like Carthage, completely destroyed.

Jacopone was clapped in prison, a subterranean cell in some friary.[94] To his incarceration we are indebted for the first genuine prison poem of modern times, *Lauda* LV. Prisoners, like Re Enzo, had written poems before Jacopone, but such well-born poets underwent merely what we would call house arrest. Deprived of the sacraments, Jacopone was in solitary confinement for nearly five years. His prison poem so deeply impressed his near contemporaries that he is pictured there in a fifteenth-century manuscript, and the one good portrait of him, the fifteenth-century mural in the Cathedral of Prato,[95] shows him holding his book open to the *incipit* of this *lauda:* "Que farai, fra Iacovone? - se' venuto al paragone [What will you do, Fra Jacopone? You have come to your trial]." The parallel between this *incipit* and that of the *lauda* to Pietro da Morrone is striking. Just as he sympathized with the old hermit in his time of trial, so he felt sorry for himself. But his self-pity is only skin deep, for behind it lies an indomitable courage. He shows it in the harsh, ironic realism with which he portrays the circumstances of his fall and the cold facts of his jail:[96]

Prebendato en corte i Roma, - tal n'ho redutta soma;
omne fama mia s'afoma, - tal n'aggio maledezione.

So arvenuto prebendato, - chè 'l capuccio m'è mozato,
perpetuo encarcerato - encatenato co lione.

La pregione che m'è data, - una casa sotterata;
arescece una privata, - non fa fragar de moscone.

Nullo omo me pò parlare, - chi me serve lo pò fare;
ma èglie oporto confessare - de la mia parlazione.

Porto getti de sparvire, - sonagliando nel mio gire;
nova danza ce pò udire - chi sta presso a mia stazone.

Da poi ch'i me so colcato, - revoltome ne l'altro lato,
nei ferri so zampagliato, - engavinato en catenone.

Agio un canestrello apeso - che dai sorci non sia offeso,
cinque pani, al mio parviso, - pò tener lo mio cestone.

As a prebendary of the court of Rome, this has been my reward; all my
fame has been darkened, such has been my curse. I have got my living and
my cowl has been taken from me, imprisoned forever, chained like a lion.

The prison that has been given me is an underground cell; there is an
open latrine that does not smell of musk. No one may speak with me except
the jailer, but he must report all I say.

I wear as scourges the leather straps that hawks have on their talons; they
jingle when I walk; whoever is near my perch can hear a new dance. When I
lie down and then turn over, I find my legs confined in irons, kneaded by
the chains. I wear a rope belt that is not repulsive to the rats. My cell could
hold, by my calculation, five loaves of bread. [Lines 4–17]

The contrast between the rich clergy and his own state forms the kind of
absolute contrast to which his black-and-white mind was attracted. Yet
he still thinks of himself as a lion, the symbol of courage and power, or as
a great bird of prey, the symbol of freedom and aggressiveness. The
prison itself he pictures with a wry humor; even today rural *carceri
giudiziarii* stink of excrement and urine and also contain rats that run over
one's face at night.[97] His description of himself as dancing a jig in his
goads and chains is full of that black humor which has a strangely
contemporary ring.[98] For his chains he shows the contempt of Socrates.
He probably would like to eat the five loaves of bread by which he
measures his cell. And, of course, the feeling of utter separation from all
mankind is the common experience of all who have undergone solitary
confinement.

Jacopone then turns to the matter of food, the soup, bread crusts, and
onions that are thrust at him through the hatch in the door. Here again he
strikes exactly the right note:

La cocina manecata, - ecco pesce en peverata;
una mela me c'è data - e par taglier de storione.

Mentre mangio ad ura ad ura - sostegno grande freddura,
lèvome a l'ambiadura - stampando el mio bancone.
Paternastri otto a denaro - a pagar Dio tavernaro;
ch'io non agio altro tesaro - a pagar lo mio scottone. . . .
Iaci, iaci en esta stia - come porco da grassìa!
lo natal non troverìa - chi de me lieve paccone.

Having eaten my soup, here is a fish in pepper sauce—it looks like a
piece of sturgeon; then I am given an apple. While I eat from hour to hour, I
am terribly cold; I get up and pace around like a horse in his stall. Paternos-
ters, eight for a penny, to pay God my innkeeper, for I have no other money
to pay the bill. . `. .
Lie, lie in this stye like a fattening pig! But you won't find much bacon on
me at Christmastime. [Lines 26–31, 48–49]

Jacopone knows the penetrating cold of prison that gets in the bones, a
cold arising out of sunless dankness, malnutrition, and enforced inactiv-
ity. Usually mealtime is the only time of day when one is less cold; so
Jacopone stretches it out as long as possible not only to preserve the
fleeting warmth of food but also to use up time. Then he stamps around
like a horse or lies like a pig; such animal parallels spring naturally to
mind, because nothing is so dehumanizing in prison as to have one's
victuals dealt out through a hole in the door. But Jacopone is by no means
defeated:

Faite, faite que volite, - frati che de sotto gite;
ca le spese ce perdite, - prezo nullo de prescione.
Ch'aio grande capitale, - chè me so uso de male,
e la pena non prevale - contro lo mio campione.
Lo mio campion è armato, - del mio odio scudato,
non po'esse vulnerato - mentra ha a collo lo scudone.
O mirabel odio mio, - d'omne pena hai signorìo,
nullo recepi engiurìo, - vergogna t'è esaltazaione.
Nullo te trovi nemico, - onnechivegli hai per amico;
io solo me so l'inico - contra mia salvazione.
Questa pena che m'è data - trent'ann' è che l'agio amata;
or è gionta la giornata - d'esta consolazione.

Do, do what you will, brothers who wander here below; you have lost
your expenses because I am not paying for this prison. I have great capital
in that I am accustomed to suffering, and punishment does not overcome
my champion. My champion is armed with the shield of my hate and
cannot be wounded as long as he has the shield on his neck.
O my marvelous self-hate, you overcome all punishment; you receive no
wound, for shame is exaltation to you. No one is your enemy, you have
every one for a friend. I alone am the enemy, the opponent of my salvation.

This suffering that has been given me I have loved for thirty years, and now
has come the day of this consolation. [Lines 52–63]

By a strange and true paradox, the poet is actually happy. The external
circumstances of the prison are merely an extension of the ascetical life of
the previous thirty years—ten years, as he says in line 65, as a *bizocone*
and twenty years as a friar. But there is an important difference between
the self-imposed asceticism of his penitential period and the deprivation
laid on him by outside forces. In the former his soul and his unconscious
were under the stress of guilt, and he expressed his nightmares in the
wild exaggerations of his penance. In the latter, outside forces have
caught up with his self-condemnation and by torturing his body and his
reputation have released him from the torture of his soul. Nothing that
the brothers can do can come up to the punishments that he has been
accustomed to inflict on himself; hence Jacopone has no rancour against
them. They are neither cruel nor threatening in his eyes—only indiffer-
ent. This indifference is his consolation—not, be it noted, an ironical
statement but an accepted fact. No doubt his dreams were full of happy
fancies of wish fulfillment, for as the surrealist Philippe Soupault has
written of his own prison experience, the dream world is "le théâtre des
prisonniers."[99] In an odd way, Jacopone was almost at peace.

But not quite. There was one consolation that was denied to him—the
sacraments. As he sat through the long hours of dark silence in his cell, a
gradual change took place in his soul, preparing him for the last period of
his spiritual development. He must have pondered the injunction of
Francis to obedience: "Then the Lord gave me, and continues to give me,
such faith in the priests who live according to the form of the Holy Roman
Church and in its order that even if they were to persecute me, I would
have recourse to them."[100] Benedetto Gaetani was a mere grasping man,
but might he not also be, regardless of his human traits, the legitimate
high priest, the true servant of servants? Unlike the heretics of his own
time and of succeeding centuries, Jacopone needed the sacraments. This
need was so great that he no longer wanted to sift out, as Ubertino and
Clareno were to do, just what a pope could or could not do—whether he
could abrogate the Franciscan Rule or fly in the face of the clear mandates
of the Gospels.[101]

It has been suggested that this turning point in his life came out of the
fear of death, that he was defeated by his imprisonment, and that he was
old and tired and just wanted to end his days in peace.[102] Such an
interpretation reads into Jacopone's mind the concept that the sacraments are a mere form to which he was driven by human weakness, in
the manner of Boccaccio or Carducci. It overlooks the fact that Jacopone's
greatest days were ahead of him and the genuine need expressed in his
moving plea to Boniface, *Lauda* LVI:

O papa Bonifazio, - io porto el tuo prefazio
e la maledizione - e scomunicazione.
  Colla lengua forcuta - m'hai fatta sta feruta,
e colla lengua ligni - e la piaga me stigni.
  Chè questa mia feruta - non può essere guaruta
per altra condizione - senza assoluzione.
  Per grazia te peto - che mi dichi: "Absolveto"
e l'altre pene me lassi - fin ch'io del mondo passi.

O pope Boniface, I suffer under your sentence, curse, and excommunica-
tion. You have given me this wound as with the forked tongue of a serpent;
lick and cure this laceration of mine with the same tongue. This injury of
mine cannot be cured by any other balm than absolution.
  I beg you for grace, that you say to me: "I absolve you." Leave me the
other punishments until I pass from the world. [Lines 1–8]

Such a prayer is not the craven cry of a defeated humanist; Jacopone does
not want to escape from the physical punishment that has been put on
him. That he can accept. What he cannot endure is to live without the
contact with God through the reality of the sacraments and to die outside
of the church. The man who had earlier seemed to him the serpent of the
Apocalypse is now asked to lick his wounds like a kindly lion. In the next
lines he urges the pope to come and try him, examine him for heresy. He
is confident, for now he has two shields to protect himself:

Ch'aio doi scudi a collo - e, se io non me li tollo,
per secula infinita - mai non temo ferita.
  È 'l primo scudo sinistro, - l'altro sede al diritto;
lo sinistro scudato - un diamant'è aprovato.
  Nullo ferro ci aponta - tanto c'è dura pronta!
Questo è l'odio mio, - ionto a l'onor di Dio.
  Lo diritto scudone - d'una pietra en carbone,
ignita como fuoco - d'uno amoroso iuoco.
  Lo prossimo en amore - d'uno enfocato ardore;
se te vuol fare enante, - puòlo provar 'nestante.

For I have two shields around my neck, and if I do not take them off, I will
never fear wounds until the end of time.
  The first is on the left side, the second on the right; the right shield is a
tested diamond; no iron will ever pierce it, since it is so hard. This is my
self-hatred joined to the love of God.
  The right-hand shield is a carbuncle, burning like a fire with the flame of
love. I love my neighbor with a burning love; if you will come and see, you
may test it immediately. [Lines 13–22]

It will be remembered that in his first prison poem, Jacopone had only

the first shield, that of guilt and fear, which had been with him throughout his penitential period. Now in the silent darkness, he has been given
a second shield, that of love, and no one who has read the mystical poetry
of his last years can doubt the reality of this divine gift. Like the Sicilian
poets, he thinks of it as a divine fire, and in this fire he transcends the
hatreds of his political life, truly forgiving his greatest enemy. "Father,
forgive them; for they know not what they do" (Luke 23:34).

Jacopone concludes his appeal on a realistic note of true friendliness:

> E, quanto vol, t'abrenca, - ch'io co l'amar non venca;
> volentiere the parlàra, - credo che te iovàra.
>   Vale, vale, vale, - Dio te tolla omne male,
> e dielome per grazia - ch'io 'l porto en lieta faccia.
>   Finisco lo trattato - en questo loco lassato.

> And if you wish, come to fight; but I will not fight because of love. I
> would like to speak with you, and I think that you would like it too.
>   Farewell, farewell, farewell, God keep you from all harm and grant me
> grace which I will wear with a happy face. The tract is finished left at this
> point. [Lines 23–27]

The prosaic ending, a reminiscence of Jacopone's life as a notary, and the
elegant Latinisms so suited to an address to the pope serve to give a final
realistic touch to this simple plea. The whole burden of his tale, carrying
the message of his change of heart, is condensed into twenty-seven
ringing lines.[103]

It is not known that Boniface even saw the poem, but even if he had, he
remained untouched. The great year of the jubilee arrived in 1300, a
surge of popular devotion encouraged by Boniface. In the fullness of his
power and glory, the pope gave out pardons on all sides—to every one
except the Colonna and their partisans. It was, as Jacopone said, a time of
"tanta perdonazione [so much pardoning]," (*Lauda* LVIII, line 20).

Jacopone seized the occasion to address a second plea to Boniface.
Ludicrous as it might seem from what he knew of Gaetani, the man, he
cast the pope in the role of the Good Shepherd:

> Lo pastor per mio peccato - posto m'ha fuor de l'ovile,
> non me giova alto belato - che m'armetta per l'ostile.

> The shepherd has put me out of the fold for my sins; my loud bleating has
> not succeeded in gaining me entrance. [*Lauda* LVII, lines 1–2]

His bleating is pathetic, but neither self-pitying nor cringing. The appeal
is to the Holy Father, the representative of Christ on earth, and not to the
mere human who happened to wear the papal crown. He begs for

salvation, likening himself to those whom Jesus saved—the blind man who was given his sight, the servant of the centurion, the cripple at the spring of Bethesda, the girl who was raised from the dead, and lastly, Lazarus. It is a balanced, almost classical composition and lacks the fervor of the earlier poems; perhaps Jacopone was becoming almost reconciled to his lot. Sent by the hand of Fra Gentile, the message may or may not have reached its destination; and well did Jacopone need his resignation and patience, as his imprisonment was to go on for three more years. Boniface remained adamant.

But the headstrong politician was rushing on to his doom. His enemies were gathering against him. Plotters, led by the French ruffian Nogaret, Sciarra Colonna, and the papal captain of Ferentino, seized Anagni on September 7, 1303, and cornered the pope in his own palace. Even the citizens of his natal town did not lift a finger to protect him. Flanked by the only two cardinals still loyal to him, Boniface sat on his throne and faced his attackers with courageous impassivity. Nogaret dragged him off, while Sciarra Colonna screamed threats. Though the pope was not injured, the shock of the insult rang through Christendom and broke Boniface's spirit. For three days he would not eat for fear of poison. Then he was removed to Rome under the charge of the Orsini cardinals, and after futile efforts to intrigue with Charles of Naples and the Annibaldi, Boniface took to his room, with terrors of imprisonment—or worse— clouding his mind. "The 'great hearted sinner' . . . died on the thirty-fifth day of his imprisonment; he was out of his mind; he believed that every one who came near him would take him to prison." As a contemporary remarked: "He entered like a wolf, reigned like a lion, and died like a dog."[104]

The gentle Cardinal Niccolò Boccasini was elected pope, taking the name of Benedict XI. He freed Jacopone.

V ∞ Donna del Paradiso

O f all the poems of Jacopone, the "Donna del paradiso" has been by far the best known since the day it was written. It is included in high-school anthologies, and every high-school student in Italy is presumably exposed to it.[1] Often enough the reader is led on to a further study of Jacopone through this one poem. If, however, he goes to seek more of the same in the body of Jacopone's work—as well he might, for the life of the poem lies in its communication of a universal human experience valid for all times and places—he will be disappointed. The "Donna del paradiso" is unique.

It is Jacopone's only dramatic poem. This statement is not to imply that no dramatic element exists in the intense dialogues of Jacopone's penitential *laude*, notably the "Quando t'alegri"; for there is, as the classical historian of the Italian theater has pointed out.[2] But in the "Donna del paradiso" Jacopone has broken out of the dialogue form by the addition of a third persona and a chorus. Just as Aeschylus created the classical Greek tragedy by the addition of one more persona to the leader and chorus of the Dionysiac festival, so Jacopone takes in the "Donna del paradiso" a giant step toward the evolution of the sacred drama of the later Middle Ages in Italy. As we have seen,[3] he used three persons once before in the *laude* but then the third person was himself. Now he tells in direct discourse the story of three other people framed by the presence of the chorus.

At first glance the "Donna del paradiso" does not fit into the rest of Jacopone's production. It is an isolated mountain peak. The rest of the range lies elsewhere and forms a lyrical exploration of his inner life with just as much consistency as the *Canzoniere* of Petrarch, with which it has been compared.[4] Jacopone's first editor, Buonaccorsi, was fully conscious of the isolation of this single dramatic masterpiece and in effect did not know where to place it within the coherent body of essentially autobiographical spiritual songs. So he placed it on the outside. By subject matter this lament of the Virgin is related to the two prayers to the Virgin in the *laude,* and so Buonaccorsi decided to frame the whole by placing the Virgin poems at the beginning and at the end. "As for the order of these laude," he wrote, "it is various and uncertain in many books, though the ones at Todi have almost all the same order; yet it has not seemed inconvenient to start with these two about the Madonna, since she is the bearer and instigator of so much grace." Later in a note on the "Donna del paradiso," he said that it was "put in this place to end the work, the beginning of which is also for her."[5] Modern editors have almost all followed Buonaccorsi's order, thus agreeing with his appreciation both of the body of the *laude* as the history of a spiritual journey and of the "Donna del paradiso" as unique.

Despite its unique nature, this prototype of the Passion play did not spring full-grown like Athena out of the head of its creator. It represents the culmination of several strains in the Jacoponian experience: his relationship with his own mother, his welcoming of the feminine aspect of divinity as a channel for overcoming his guilt, his acceptance of conventional forms of the worship of the Virgin, and even his finely attuned musical ear.

Recent research has conclusively shown that the Virgin poems are closely related to the penitential ones and that thus they belong to the earlier part of his work, composed probably between 1278 and the time of his imprisonment in 1298. Heretofore, most modern students have placed the composition of the "Donna del paradiso" after 1298, on the grounds that the perfection of its style reflect the full maturity of the artist.[6] But several of the penitential *laude* show an equally firm command of poetic power, and the mystical poems of the last period have little in common with the dramatic masterpiece.

No spiritual neophyte, to be sure, composed the "Donna del paradiso," for the power of the inner light is manifested in it. As Aristotle said in the *Poetics,* neither the dramatic author nor the spectator of the drama can bring a tragedy to life without identification with the protagonist. Jacopone feels pity and terror in the presence of Mary at the foot of the cross, and he has come to his understanding of the mother of Christ through his experience with his own mother.

In the autobiographical *Lauda* XXIV, "O vita penosa, continua battaglia," Jacopone reveals that the influence of his mother in his life was both deep and formative. Saints, from Augustine down, have often had deep maternal attachments. While his father remains a distant and shadowy taskmaster, he gives us an intimate picture of his mother, recollected in a passion of both guilt and love. In fact the picture is so intimate as to seem almost ludicrous to modern tastes, since like Jeremiah, he begins his autobiography by telling of his prenatal life. Jeremiah had written: "The word of the Lord came unto me, saying, Before I formed thee in the belly,

I knew thee; and before thou camest forth out of the womb I sanctified thee, and I ordained thee a prophet unto the nations" (1:4–5). Jacopone has been formed in the lowest parts of the earth, and he looks back to his beginning with the same horror as was expressed by Innocent III:

Mentre sì stette en ventre a mia mate,
presi l'arrate - a deverme morire;
como ce stette en quella contrate
chiuse, serrate - non so reverire;
venni a l'uscìre - con molto dolore
e molto tristore - en mia comitata.

    Venni renchiuso en un saccarello
e quel fo el mantello - co venni adobato;
operto lo sacco, co stava chello
assai miserello - e tutto bruttato,
da me è comenzato - un novo pianto;
esto 'l primo canto - en questa mia entrata.

    Venne cordoglio a quella gente
che stava presente; - sì me pigliâro;
mia mate stava assai malamente
del parto del ventre - che fo molto amaro.

    When I was in the belly of my mother, I had already contracted to die; I cannot describe how I lived in that place, all closed in and locked up. I came forth and there was great pain and grief at my presence. I came in a sack and this was the coat I had on. When the sack in which I lay was opened, I was a wretched little thing, all dirty. Then I began to cry for the first time, and this was my first song as I entered the world.

    Those who were there took pity on me and picked me up. My mother was in a very bad way because of the birth from her womb, which was very painful. [*Lauda* XXIV, lines 3–18]

In his characteristic manner Jacopone paints realistically the sordid details of the nursery. It is clear that this poem comes from the earliest period after his conversion, when he was overwhelmed with the consciousness of his sin, and Jacopone continues in the same vein of horror at his guilt in relation to his mother and of pity and love for her at the same time—the theme classically illustrated by Oedipus in his relations with Jocasta.

    Se mamma arvenisse che racontasse
le pene che trasse - en mio nutrire!
la notte ha bisogno che si rizasse
e me latasse - con frigo suffrire
staendo a servire; - ed io pur plangea;
anvito non avea - de mia lamentata.

Ella pensando ch'io male avesse,
che non me moresse - tutta tremava;
era besogno che lume accendesse
e me scopresse, - e poi me mirava
e non trovava - nulla sembianza
de mia lamentanza - perchè fosse stata.
    O mammia mia, ecco le scorte
che en una notte - hai guadagnato!
portar nove mesi ventrata sì forte
con molte bistorte - e gran dolorato,
parte penato - e pena en nutrire;
el meritire - male n'èi pagata.

If mother should come and tell the trouble she had in feeding me! She had to get up at night and give me the breast, suffering with cold and standing at her service, and I was crying. I had no reason to cry. She, thinking that I was sick and might die, trembled all over; she had to light a light to see me, and then she examined me and found no reason for my crying—why it should have been.

O my mother, here is the reward which you earned in one night! To carry me nine months in your belly with such strong and frequent spasms of great pain, to have a painful delivery, to have troubles in feeding—you paid a bad price for that reward. [Lines 27–44]

Those with a penchant for psychological analysis might speculate at length on Jacopone's Oedipus complex, using the rather limited evidence that has survived, but it seems at least likely that his feelings for his own mother gave him the understanding and passionate commitment that enabled him to write so movingly of the mother of Jesus.[7]

This point can be clearly illustrated by contrasting his emotional involvement with motherhood with his lack of interest in that related symbol, the infant Jesus. Both symbols had become commonplaces of Franciscan spirituality in Jacopone's day, and the annual Christmas pantomime of the crèche at Greccio, one of the sources from which the Nativity plays sprung, was well on its way to becoming one of the favorite Christian tableaux.[8] Francis's inspired invention of the crèche answered to his childlike spirit because he was one who welcomed with joy Jesus' statement: "Suffer little children . . . to come unto me: for of such is the kingdom of heaven" (Matthew 19:14). But it is doubtful that little children came to the childless old widower, Jacopone. If the symbol of the infant Jesus did not leave Jacopone cold, it left him tepid.

He wrote two poems on the Nativity, *Laude* LXIV and LXV. The first might almost be called a Christmas carol, for in it Jacopone breaks from his usual ballad form into a more lilting verse. He opens it with the rather self-conscious statement that he has seen the sheet music of the angelic choirs:

O novo canto - c'hai morto el pianto
de l'uomo enfermato.
   Sopre el "fa" acuto - me pare emparuto
che 'l canto se pona;
   e nel "fa" grave - descende suave
che 'l verbo resona.
Cotal desciso - non fo mai viso
sì ben concordato.

O new song that has overcome the lament of sick mankind. It seems clear
to me that the song is set on "fa" sharp and it descends on "fa" flat smoothly
and makes the words sing. Such a melodic descent has never been heard so
well modulated. [*Lauda* LXIV, lines 1–8]

Despite the analysis of our amateur musicologist, Jacopone almost
breaks into song in the next lines.

   Li cantatori - iubilatori
che tengon lo coro,
son li angeli santi, - che fanno li canti
al diversoro,
davante 'l fantino, - che il Verbo divino
ce veggio encarnato.
   Audito è un canto: - "Gloria en alto
a l'altissimo Dio;
e pace en terra, - ch'è strutta la guerra
ed onne rio;
onde laudate - e benedicate
Christo adorato!"

   The rejoicing singers making up the chorus are the holy angels who sing
their songs at the crèche before the infant, for they see there the divine
Word incarnate.
   A song is heard: "Glory to God in the highest and peace on earth, for war
and all evil have been destroyed. So praise and bless the adored Christ."
[Lines 9–20]

But the musicologist wins out, as Jacopone turns to describing the
parchment containing the score written by God through the hand of the
composer. It becomes evident that Jacopone is writing about a song,
rather than writing one. He arranges the different choirs: martyrs,
evangelists, and innocents join in the hymn: "Te Dio laudamo, - con voce
cantamo, chè Christo oggi è nato [We praise thee, O God, and sing with
our voices that today Christ is born]," (Lines 55–56). How far Jacopone
has missed the joyful message of Christmas is indicated by his closing of

the "carol" with a calling of various types of sinners to repentance.

The second of Jacopone's *laude* on the Nativity has even less of the Christmas spirit. In it he uses the crèche only as a starting point to launch into a long theological dialogue on the meaning of the incarnation and the power of divine love. It is hard to imagine that such a poem could become a hymn or carol; yet one very much like it, *Lauda XLI*, "O Cristo omnipotente," is the only one of Jacopone's *laude* known to have been set to music.[9] The tune is a lively one, full of melismas and probably sung rather fast like the contemporary French chansons.[10] Of a collection of 126 songs taken from the hymnbooks of the *disciplinati* this is the only one by Jacopone; one other comes from the laudario of Urbino, so closely associated with Jacopone; six more are enough like the work of Jacopone to have been attributed to him at one time or other.[11] Here is another indication that the *disciplinati* did not often use the *laude* of Jacopone. Their music consisted entirely of monophonic melodies, probably sung without instrumental accompaniment—distinctly unpretentious musical fare when compared with the great polyphonic motets of the liturgical composers of the contemporary school of Perotinus.

Because so very much of the music of this period has not survived or at least has not yet been discovered, there is every reason to suppose that some of Jacopone's *laude* were sung. He himself was most conscious of music and makes frequent reference to song in his poetry.[12] Furthermore, he was equally conscious of verbal rhythms, and many of the compositions of his last period, his songs of divine love, could be effectively set to music. The "Donna del paradiso" itself was almost certainly recited by several speakers and would have made an excellent text for opera or oratorio—if opera or oratorio had existed in 1290.

Like the *disciplinati*, Jacopone closely associated the worship of the Virgin with the need for penitence, and nothing illustrates this connection more clearly than *Lauda I*, "O Regina cortese." As we have seen,[13] Jacopone appeals in it to the love of the Virgin for her son, praying that this love be extended to him as another son and that she come to cure his sick soul. The same theme is taken up in a different context in *Lauda II*, "O Vergen più che femina - santa Maria beata [O Virgin more than woman, holy blessed Mary]." This is a public invocation and prayer, rather than the plea of an individual. In the invocation, which takes up most of the poem, Jacopone draws an intensely human picture of the mother, beginning with her humility at the Annunciation. Then he revels in the miracle of the virgin birth, elevating the mother above the sordidness of the sex act as sons do. Her "body is pure, not having been touched . . . she conceives without corruption . . . has milk without seed" (Lines 31–35). Being a realist, Jacopone describes the actual birth in terms so literal as to seem almost naïve:

Lauda XLI
O Cristo Onnipotente

O Cri — sto 'ni-po — ten — te, do —
ve sie — te in -vi – a — to, che
sì po – ve — ra — men — te
gi — te pel-le — gri — na — to? U —
na spo-sa pi — gla — i, che, da-tol'
il mio co — re, di gio-ie l'a-dor-nà —
i per a -ver-ne ho — no — re; la-sciom-
mi a dis — o — no — re, fa —
mi gi — re pe — na — to.

Rendered from Liuzzi, *La lauda* (Istituto Poligrafico dello Stato), II, 97–98.

O parto enaudito, - lo figliol partorito
entro del ventre uscito - de matre segellata!
 A non romper sogello - nato lo figliol bello,
lassando 'l suo castello - con la porta serrata!

O unheard of birth—the son comes out of the belly of a sealed mother!
The beautiful son is born without breaking the seal, leaving his castle with
the gate locked. [*Lauda* II, lines 42–45]

What a difference between this castle and the dirty sack he himself was
born in! The poem continues with another picture, one that was later to
be spread over all the world by hosts of medieval, Renaissance, and
Baroque painters. It is the picture of the adoring mother with her lovely
baby:

O Maria, co facivi - quando tu lo vidivi?
or co non te morivi - de l'amore afocata?
 Co non te consumavi - quando tu lo guardavi,
chè Dio ce contemplavi - en quella carne velata?
 Quand'esso te sugea, - l'amor co te facea,
la smesuranza sea - esser da te lattata?
 Quand'esso te chiamava - e mate te vocava
co non te consumava - mate di Dio vocata?

O Mary, how could you stand it when you saw him? How is it you did not
die smothered by love? How is it you were not consumed when you looked
at him, when you contemplated God veiled in that flesh? When he sucked
you, how could you bear the love, its immensity being nursed by you?
When he called you and named you mother, how is it you were not
consumed to be called the mother of God? [Lines 48–55]

The passion of the invocation is broken in two places with prayers to
help suffering mankind, the first at about the middle of the poem and the
second at the end. Here Jacopone shows the same didactic urgency that
he used, for example, in *Lauda* VI, "Guarda che non caggi."[14]

Accurrite, accurrite, - gente; co non venite?
vita eterna vedite - con la fascia legata.
 Venitel a pigliare, - chè non ne può mucciare,
chè deggi arcomperare - la gente desperata.

Run, run! People, why don't you come? See eternal life, bound up in
swaddling clothes. Come get it, for you cannot do without it, and it has
come to redeem despairing people. [Lines 70–74]

Such themes were anything but original with Jacopone. They were
about the most common form of religious expression in his time. The

hymnbooks of the *disciplinati* all over Italy contain only two major themes: that of penitence and that of the worship of the Virgin.[15] So Jacopone was merely following the accepted patterns of popular devotion. Already in his day, the worship of the Virgin, and specifically the lament of the Virgin at the cross, had a considerable history. A fragment of such a lament, written in Italian, has been found at Montecassino and dated at the end of the twelfth century;[16] and similar laments, used by the *disciplinati* on Good Friday, probably spread widely through the Abruzzi and the Marches during Jacopone's lifetime.[17] In 1254, Innocent IV granted an indulgence for the singing of what was probably a well-known Umbrian *lauda*, "Rayna potentissima, sovra el ciel siti asalatata [Most powerful Queen, may you be exalted over the heavens]."[18] The early composition of this *lauda* is clearly indicated by its archaic form; it is a declamatory invocation, almost a litany in sixty-odd monorhymed lines. The effect of singing it must have been both august and monotonous.

Furthermore, the *laudario* of Cortona contains several laments of the Virgin, one of the best of which is the "Ave vergene gaudente," of Garzo.[19] The latter develops nearly all the themes of the "Donna del paradiso," expressed, however, in the form of both invocation and prayer, rather than in a dramatic setting. In the Urbino collection, the importance of the subject was so great that no less than sixteen, or about one quarter of all the *laude*, are laments of the Virgin.[20]

A strong impulse was given to mariolatry in general and to the lament in particular by one of the most widely used books of devotion in Jacopone's lifetime, the *Meditations on the Life of Christ*. Originally attributed to Bonaventure, this homely guide to scriptural meditations is now thought to be the work of a Franciscan of San Gimignano, one Giovanni de' Cauli, writing sometime between 1256 and 1263.[21] Just as the *disciplinati* were adding their own poetry to the Latin liturgy, so the good Franciscan adds his own human interest stories to the body of scripture. "The evangelists left out many things," he informs us; so "for the sake of greater impressiveness, I shall tell you them as they occurred or as they might have occurred according to the devout belief of the imagination and the varying interpretations of the mind. . . . as if I had said: 'Suppose this was what the Lord Jesus said and did.' "[22] Following out this typically Franciscan concept of biblical exegesis, the author retells the whole life of Jesus and popularizes it by relating it to the commonplace, everyday experience of the people of his own time. Perhaps the most significant addition to scripture is the creation out of whole cloth of a positive role for Mary in the Passion. Even before the Passion, Mary is given an active role, when the friar introduces Meditation LXXII by writing: "Here one may interpolate a very beautiful meditation of which Scripture does not speak." There follows a touching scene in which Mary and Mary Magdalen plead with Jesus not to go up to Jerusalem for the Passover, knowing that the Jews will kill him there. "Oh, if you could see the Lady weeping between these words, but moderately and softly, and the Magdalen frantic about her Master and crying with deep sobs, perhaps you too would not restrain your tears!"[23] This thought is in the famous passage in the "Stabat Mater," which begins: "Quis est homo, qui non fleret, / Matrem Christi si videret / in tanto supplicio? [Who is the man who would not weep to see the Mother of Christ in such distress?]."[24]

In the same vein, the role of the mother is magnified throughout the entire Passion:

> Now for the first time the Mother beholds her Son thus taken and prepared for the anguish of death. She is saddened and shamed beyond measure when she sees Him entirely nude: they did not leave Him even His loincloth. Therefore, she hurries and approaches her Son, embraces Him and girds him with the veil from her head. Oh, what bitterness is in her soul now! . . . And all this [the Crucifixion] is said and done in the presence of the most sorrowful Mother, whose great compassion adds to the passion of her Son, and conversely. She hung with her Son on the cross and wished to die with Him rather than live any longer. . . .[25]

There was a whole cast of characters around the cross: "John and the Magdalen and the Lady's two sisters, Mary Jacobi and Salome, and perhaps others as well." Mary defends the body of the dead Jesus from the soldiers who have come to break his legs, and the whole scene of the Deposition is described.

It can be easily understood how important such a work was both in the development of contemporary pictorial art and in the origins of the sacred drama. It is the plot line of the "Donna del paradiso."

While this theme was as familiar to Jacopone as to his listeners, now it can be seen through the research of Bettarini on the *laudario* of Urbino as forming a substantial part of the corpus of his work. Four of the laments of the Virgin can now be safely attributed to Jacopone's pen, and they have in common this aspect: they are dialogues suitable to dramatic presentation.[26] One of the most notable and certainly the most musical is the lament that opens with Mary calling upon all nature to share in her grief:

Planga la terra, planga lo mare,
planga lo pesce ke sa notare,
plangan le bestie nel pascolare,
plangan l'aucelli nel lor volare.

Plangano flumi e rrigarelli,

plangano pietre et arvoscelli;
tucti facçamo planti novelli
edd io dolente plu ke kivelli.

Planga lo sole, planga la luna,
planga planeta onenessuna,
l'aire, lo foco cun facça bruna
siano a lo planto kess'araduna.

Planga lo bene, planga lo male,
planga la gente tucta ad uguale:
mort'è lo rege celestiale,
e nno de morte sua naturale.

Mort'è lo lume e lo splendore,
mort'è la manna del gran dulçore,
d'ambra e mmoscato mort'è ll'odore,
de neve e rrose mort'è el colore.

Mort'è lo bello a rremirare,
mort'è ll'oglioso ad odorare,
dolçe ad audire et a ssaporare,
süavetoso ad abbraçare.

   The earth weeps, the sea weeps, the fish who know how to swim weep,
the cattle weep in their pastures, the birds weep in their flight. The rivers
and brooks weep, the rocks and saplings weep—all make fresh laments,
and I grieving more than any of them.
   The sun weeps, the moon weeps, each planet weeps; the air, the fire with
its brown face are among the gathered mourners. Good weeps, evil weeps,
all men equally weep. Dead is the heavenly king and not from a natural
death.
   Dead is the light and the splendor, dead is the manna of great sweetness,
dead is the scent of ambergris and musk, dead is the color of snow and
roses. Dead is the beautiful to see, dead is the scent to smell, the sweet to
hear and to taste, the lovely to embrace. [Bettarini, *Recuperi Jacoponici*, III,
lines 1–24]

In this deceptively simple *lauda*, Jacopone uses the dull repetition of
key words, first "planga" then "mort'è," to project the grief of Mary. He
hammers it out. It is the voice of mother—any mother—repeating over a
dead infant "Oh my baby" again and again for hours on end to release
some little of the terrible hurt. Mary finds that all creation and the whole
world of the senses reflect her grief, just as any grieving parent finds that
every perceived thing becomes gray and dead as the inner load engulfs
and depresses all outward life. Time itself slows down to a hopeless
monotonous crawl, and the chant should be sung "lento" to the rhythm

of those deep-voiced cathedral bells that are still struck in Italy once a minute during the day of the death of a universally mourned person. As Jacopone said, one has to experience it to know what it is like.

The *lauda* is deceptively simple too in its use of seemingly endless repetition, which at first sight looks naïve. Perhaps drawing his model from the work of the Goliardic poets, Jacopone raises the form to high art. Here repetition expresses grief. In Lady Poverty's rollicking listing of her domain in *Lauda* LIX, it expresses joy. In the "Amor de caritate," *Lauda* XC, it expresses love.[27]

The other three of Jacopone's *laude* in the hymnbook of Urbino are dialogues between Mary and those sisters, with whom the author of the *Meditations on the Life of Christ* has provided her. In one, the most pessimistic and didactic, Mary seems to call for vengeance on the whole human race for the murder of her son:

> Et ove fo lo pesce de lo mare,
> le bestie, l'aucelli e li serpenti
> ke ffossero venuti ad aiutare
> lo lor Signore de le false genti?
> Da ke nno se cçe volçer retrovare
> l'amici, li vicini e li parenti,
> bene averanno de ke vergognare
> si de lo repentir fossero osenti!

> And where were the fishes of the sea, the beasts, the birds, and the reptiles that they did not come to save their Lord from false men? So I do not want to go and search out friends, neighbors, and relatives; they will certainly have a lot to be ashamed of if they do not repent! [Bettarini, *Recuperi Jacoponici*, I, lines 81–88]

It is interesting that this lament, like some other *laude*, is written in eight-line stanzas of alternate rhymes (abababab). It is the form which Jacopone preferred for particularly august statements and is the metrical ancestor of the *ottava rima* of Boccaccio and Ariosto.

The second dialogue with the sisters opens with Mary calling on them to join the wake: "Sorelle, prègovo per mi' amore [Sisters, I beg of you for your love of me]." Mary develops the theme of her loss, and addressing her son, petitions that she may die with him:

> Fillo, permicti lo mio murire
> ke tt'acompangni al sepellire:
> non me lassare da te partire,
> kè ià nno sacço dove me gire!

> Son, allow me to die and to accompany you to the grave; don't let me be separated from you, for I don't know where to go! [Bettarini, *Recuperi Jacoponici*, II, lines 61–64]

The idea of Mary's dying with Jesus not only comes from the *Meditations on the Life of Christ,* but also is incorporated in the "Donna del paradiso." Ever closer to both these works is the third dialogue with the sisters, in which the latter report the events of the Passion to Mary, and she expresses her grief. Here the dramatic element becomes very strong indeed. At the beginning Mary tells how beautiful Jesus is, describing his body with a richness of detail and an aura of love reminiscent of the oriental splendors of the *Song of Songs.* The sisters interrupt with harsh realism:

> "Sora, veduto avemo
> uno omo ke credemo
> ke aia nome Cristo,
> ma è ssì bactuto e ppisto,
> alliso e 'nsanguenato,
> ke ssi fo dilicato
> or non se pò parere,
> nanti sembla a vedere
> sì terribile cosa,
> k'appena dire s'osa."

"Sister, we have seen a man whom we think had the name of Christ, but he was so beaten and pounded, struck and bloody that we can't tell whether or not he was delicate. We have never before seen such a terrible thing and hardly dare speak of it. [Bettarini, *Recuperi Jacoponici,* IV, lines 105–114]

The sisters continue to describe the harrowing details of the violent breaking of Jesus's body, details that, repugnant though they are to modern taste, no doubt were almost commonplace in that age of public executions. The lament of Mary follows through hundreds of lines to express her grief.

There are two important differences between these four laments in the Urbino hymnbook and the "Donna del paradiso." First, they were little known, for in every case only this one copy has survived—in the original hymnbook. Here at Urbino evidently gathered a group of poets who for a long time followed the inspiration of Jacopone and continued to write and sing *laude* in his style long after the rest of Italy had adopted newer forms. Second, almost all the laments, both at Urbino and elsewhere, were either monologues or dialogues and did not take the final step into true drama.

Jacopone's "Donna del paradiso" towers above the many hymns to the Virgin sung by the *disciplinati,* just as the "Deposition from the Cross" by Giotto in the Scrovegni Chapel is overwhelming in its grandeur and far outshines the hundreds of *pietà* painted at that time. "Of this period of the very origins of our dramatic poetry, it is the true masterpiece," wrote

The descent from the Cross. Detail from the fresco by Giotto in the Scrovegni Chapel, Padua, 1306

one of the most penetrating of modern scholars.[28] Another wrote that Jacopone came to the theater "ex abundantia cordis [out of the fullness of his heart]."[29] A third: "This was an event of capital importance in religious history. . . . perhaps the one subject of the first dramas composed by the *disciplinati*."[30]

In the many manuscript copies of the poem, the parts of the different personae are not separated out, though they were probably spoken by different people; but many modern printed editions do so separate the parts for easier reading.

The "Donna del paradiso" opens with a prologue, like the great chorus, "Come, ye daughters," in the "Saint Matthew's Passion" of Bach; but the Baroque master has over three hours to tell his story. Jacopone is in a hurry. In breathless haste, the messenger announces the shattering news to Mary:

> Donna del paradiso, - lo tuo figlio è priso,
> Iesù Cristo beato.
> Accurre, donna, e vide - che la gente l'allide;
> credo che llo s'occide, - tanto l'on flagellato.

> Lady of Heaven, your son is taken, blessed Jesus Christ. Run, lady, and see how the people are beating him; I think they are going to kill him, they have beaten him so much. [*Lauda* XCIII, lines 1–4]

The urgency of the message is overwhelming, and into it Jacopone has poured all the anxiety of his guilt-tortured soul. The news is greeted with absolute incomprehension by Mary, who, as in the Urbino lament IV, has in her mind the incomparable beauty and perfection of Jesus and cannot grasp the enormity of the disaster. So the messenger must tell his story until Mary, the symbol of the hope and love of all mankind, is convinced and drawn into the eye of the storm:

Mary:	Como esser porrìa - che non fece follia,
	Cristo, la spene mia, - om l'avesse pigliato?
Messenger:	Madonna, egli è traduto, - Iuda sì l'ha venduto,
	trenta danar n'ha 'vuto, - fatto n'ha gran mercato.
Mary:	Succurri, Magdalena, - gionta m'è adosso piena!
	Cristo figlio se mena, - como m'è annunziato.
Messenger:	Succurri, donna, aiuta! - ch'al tuo figlio se sputa
	e la gente lo muta, - hanlo dato a Pilato.
Mary:	O Pilato, non fare - 'l figlio mio tormentare,
	ch'io te posso mostrare - como a torto è accusato.

Mary:	How can that be, for Christ, my hope, has done nothing that men should arrest him?

Messenger: Lady, he is betrayed. Judas has sold him and got
thirty coins. He made a great bargain.
Mary: Help, Magdalen! Full suffering has come upon me.
Christ, my son, has been taken away, as it has been told to me.
Messenger: Help, help, lady! For they are spitting at your son, they gang
up on him, they have turned him over to Pilate.
Mary: O Pilate, don't do it, don't torture my son, for I can show you
he is wrongly accused. [Lines 5–14]

The piling on of imperative commands conveys the action in desperate
cries, and the curt sentences make it race on, when the chorus interrupts.
The people utter their fierce judgment in cutting words with the staccato
blows of many consonants:

People: Crucifige, crucifige! - Omo che se fa rege,
secondo nostro lege, - contradice al senato.
Mary: Priego che m'entendati, - nel mio dolor pensàti;
forse mò ve mutati - de che avete pensato.
Messenger: Tragon fuor li ladroni - che sian suoi compagnoni:
People: De spine se coroni! - chè rege s'è chiamato.

People: Crucify him, crucify him! A man who makes himself king
contradicts the elders according to our law.
Mary: I beg you, listen to me. Think of my grief. Perhaps now you
will change your minds from what you have thought.
Messenger: They have dragged forth the robbers who are to be his companions.
People: Crown him with thorns, since he called himself king. [Lines
15–20]

As the messenger continues to tell of the awful events, Mary breaks in
with her laments, which gradually build up to a state of frenzy, marking
the first climax of the *lauda:*

Mary: O figlio, figlio, figlio! - figlio, amoroso giglio,
figlio, chi dà consiglio - al mio cor angustiato?
Figlio, occhi giocondi, - figlio, co no respondi?
figlio, perchè t'ascondi - dal petto o' si lattato?
Messenger: Madonna, ecco la cruce, - che la gente l'aduce,
ove la vera luce - dèi essere levato.
Mary: O croce, que farai? - el figlio mio torrai?
e que ci aponerai, - chè non ha en sè peccato?
Messenger: Succurri, piena de doglia, - chè 'l tuo figliuol se spoglia;
la gente par che voglia - che sia en croce chiavato.
Mary: Se i tollete 'l vestire, - lassatemel vedire
come 'l crudel ferire - tutto l'ha 'nsanguinato.
Messenger: Donna, la man gli è presa - en ella croce è stesa,
con un bollon gli è fesa, - tanto ci l'on ficcato!

L'altra mano se prende, - nella croce se stende,
e lo dolor s'accende, - che più è moltiplicato.
Donna, li piè se prenno - e chiavellanse al lenno
onne iontura aprenno - tutto l'han desnodato.

Mary: Ed io comencio el corrotto: - figliolo mio deporto,
figlio, chi me t'ha morto, - figlio mio delicato?
Meglio averìen fatto - che 'l cor m'avesser tratto,
che, nella croce tratto, - starce desciliato.

Mary: O my son, my son, my son,—my son, my beloved lily! My son,
who will give solace to my straightened heart? My son with
the laughing eyes, my son, why don't you answer? My son,
why do you hide from the breast that nursed you?

Messenger: Lady, here is the cross which the people have brought, where
the true light must be raised.

Mary: O cross, what can I do? Are you taking my son from me? For
what can you condemn him, since he has no sin in him?

Messenger: Help, lady of sorrow! For they are undressing your little boy. It
seems that the people want him to be nailed to the cross.

Mary: If you are undressing him, let me see how cruelly he has been
wounded. He is all bloodied.

Messenger: Lady, they take his hand and stretch it on the cross. They fix it
with a nail and hammer it right in. They take the other hand
and fit it on the cross, and the pain lights up and is much
increased. Lady, they take his feet and nail them to the wood.
They take every joint and pull them apart.

Mary: And I begin my wailing: O my little son taken from me. O my
son, my tender son, who has killed you? They would have
done better to cut my heart out than for me to see you stretched
on the cross. [Lines 21–42]

Jacopone has superimposed on the figure of the man that of the baby and
little boy, as indeed the mother might well see her son, both facing the
present horror and harking back to the intimate memories of his early
life. The seeing of a child in a grown man is always a shocking experience, leading one to see innocence and feel compassion for the most
hardened criminal.[31] Here the contrast is drawn to the fullest extent as
the mother who bound up childish scratches fusses futilely over the
gaping wounds. Queasy critics have accused Jacopone in this passage of
Gothic exaggeration in his harsh realism, but is he not just telling the
facts? His picture is a foretaste of the weeping Madonnas and the bleed-
ing Jesuses of late medieval and Baroque statues and paintings.

At this point, Christ addresses his mother in august language, which is
both human and divine. The calm power of the crucified Christ is
contrasted with the human agony of Mary, as each asks the other rhetorical questions for which they know only too well the answers. The sub-

lime pathos of the scene is such that is raises the commonplace questions to an epic level:

Christ: Mamma, o' sei venuta? - mortal me dai feruta,
        chè 'l tuo pianger me stuta, - chè 'l veggio sì afferato
Mary: Figlio, che m'agio anvito, - figlio, patre e marito,
        figlio, chi t'ha feruto? - figlio, chi t'ha spogliato?
Christ: Mamma, perchè te lagni? - voglio che tu remagni,
        che serve i miei compagni - ch'al mondo agio acquistato.
Mary: Figlio, questo non dire, - voglio teco morire,
        non me voglio partire, - fin che mò m'esce 'l fiato.
        Ch'una agiam sepoltura, - figlio de mamma scura,
        trovarse en affrantura - matre e figlio affogato.
Christ: Mamma, col core affletto, - entro a le man te metto
        de Ioanne, mio eletto; - sia il tuo figlio appellato.
        Ioanne, esta mia mate - tollela en caritate,
        aggine pietate - ca lo core ha forato.

Christ: Mother, why have you come? It gives me a mortal wound to see you weeping and so tormented.
Mary: Son, I had to come—son, father, and husband. Son, who has wounded you? Who has undressed you?
Christ: Mother, why are you wailing? I want you to stay and serve my companions whom I have gathered in the world.
Mary: Son, don't say that. I want to die with you. I will not leave you until my breath leaves me. May we have one grave, o son of a desolate mother. May we be buried together, mother and son.
Christ: Mother, with an afflicted heart, I put you in the hands of John, my chosen one; may he be called your son. John, here is my mother, treat her with love, have pity on her, for her heart is broken. [Lines 43–56]

The close dependence on the very words of the Gospel lends both authority and power to the scene, which must have been overwhelming to people who may have been hearing these words for the first time in their own everyday language.

The moment of death arrives. Mary meets it in the manner of a peasant woman—which she was. Even today in Lucania, and they say also in Corsica, Calabria, and Sicily,[32] a widow meets the moment of death with an unearthly scream that splits the throat and shakes the entire body. I have heard it once, twenty-five years ago, and can hear it still. The screams come again and again. Eventually words can be distinguished, neighbors come in to hold the writhing body of the widow. The words gradually form into a wild ululation drawn from the heart of the bereaved—a chant that seems to come from the very dawn of the life of the Italic peoples, the age of Homer. Such is Jacopone's lament of the Madonna:

Figlio, l'alma t'è uscita, - figlio de la smarrita,
figlio de la sparita, - figlio attoccicato!
  Figlio bianco e vermiglio, - figlio senza simiglio,
figlio, a chi m'apiglio? - figlio, pur m'hai lassato.
  Figlio bianco e biondo, - figlio, volto iocondo,
figlio, perchè t'ha el mondo, - figlio, cusì sprezato?
  Figlio, dolce e piacente, - figlio de la dolente,
figlio, hatte la gente - malamente trattato!
  Ioanne, figlio novello, - morto è lo tuo fratello,
sentito aggio 'l coltello - che fo profetizato.

Son, your soul has departed. Son of the desolate one, son of the beaten one,
dead son! Son, white and rosy, son without compare; son, to whom shall I
turn, son, now that you have left me? Son, white and blond, son with the
happy face; son, why has the world so disdained you? Son, sweet and
pleasing, son of the grieving one; son, men have treated you badly.
  John, my new son, your brother is dead. I have felt the knife that was
prophesied. [Lines 57–66]

The messenger ends the tragedy with a brief statement of what is so often
the case when a deeply loved one dies. The mother no longer really lives,
only waits, after the son is dead.

Che morto ha figlio e mate - 'n dura morte afferate
trovarse abbraccecate - mate e figlio a un cruciato.

Death has killed both mother and son. Seized in harsh death, both
mother and son embrace on the same cross. [Lines 67–68]

The "Donna del paradiso" begs comparison with the roughly contemporary "Stabat Mater."[33] As far as the ideas expressed are concerned,
they appear to be very close, and the latter was also probably a Franciscan
composition. But here the similarity ends, for the stately Latin hymn is a
masterpiece of a different order. It contains no direct discourse, except
the fervent prayer of the writer for salvation, and it is, of course, in Latin
and so does not reflect the style of Jacopone. In the eighteenth century,
when the "Stabat Mater" achieved an international fame by being incorporated in the liturgy of the Roman Catholic Church, it was frequently
attributed to Jacopone, the author of that other famous lament. Such
attribution is now considered to be far-fetched, and even if it had been
made in or shortly after Jacopone's lifetime, the credit would have
scarcely added to his fame, since the Latin hymn was relatively little
known until much later.
  By contrast, the "Donna del paradiso" had an immediate fame. According to de Bartholomaeis: "The masterpiece of this very first period of
Italian drama is the 'Donna del paradiso' of Jacopone. Of the religious

poetry produced in Italy during all the Middle Ages, this is one of the most popular, if not the most popular. Numerous manuscripts have preserved it, in the widest variants and with the most different dialectical settings: both dramatic and non-dramatic collections, both Franciscan and non-Franciscan."[34] As is self-evident, the life of this *lauda*—and of the "Quando t'alegri" as well—is attested by the fact that Italians wanted to put it each in his own dialect and adapt it each for his own uses. These variants are to be found all over central and north Italy up to the very frontiers of the Italian language at Pieve di Cadore.[35] Sometimes it appears in collections made for the "battuti" or companies of actors, sometimes in the hymnbooks of the *disciplinati,* but most often in the devotional books of the Franciscans and the Order of the Gesuati.

That the *disciplinati* used it as their first dramatic representations, in the Good Friday services, can hardly be doubted, and it was among these groups that the next step in the creation of the Italian theater was taken.[36] At Perugia, the company of *disciplinati,* which was so large that it was later split up into several parochial units, began to want to add costumes and scenery, and eventually to write plays of their own. By the early years of the next century, a whole collection of nearly 200 such playlets was gathered together in the "Libro de Laonde." They were mostly very short, but "true jewels in their brevity, simplicity, clarity, and precision."[37] Written in the ballad form, which Jacopone preferred and which made the best musical settings, the plays dealt with the events of the church year and formed a running commentary on the liturgy. Some few dealt with the lives of saints. Occásionally, the eight-line stanza, which Jacopone used for sad themes, appears, as is notably the case in the Perugian play for the dead based on the "Quando t'alegri." Only slowly did the idea of stage performance spread, because it had to be seen to be reproduced, and the next centers of theatrical activity were first at Orvieto and later at Aquila.

The direct influence of the "Donna del paradiso" is most clearly seen at Aquila. Three of the dramatic *laude* of the Abruzzese *disciplinati* have survived and tell the very same story, but in a more diffuse manner. Quite a few speaking parts have been added: the sisters of Mary, the Magdalen, John, Pilate, and Joseph; the material in the *Meditations on the Life of Christ* seems to have been used again. Though these poems do not have much artistically to offer a reader, they must have come to a vigorous life when they were staged in an increasingly elaborate manner.[38]

Good Friday Passion plays also survive from such lesser centers as Assisi and Gubbio, where the derivation from the "Donna del paradiso" is equally clear.[39] The smaller towns had much less ambitious mise en scènes and much simpler tastes, so the old-fashioned Jacoponian *laude* kept on being performed well into the fifteenth century—long after the great cities of Rome, Siena, and Florence had developed their own splendid variety of *sacre rappresentazioni*. The vitality of Jacopone's dramatic masterpiece is further confirmed by the fact that it has been revived and given open-air performances in our own day.[40]

But what is even more significant for the history of the Italian people is that the Franciscans went out into the countryside. Historians have so long thought of the order as a manifestation of the religious life of the towns that it comes almost as a surprise to discover the Franciscans penetrating into the deepest fastnesses of the country—for many centuries and even today. The rural areas were where most of the Italian people lived. Even at Todi, which lay in a particularly heavily settled part of Italy, the rural population outnumbered the town population in 1300 by about three to one. And when they went into the country, the Franciscans took the "Donna del paradiso" with them. Three manuscripts have been discovered in the Abruzzi, which include the poem in Good Friday sermons, and probably the friars divided the parts among themselves and presented a simple drama. Thus the genius of Jacopone penetrated into the high Appenines. As an Abruzzese historian has written: "The Franciscans spread out in all directions, even to the villages and hamlets of the most alpine regions. From these friaries, planted among the thickest forests or hanging over steep cliffs, they spread the joy of knowledge with the light of faith among the most humble—even peasants and shepherds."[41]

VI ∞ The Fool of God

Upon being freed from prison in 1303, Jacopone retired to the little village of Collazzone, standing on a hill some eight miles up the Tiber Valley from Todi. Here he lived out the last three years of his life among the several friars attached to the convent of San Lorenzo di Collazzone. Small groups of friars were often sent to take care of the spiritual needs of the sisters, and conversely the sisters saw to the physical needs of the friars. Such an arrangement would have been convenient, since Jacopone was now an old man nearing seventy. He could not well return to his former house at San Fortunato, as that respectable community was now deeply involved in the building of the great church and would not have welcomed the former rebel. It is even possible that he had been imprisoned at San Fortunato; in any case, the prophet was not honored in his own country. When Jacopone had been safely dead for over a hundred years and was revered by some as a saint, Todi began to make up for its neglect. In 1433, his remains were discovered in the convent of Santa Maria di Montecristo, whither the sisters had taken them, probably around 1365, after the decline of the house at Collazzone; not until 1596 was the existing tomb in the crypt of San Fortunato dedicated with suitable ecclesiastical fanfare.[1]

But it would be a mistake to think of Jacopone as a rejected and broken old man. He was not to die like a dog in the manner of Boniface VIII but was to progress in holiness and poetic creativity right up to the time of leaving this life. The record of his apotheosis is contained in the poems of divine love that make up the last quarter of the Buonaccorsi edition. By reading them it can be seen that Jacopone's last years were, like those of Francis, the best years of his life. In the words of a perceptive modern critic: "What lives especially in Jacopone and makes him great is his original mystical experience; and one must tell the history of this experience . . . to give value to that which is the poetry of Jacopone."[2]

Probably most of the poems of divine love were written after the period of political activity, both in prison and at Collazzone. But since the dating of all except the political poems is based on internal evidence, wide divergencies of opinion on the subject among scholars are to be expected. Mostly, the poems are dated earlier, and a situation is visualized in which contemplation and social action alternate.[3] Such a pattern of withdrawal from the world and then reentry into it in activist conflict was and is common; it is certainly in the Augustinian tradition, strikingly exemplified by Bernard and later by Luther. Bernard, who in Jacopone's day was considered to be the hero of the contemplative life and was so pictured by Dante (*Paradiso*, xxxi–xxxii), could leave the quiet meditations of his Cistercian cloister and enter into the most murderous and bigoted political activity. His preaching of the crusade activated the militaristic elements in a church that prior to his time was largely dedicated to peacemaking. Such a course was possible for Bernard, since even in his highest moments of contemplation he thought of the world as full of conflict between good and evil. For Bernard loving God implied hating sin and fighting against it. He conceived of the fourth and perfect state of the love of God, in which the soul of man is identified with God in perfect union, as being unattainable on this earth; in other words it was beyond his experience except, as he reports, in occasional moments of rapture.[4]

Jacopone progressed on the path of divine enlightenment beyond Bernard. Despite the misreading of some modern scholars,[5] it is clear that he ceased being embattled and reached in his last days a state of being beyond both good and evil. Hence, a good portion of the *laude* of divine love must have been written after his imprisonment, for it is inconceivable that the author of such poems as the "Amor de caritate," *Lauda* XC, and the "Sopr'onne lengua amore," *Lauda* XCI, could have regressed enough to descend into the political arena and write invectives against Boniface. This supposition is not to say that Jacopone withdrew from life in the manner of an Indian mystic; in any case, the dichotomy between the contemplative and the active life did not then exist in men's minds.[6] Rather it is to be supposed that he reached a state comparable to that of Francis, about whom it has been written: "When contemplation rises to this degree of perfection, it acts like a real force with effects immediately perceptible: the contemplative who comes back from these celestial regions to life among men, comes back with virtues beyond the human, he passes in the midst of things as an angel might pass—radiating extraordinary forces, seeing into what is fundamental in being, entering into communion through the wrappings of matter with whatever of divine lies at the heart of each."[7]

Like almost all mystics, Jacopone could reach such a state of blessedness only after a long struggle and a long experience of meditation, but the poles of the struggle had changed. During his penitential and political period the battle was between sin and virtue, good and evil, guilt and expiation, salvation and damnation, life and death. Gradually these conflicts were resolved, and Jacopone could look back on them with indifference. Now the struggle was between the consciousness of God's love and the sense of being deprived of it—God's presence or absence. This kind of conflict is the problem of Brother Lawrence and Thomas R. Kelly,[8] and not that of Bernard. Jacopone's consciousness of God's love starts as a trickle in the early poems and swells to a great river that carries everything away with it in its mighty course. To select a few examples, hints of the power of divine love are found in the last lines of the penitential *Lauda* XXXIX, when he is "overcome with the abundance of his sweet Lord." Or, again, he rises above the problems of wealth and poverty in loving union with Christ—*Lauda* LX, lines 34–41. Or, he reflects on the power of love as shown in the Incarnation—*Lauda* LXV.

Though this growth was gradual and for a man so impatient as Jacopone depressingly slow, the prison experience represents a decided turning point. Here he acquired his second shield, that of love; here Boniface was transformed by the power of love in Jacopone from the representative on earth of the Anti-Christ to that of the Christ; here sheer physical deprivation released him from the furies of guilt.[9] For a soul so tortured as that of Jacopone, it was easier to learn of God's love through suffering than through happiness, and he may have been intellectually aware of the usefulness of adversity in spiritual growth, since Richard of St. Victor had written extensively on the subject.[10] Prison may have been Jacopone's "cell of self-knowledge,"[11] where he learned that it is only through the death of his human individuality that he can share in the universal life of God. The death of the individual historical Jesus on the cross and the continuing life of the eternal Christ brought this truth home to him. In *Lauda* LXXXIII, Jacopone shows how he has mastered this difficult lesson:

O dolce amore - c'hai morto l'amore,
prego che m'occidi d'amore.
    Amor c'hai menato - lo tuo enamorato
ad cusì forte morire,
perchè 'l facesti - che non volesti
ch'io dovesse perire?
Non me parcire, - non voler soffrire
ch'io non moia abracciato d'amore. . . .
    L'amore sta appeso, - la croce l'ha preso
e non lassa partire.
Vocce currendo - e mo me cce appendo,
ch'io non possa smarrire.
Ca lo fugire - farìame sparire,
ch'io non serìa scritto en amore.
    O croce, io m'apicco - ed ad te m'aficco,

ch'io gusti morendo la vita.
Chè tu ne se' ornata, - o morte melata;
tristo che non t'ho sentita!
O alma sì ardita - d'aver sua ferita,
ch'io moia accorato d'amore.
    Vocce currendo, - en croce legendo
nel libro che c'è ensanguinato.
Ca essa scrittura - me fa el natura
ed en filosofia conventato.
O libro signato - che dentro se' aurato
e tutto fiorito d'amore!
    O amor d'agno - magior che mar magno,
e chi de te dir porrìa?
A chi c'è anegato - de sotto e da lato
e non sa dove sia,
e la pazia - gli par ritta via
de gire empazato d'amore.

O sweet love, who has killed love [Jesus], I pray that you kill me with love. Love, you have brought your beloved to such a bitter death. Why did you do it if you did not wish that I should perish? Do not spare me, for I do not want not to die embraced by love. . . .

Love [Jesus] is nailed on the cross, which has seized Him and will not let Him go. I go running to it and am nailed there too so that I cannot go astray, for to flee from it would make me disappear and not be inscribed among the beloved.

O cross, I am hanging on you and am nailed to you, so that I, dying, may taste the life with which you are adorned. O honeyed death, sad for one who has not undergone it! O my soul, so burning to receive its wound that I may die with my heart overcome with love.

I go running to it, and bloodied on the cross, read in the book of life, and in this scripture I become learned in science and philosophy. O book of signs, which is full of gold and all flowering with love.

O love of the lamb, greater than the wide sea, who can tell of you? Whoever is drowned in it and has it on all sides does not know where he is, and madness, walking driven mad with love, seems the straight way to him. [Lines 1–8, 15–38]

This is the straight way which Dante found out of the dark wood (*Inferno*, i, 1–6); but Dante's voyage was through an ordered cosmos ruled by human reason and divine love, while Jacopone's was into a chartless infinity entirely beyond human reason. Herein lies the madness of the fool of God.

It is hardly surprising that Jacopone should have found his way through the symbolism of the cross, as he expresses it in this *lauda*, for the cross was deeply embedded in the Franciscan imagination. Francis's experience of the stigmata was the beginning of a strong tradition of concentration on the cross as a theme for meditation, a tradition that was especially dear to the spirituals, as the little work, "Considerations on the Stigmata," shows.[12] Furthermore, Bonaventure had used almost the same words as Jacopone: "Now there is no path but through that most burning love for the Crucified which so transformed Paul the apostle that when he was carried up to the third heaven, he could say: 'With Christ I am nailed to the Cross. It is now no longer I that live but Christ in me.' (Galatians, ii, 20.)" This passage comes from Bonaventure's *The Journey of the Mind to God,* perhaps his most famous devotional work and one which Jacopone certainly knew. He probably also knew Bonaventure's *The Tree of Life,* another very popular manual for meditation, which opens with the simple statement: "With Christ I am nailed to the Cross."[13]

Yet despite the fact that Jacopone's spirituality closely followed Franciscan tradition, this *lauda,* "O dolce amore," unquestionably reflects his own experience and his own personality. We have already seen how the Savior was the primary influence in his rising from the depths of depression in his penitential period,[14] and now he is beginning to develop that resolution of opposites in divine love that was the hallmark of his last period. The *lauda* is full of almost Erasmian paradoxes. In it he rapidly changes the meaning of "love" and "death": divine love kills the physical and human "love" or the man Jesus; physical death is sweet because it leads to eternal life, while physical life is abhorred because it leads to eternal death. The use of the double negative—he does "not want not to die"—serves to confuse the polarities still further, and the extreme condensation of the thought, characteristic of the notary, makes it hard for the reader to sort out the opposites. Difficult as this makes the poem, Jacopone must write it in such a way, for only through the overcoming of the conventional dialectical thought of his time can he rise to the understanding of divine love. Thus Jacopone has gone beyond Bonaventure, who remained trapped in scholasticism. His madness does not stem, as Sapegno has supposed,[15] from the irreconcilable tension between his light and dark side, but from the exact opposite—the loss of all sense of polarities, all external landmarks, in the sea of divine love.

Like all forms of madness, it was terrifying. The giving of oneself in love is a fearful and dangerous thing. In our modern world, so expert in the realm of Eros, we can easily understand the reticences and psychological scar tissue with which the human lover protects himself from the hurts administered by his human beloved; but being less experienced in the realm of Agape, which the thirteenth century knew well, and especially from the works of the Victorines,[16] we do not so easily understand that the same fears beset the lover of God.

Jacopone recoiled in horror:

Fuggo la croce che me devura,
la sua calura non posso portare.

Non posso portare sì gran calore
che getta la croce, fuggendo vo amore;
non trovo loco, ca porto nel core
la remembranza me fa consumare.

I flee the cross that devours me; I cannot stand its heat. I cannot stand the
so great heat that the cross projects; I go fleeing from love. I cannot find a
place to hide, for I carry it in my heart and the memory of it burns me up.
[*Lauda* LXXV, lines 1–6]

The poem develops into a dialogue with another friar, so realistic that
it might actually have taken place. Note that in falling from grace, the
poet has relapsed into his former dialectical pattern. Jacopone's friend is
a typical, "normal" Franciscan, full of joy and delight in the love of
Christ. One is cured by the cross, the other is wounded; one sees flowers
on the cross, the other, arrows piercing his heart; one sees by the light,
the other is blinded by it; one wants to preach, though he had not been
articulate, the other is struck dumb with awe, though he had been highly
articulate. Finally, the relentless dichotomies are too much for Jacopone
and he explodes:

"Tu stai al caldo, ma io sto nel fuoco;
a te è diletto, ma io tutto cuoco;
co'n la fornace trovar non pò loco,
se non c'èi entrato non sai quegn'è stare."
"Frate, tu parli che io non t'entendo,
como l'amore gir vòi fugendo,
questo tuo stato verrìa conoscendo,
se tu le me potessi en cuore splanare."
"Frate, el tuo stato è en sapor de gusto,
ma io c'ho bevuto, portar non pò el musto,
non aggio cerchio che sia tanto tusto
che la fortura non faccia alentare."

"You are in the warmth, but I am in the fire; it is a delight to you, but I am
all scalded. I have no place to stand in this furnace; if you have not entered
it, you don't know what it's like."
"Brother, you are saying something I don't understand, this wish of
yours to flee from love. I would like to know of this your state, if you can
explain it to me, heart to heart."
"Brother, in your state you are enjoying the taste of fine wine, but what I
have tasted is the fermenting juices that I can't stand. I do not have a bottle
that is strong enough to hold the new wine." [Lines 50–62]

The last figure obviously refers to Jesus' injunction that new wine cannot
be put into old bottles (Matthew 9:17). It is an apt symbol from several

points of view: wine is the substance of the Eucharist, where it becomes the very blood of Christ; new wine, especially that called "frizzante," the incomplete fermentation of which plays hob with the digestion, was well known to every resident of a wine-producing country like Todi. Jacopone's fear of exposing himself further to divine love is, like bad wine, in his guts.

This new stage in his spiritual growth separated him even more from the conventional religious of his time. Even the Blessed Angela da Foligno, Jacopone's contemporary and near neighbor, rarely rises above the commonplace in her remarkable journal. Her *Book of Divine Consolation* is remarkable because it is one of the first attempts to use autobiography as a tool in the spiritual life and is thus the forerunner of those many spiritual journals that graced the history of Christianity in later centuries both within the Catholic Church and among the followers of the Inner Light.[17] Jacopone's new state unavoidably separated him from the vast majority of mankind, as so few could understand the route he was following. This separation has led him to be accused of being "solitary and proud"—full of the stiff-necked arrogance characteristic of heretics.[18] There is some ground for the charge, but not much. Certainly those charming tales of humble human companionship that so bring Francis to life in the *Fioretti* did not cluster around his memory; as he became more conscious of the power of divine love, he became more sensitive to the inadequacies of human love. Even in this last period, Jacopone could have his moments of pessimistic didacticism. For example, in *Lauda* LXXII, he begins: "Vorrìa trovar chi ama: - molti trovo che sè ama [I would like to find one who loves; I find many who love themselves]." He then proceeds to describe with considerable subtlety the various ways in which human beings use each other through "false love" to achieve their own selfish purposes. One feels an element of Dantean judgmentalism or disdain.

But to conclude from this *lauda* that Jacopone stood apart from his fellow men in sour pride is to overlook the fact that he was attacking the sense of self in himself as well as in others. Hence his reflections on "false love" represent only another step in the progress of his victory over self. He makes this clear in the first of his *Detti:*

> Of the love of my neighbor I have this sign: that if he offends me, I do not love him less. In fact, if I did love him less, it would be a sign that before I did not love him, but me. I should in fact love my neighbor for himself, and not for me, and take pleasure in his good and his advantage. And doing this, I seek for his good more than he does himself.[19]

If Jacopone succeeded, he would indeed have been a true and sensitive friend to men as well as to God, and there is every reason to believe that he did so succeed. Not only is there the evidence of his friendship with Giovanni de la Verna, but also there is the imposing monument of his pure joy, the *lauda* in which he rushes out to his fellow men in ecstatic euphoria. Unalloyed fun bursts forth from his little masterpiece, *Lauda* LXXVI:

> O iubilo del core, - che fai cantar d'amore!
> Quando iubilo se scalda, - sì fa l'uomo cantare;
> e la lengua barbaglia - e non sa que parlare,
> dentro non pò celare, - tanto è grande el dolzore!
> Quando iubilo è acceso - sì fa l'omo clamare;
> lo cor d'amore è preso - che nol po' comportare
> stridendo el fa gridare - e non vergogna allore.
> Quando iubilo ha priso - lo cor enamorato,
> la gente l'ha en deriso, - pensando suo parlato,
> parlando smesurando - de que sente calore.
> O iubil, dolce gaudio, - ched entri ne la mente,
> lo cor deventa savio - celar suo convenente,
> non può esser sofferente - che non faccia clamore.
> Chi non ha costumanza - te reputa empazito,
> vedendo svalianza - com omo ch'è desvanito,
> dentro lo cor ferito - non se sente de fuore.

O joy of the heart that makes one sing of love! When joy heats up, a man must sing, and the tongue babbles and knows not what it is saying, and joy cannot be hidden inside, so great is its sweetness.

When joy is lit up, a man must shout. The heart is seized with love that it cannot bear and makes him yell and scream and not be ashamed of it.

When joy has captured the loving heart, folk make fun of him, thinking his speech the unbalanced prattling of an overheated spirit.

O joy, sweet gladness, when you enter the mind, the heart becomes wise in hiding what should be hidden, but it cannot keep from making a cry.

Whoever hasn't experienced it thinks you are crazy, seeing the eccentricities of a man who is unbalanced, has a wounded heart, and has lost touch with external reality.

If a musician were to select just one of Jacopone's *laude* to set to music, this would be it. The melodious verses seem to clamor for that heightened sense of passion conveyed by music. Jacopone has reached a "high" and on this eminence can dance and yell and sing only slightly inhibited by the knowledge that his behavior will excite amusement among others. One of the friars' stories about Jacopone has passed on what these transports might have looked like:

> Sometimes finding himself in the country and considering the great love which God had shown to man and all drunk with this great divine love, he

went running about like one who was seeking to embrace some one and took to embracing a tree, pressing it close as though he were embracing Jesus. He shouted and said: "O my sweetest Jesus, O Jesus my dear friend," and other such loving words to his Redeemer. [At other times] when he received the holy sacrament, he was seen and heard to utter the same loving expressions and to have his face light up as with a flame of fire, without remembering that he was in church and could be overheard.[20]

Such transports express "perfect joy"—the "highest gift and grace of the Holy Spirit that Christ concedes to His friends," which Francis had preached so eloquently.[21] Those modern critics who persist in thinking of Jacopone as always imprisoned in pessimistic moral struggles, always embattled, never understanding the happy Franciscan spirit—and unfortunately they are in the majority[22]—have not read aright this little gem of a *lauda*. If this hymn to joy were unique, such a misapprehension might be more understandable, but it is not. Listen to the smooth-flowing measures of *Lauda* LXXXVI:

> Amor dolce senza pare - sei, tu, Cristo, per amare.
> Tu sei amor che coniugni, - cui più ami spesso pugni;
> onne piaga, poi che l'ugni, - senza unguento fai sanare.
> Amor, tu non abandoni - chi t'offende, sì perdoni;
> e de gloria encoroni - che se sa umiliare.
> Amor grande, dolce e fino, - increato sei divino,
> tu che fai lo serafino - de tua gloria enflammare.
> Cherubin ed altri cori, - apostoli e dottori,
> martiri e confessori, - vergene fai iocundare.
> Patriarche e profete - tu tragisti de la rete;
> de te, amor, àver tal sete, - non se crèdor mai saziare.

> Sweet, incomparable love, you are, Christ, to love. You are the love that often joins friends who fight; you anoint every wound and cure it without ointment. Love, you do not abandon but pardon the one who offends you and crown with glory the one who knows how to humble himself. . . .
> Great, sweet and delicate love, you are the increate divine, you who make the seraph flame with your glory. Cherubim and other singers, apostles and doctors, martyrs and confessors, virgins—you make them all happy. Patriarchs and prophets you draw from the devil's net. They have such thirst for you, love, that it never will be slaked. [Lines 1–5, 10–15]

Such was the living water of Jacob's well (John 4:14). Here again joy bubbles forth and expresses itself in the rollicking listing of all the blessed, reminiscent of the listing of poverty's subjects in the "Povertade enamorata."[23]

But no one can live long on such heights. "And as the height to which the soul's boldness raises it," wrote Richard of St. Victor, "is far above man; so the depths to which its patience depresses it is far below man."[24] Mystic pains follow the ecstatic periods. The more intense the state of ecstasy, the deeper the depression that is likely to follow. For Jacopone, as for others, measureless love is followed by measureless sorrow, and he expresses the Victorine polarity with a wail:

> Or chi averà cordoglio? - vorrìane alcun trovare
> che vorrìa mostrare - dolor esmesurato. . . .
>   Signor, io vo cercando - la tua nativitate,
> e mettome a vedere - le tue penalitate,
> non ci ho suavitate, - chè l'amor è arfreddato.
>   Vedendo el mio cordoglio, - sì me move pianto,
> ma è un pianto sciucco - che vien da cor affranto;
> ed ov'è 'l dolzor tanto - che me s'è sì encarato.

> Now who will take pity? I must find some one to whom I can show my measureless grief. . . .
>   Lord, I go seeking for the meaning of your nativity and your sufferings, but I do not find consolation in them, for my love has gone cold. Seeing my grief, I am moved to tears, but it is a dry complaint that comes from a broken heart. And where is the great sweetness that has become so dear to me? [*Lauda* LXVI, lines 1–2, 30–35]

Jacopone is bored, finding that he cannot weep or sigh, read or pray. For both the worshiper and the artist the absence of inspiration can be complete and is more keenly felt in proportion to the greatness of the inspiration. Mystics and creative artists of all times go through such periods of sterility, when inner power is cut off and the reaction is the form of fear called boredom. Realizing that dryness has been experienced by others and hence is to be expected, can be consoling; so the analysis of Richard of St. Victor may have been helpful to Jacopone.

He might have turned for consolation also to Bernard, for Bernard understood the problem when he wrote: "The mind experiences affection like this, so that inebriated with divine love, forgetful of self, . . . it may utterly pass over into God, and adhering to God, become one spirit with Him. . . . Blessed and holy should I call one to whom it has been granted to experience such a thing in this mortal life at rare intervals. . . . Alas, he is compelled to return to himself, to fall back on his own, and miserably to exclaim: . . . 'Unhappy man that I am, who shall deliver me from the body of this death?' "[25] Such relapses are common in the early stages of the meditative life, especially when the worshiper is concentrating his attention and will on a formal life of devotion to a God outside of himself—what Quakers have called "willful prayer." Jacopone had passed through such a stage and described his experience accurately in *Lauda* XXVIII:

Assai me sforzo a guadagnare - se 'l sapesse conservare.
Religioso sì so stato - longo tempo ho procacciato;
ed aiolo sì conservato, - che nulla ne pos mostrare.

Much have I forced myself to gain; if I only knew how to keep. I have
been a friar and for a long time have sought, but I have kept so little that I
have nothing to show for it. [Lines 1–3]

He goes on to describe his prayers, his study, his ascetical practices, and
the routines of his conventual life. But they are all for nothing.

E vil cosa me sia ditta, - al cor passa la saitta;
e la lengua mia sta ritta - ad voler fuoco gettare.
Or vedete el guadagnato, - co so ricco ed adagiato!
ch'un parlar m'ha sì turbato - ch'a pena posso perdonare.

And if a harsh word is said to me, the arrow pierces my heart and my
tongue stands ready to throw out fire. Now see my gain, how rich and at
ease I am! One word can upset me so much that I can hardly forgive it.
[Lines 12–15]

To overcome such moments of depression, Jacopone tried to use his
mind and turned to the guidebooks for the spiritual life. Here Bonaventure was Jacopone's chief helper. The poet may even have met the great
Franciscan leader, as the latter came to Todi in 1261;[26] but whether he
knew him personally or not, he was well acquainted with Bonaventure's
thought over a long period of time. Bonaventuran language has been
traced in Jacopone's poems from those of the earliest penitential period,
like Lauda IV, "O alta penitenza," and Lauda VI, "Guarda che non caggi";
through those of his life as a spiritual Franciscan, like Lauda LXI, "O
Francesco povero," which draws heavily on Bonaventure's life of Francis; to, finally, the philosophical laude of his old age.[27] There are three of
the latter, Laude LXIX, LXXXVIII, and LXXXIX, and they show how
Jacopone tried to provide a rational explanation for his experience.

Like mystics of all ages, Jacopone evinced the need for intellectual
structure in his spiritual life in the hope of making a map to avoid pitfalls.
He followed the very common practice of constructing a numerical sequence of states of the soul. This numerical sequence can in itself be both
magical and safe, as Bonaventure observed: "Since . . . proportion is first
found in numerical harmony, it must follow that all things are related to
number. Thus 'number is the foremost exemplar in the mind of the
Creator' (Boethius, 'De Arithmetica'); and in things, the foremost trace of
His wisdom."[28]

The first of Jacopone's philosophical laude, "Fede, spene e caritade"
(LXIX), follows closely the pattern laid out by Bonaventure, whose Jour-

ney of the Mind to God describes nine stages of spiritual growth, three each for faith, hope, and charity, and whose *Tree of Life* uses the symbolism of climbing a spiritual tree. Again like Bonaventure, Jacopone is didactic; he wishes to show the way to others by telling of the growth of his own inner life. He writes that three trees are each to be climbed in succession, the trees of faith, hope, and charity. Each tree has three branches representing appropriate virtues, and the three trees are also related to the three heavens as posited by Pseudo-Dionysius and passed on by Bonaventure in *The Triple Way*. Thus Jacopone's first tree is that of faith and corresponds to the first heaven, inhabited by Thrones and Virtues; Jacopone thinks that he has passed through this stage during his life as a *bizocone*. The second tree is that of hope, corresponding to the second or crystalline heaven inhabited by Powers and Principalities, and Jacopone places in this stage the conflict of good and evil in his soul. The third tree is that of love, the empyrean inhabited by the Seraphim, and it is this area that is of most concern to Jacopone in his old age.

Almost exactly the same pattern is developed in the next philosophical *lauda*, "L'omo che può la sua lengua domare" (LXXXVIII), but some significant differences indicate the progress in Jacopone's thought. He is no longer didactic but writes only to clarify his own mind, realizing that his own spiritual growth will in itself teach, without the need for evangelical preaching. Now, there is only one tree, the roots of which are in humility and faith and the height of which represents a barely achievable goal to the aspiring climber led on by hope. The nine branches follow the Bonaventuran pattern, but there is also evidence of the thought of Bernard, Hugh and Richard of St. Victor, Brother Giles, and Joachim of Fiore. It is not necessary to suppose, of course, that Jacopone read much in the voluminous works of these masters, but the latter certainly formed the intellectual atmosphere of the circles in which he lived.

By the time Jacopone wrote the last of the three philosophical *laude*, "Un arbore è da Dio plantato - lo qual amor è nominato [A tree has been planted by God, which is called love]" (LXXXIX), he has made the whole symbolism his own. In the first place, love is given primacy over faith, and then the numerical and intellectual categories are not so very definite. Furthermore, Jacopone is not so very long-winded. The *Trattato*, which either he or one of his followers wrote as a summation of his thought, probably stems from this last period and is a prose commentary on the philosophical *laude*—the same sort of spiritual guidebook as the mystical works of Bonaventure.

Most modern critics agree that these three poems are among Jacopone's worst.[29] They fail for two reasons: first, the intellectual patterns and symbolism of any historical period become quickly outdated, so verbal structures that were once meaningful lose their power and can be understood only after patient historical reconstruction; second, such intellectual structures did not mean much to Jacopone. (It is interesting to note that the intellectual structures drawn from the same sources by Dante meant so much to him as to be integrally incorporated in *The Divine Comedy*.[30] Dante could make poetry out of rigid mathematical patterns and rational cosmology; Jacopone couldn't.) The contrast between such "naturals" as Jacopone and Francis and such intellectuals as Bonaventure and the Victorines hardly needs further emphasis; it is the contrast between direct intuitive experience expressed in poetry and action and the "systematization of religious experience."[31] As Underhill wryly commented: "Christian Platonists and mystical philosophers are no more mystics than the milestones on the Dover Road are travellers to Calais."[32] Jacopone could not agree more. Manfully he tried to explain his experience through traditional philosophy, but he found that rational analysis did not help him much.

For Jacopone the liberation from depression was not by reason, but by grasping the nettle, that is, by entering into the experience of sterility and giving it complete expression. In effect, Jacopone was able to discharge through laments the desolation over the absence of God just as he had been able to discharge his sense of guilt through tears. Unconsciously perhaps, he had models in the love laments of the Sicilian poets; what was valid in the realm of Eros might also apply to the realm of Agape. When in *Lauda* LXVII, Jacopone laments the loss of God's love, he is in the same emotional position as the woman who had been abandoned by her lover in the "Già mai non mi conforto" of Rinaldo d'Aquino.[33]

> Amor, diletto amore, - perché m'hai lassato, amore?
> Amor, di' la cagione - de lo tuo partimento,
> che m'hai lassata afflitta - en gran dubitamento. . . .

> Love, beloved love, why have you left me, love? Love, tell me the reason for your leaving, for you have left me afflicted and in great doubt. . . .
> [*Lauda* LXVII, lines 1–3]

The poem develops into a dialogue with love and in terms of its thought follows closely the pattern of a typical Sicilian *tenson*, like the "Donna di voi me lamento" of Giacomino Pugliese.[34] But Jacopone has raised the discourse to a new level. Whereas Giacomino writes of the tensions between a man and a woman in love—almost a mere lovers' quarrel—Jacopone uses the form to explore the inner tensions of his soul in travail, thus infusing it with an interiority and a passionate intensity far removed from the conventionality of the Sicilian poet.

In a sense, Jacopone's spiritualizing of the concept of love in a religious context is parallel to the spiritualization of love in the protohumanist patterns of his contemporaries, the poets of the *dolce stil nuovo*. Guido Calvacanti, for example, was ridding the concept of love of the external and earthy formulations of the Sicilian school and charging it with the deeper significance of Platonic idealism. Sonnets like his "Tu m'hai sì piena di dolor la mente" and *canzoni* like his "Io non pensava che lo cor giammai" are typical love laments in the new style. It was Dante, of course, who made the whole development explicit both by the *Vita Nova* and by his definition of the *dolce stil nuovo* in the *De Vulgari Eloquentia*.[35] Jacopone almost certainly did not know of this parallel development and would not have thought of it as parallel, because Beatrice (and the other beloveds) was still a woman on earth and had not yet risen to paradise to express the idealization of love in a religious sense.

Yet Jacopone achieves the same intensity and the same precision of expression, when in *Lauda* LXVIII, he laments the loss of divine love:

> Piangi, dolente anima predata,
> che stai vedovata de Cristo amore.
>   Piangi, dolente, e getta sospire,
> chè t'hai perduto el dolce tuo Sire;
> forsa per pianto mo 'l fa revenire
> a lo sconsolato tristo mio core.
>   Io voglio piangere, chè m'agio anvito,
> chè m'ho perduto pate e marito;
> Cristo piacente, giglio fiorito,
> èsse partito per mio fallore. . . .
>   O occhi miei, e como finate
> de pianger tanto che 'l lume perdate?
> Perduto avete la gran redetate
> de resguardare al polito splendore.
>   Orecchie miei, e que ve deletta
> de udire pianto de amara setta?
> Non resentite la voce diletta
> che ve facea canto e iubilore?

Weep, my grieving harrowed soul, for you are widowed by the love of Christ. Weep, grieve, and utter sighs, for you have lost your sweet Lord. Perhaps by means of my lament, you will make it come back to my sad and disconsolate heart.

I wish to weep and I have reason, for I have lost father and husband: fond Christ, flowering lily, has left me because of my fault. . . .

O my eyes, why do you not weep so much as to lose your sight? You have lost the great gift of contemplating pure splendor. O my ears, how can you delight in hearing the lament of the bitter people? Can you not hear the beloved voice that made you sing with joy? [*Lauda* LXVIII, lines 1–10, 27–34]

This full-throated song of melancholy has gained a new directness and simplicity and makes one think of the melodic sweep of Petrarch in the sonnets "Occhi, piangete, accompagnate il core" and "Occhi mie, oscurato è 'l nostro sole."[36] Even the words of the two poets are similar, though one sings of human, and the other of divine love.

Jacopone ends his lament with a statement of his loneliness:

Non voglio mai de om compagnia,
salvaticata voglio che sia
enfra la gente la vita mia,
da c'ho perduto lo mio Redentore.

I never wish for the company of men; I wish that my life may be savage among people, since I has lost my Redeemer. [Lines 39–42]

And here again Petrarchan echoes spring to mind. The humanist poet also seeks out the savage wilderness to escape from the superficial babbling of men and to converse with love: "Solo e pensoso i più deserti campi / vo mesurando a passi tardi e lenti [Alone and pensive the most deserted strand / I tread and measure with steps slow and dark]."[37]

Jacopone even thinks to shield his love from contact with men in the hope of protecting it from loss. In one of the most original of his laude, he gives way to the fear that the very act of externalizing his love in words will extinguish its inner force.

O amor muto - che non vòi parlare,
che non sie conosciuto!
O amor che te celi - per onne stagione,
ch'omo de fuor non senta - la tua affezione,
che non la senta latrone - per quel c'hai guadagnato,
che non te sia raputo.
Quando l'om più te cela, - tanto più 'n foco abunne;
om che te ven occultando - sempre a lo foco iugne,
ed omo c'ha le pugne - de volere parlare,
spesse volte è feruto.

O silent love that will not speak so that it will not be known! O love, who hides yourself at all times, so that men will not feel externally your affection and so that the thief will not be able to take you away from the one who has gained you.
The more a man hides you, the more he abides in the fire. The man who hides you always reaches the fire, and the man who struggles to speak of you is often hurt. [Lauda LXXVII, lines 1–10]

Here Jacopone speaks almost like a Zen master, who guards the secret of his meditation from the view of outsiders and repels those who come to

learn in order to test the strength of their purpose. Jacopone is careful not
to cast pearls before swine. It often happens, indeed, that when one
speaks of divine love, its power is dissipated and leaves the speaker dry
and empty. Jacopone's originality consists in recognizing this phenomenon, an unusual and perhaps unique insight in his time. In the next
lines, he makes the point even more explicit:

> Omo che ha alcun lume - en candela apicciato,
> se vol che arda en pace, - mettelo a lo celato;
> ed onne uscio ha enserrato - che nogl venga lo vento
> che 'l lume sia stenguto.

> A man who has a lighted candle hides it if he wishes it to burn in
> peace—locks every door so that no wind will come and blow out his light.
> [Lines 15–18]

This is the exact opposite of the injunction of Jesus that men put the
candle not under a bushel, "but on a candlestick; and it giveth light unto
all that are in the house" (Matthew 5:15). It shows how far, at least at this
moment, Jacopone has come from the evangelical and activist drive to
spread the light unto all.

And he has good reason to treasure up the gift of grace in his heart:

> Tale amor ha posto - silenzio a li suspiri,
> èsse parato a l'uscio - e non gli lascia uscire;
> dentro el fa partorire - che non se spanda la mente
> da quel che ha sentuto.

> Such a love has silenced sighs and has barred the gate so that they cannot
> escape; it is born inside and the mind of one who has felt it must not
> dissipate it. [Lines 19–22]

Jacopone has realized the importance of silent meditation and felt again
the power of the inner light. The love of God has come to rest in his soul.
Talking about mysticism leads to reasoning away the reality of his experience, sullying the purity of his emotion and dispelling its power.[38]

Once having made this discovery, he threw out reason with typical
finality and found again his lyrical joy:

> Senno me pare e cortesia - empazir per lo bel Messia.
> Ello me sa sì grande sapere - a chi per Dio vol empazire,
> en Parige non se vidde - ancor sì gran filosofia.
> Chi per Gesù va empazato, - par afflitto e tribulato;
> ma è maestro conventato - en natura e teologia.
> Chi per Cristo ne va pazo, - a la gente sì par matto;
> chi non ha provato el fatto - pare che sia fuor de la via.

Chi vol entrare en questa scuola, - troverà dottrina nova;
la pazia, chi non la prova, - già non sa que ben se sia.
   Chi vol entrar en questa danza, - trova amor d'esmesuranza;
cento dì de perdonanza - a chi li dice villania.

It seems to me good sense and courtesy to go mad for the lovely Savior. It seems to me great wisdom to go mad for God. Paris has never yet seen such a great philosophy.

He who is mad for Jesus seems afflicted and disturbed, but he is a master with a doctorate in science and theology. He who is mad for Christ seems so crazy to people; whoever has never had the experience thinks him disoriented. He who wants to go to this school will find a new doctrine: madness, those who have not experienced it don't know how good it is. He who wants to join in this dance will find limitless love, a hundred days of pardon for him who speaks evil. [*Lauda* LXXXIV, lines 1–11][39]

Such is Jacopone's holy madness, which lies at the center of his spiritual life and forms his special contribution to the development of Christian mysticism. It has often been misunderstood. The first time that the title, "the Fool of God," was applied to him was by Alessandro d'Ancona in his work, *Jacopone da Todi, il giullare di Dio*, written nearly a hundred years ago. But d'Ancona meant that Jacopone was a Franciscan "ioculator Dei," a traveling popular minstrel full of the quaint eccentricities reported by the good friars in the *Franceschina*, because good scholar though he was, d'Ancona had no conception of the life of a mystic.[40] The true meaning of Jacopone's holy madness lies much deeper—in the recognition that Jacopone denied human reason, that he stilled the human mind in order to let in the flood of God's love. This insight is the central burden of his last message—and a prophetic one, for in the spirituality of the late Middle Ages, "the fool replaced the pilgrim as the 'ruling idea' of society."[41]

Jacopone approaches the experience of holy madness through reflection on the meaning of morality, finding that the nagging guilt and black pessimism of his penitential period is melting away in the warmth of the goodness of God. Thus, *Lauda* LXXIX forms a bridge between his earlier poems and the final ones expressing the fullness of divine love.

La bontade enfinita - vol enfinito amore,
mente, senno e core - lo tempo e l'esser dato.
   Amor longo fidele, - in eterno durante,
alto de speranza, - sopra li ciel passante,
amplo in caritate, - onne cosa abracciante,
en un profundo stante - de core umiliato.

Infinite goodness demands infinite love, wishes to be granted mind, sense, heart, time, and being.

Love, ever faithful, eternally lasting, high in hope, surmounting the heavens, full of charity, embracing all things, lies in the depths of a humble heart. [*Lauda* LXXIX, lines 1–6]

In this *lauda*, the jerks, kinks, and sudden changes of mood have been resolved into smooth-flowing verses, as Jacopone shows that he has surmounted the tortured intricacies of his embattled asceticism. He takes literally the command of Jesus: "Thou shalt love the Lord thy God with all thy heart, and with all thy soul, and with all thy mind. This is the first and great commandment" (Matthew 22:37–38). All human individuality, all perception of the outside world are swallowed up in the stable and pervading love of God. As Bonaventure had written: "It now remains for the soul . . . to transcend and go beyond not only this sensible world, but even its own self."[42] In the process, Jacopone shows that both will and mind are overcome:

La volontà creata, - en infinitate unita,
menata per la grazia - en sì alta salita,
en quel ciel d'ignoranzia - tra gaudiosa vita,
co ferro a calamita - nel non veduto amato.

Created will is united with the infinite, led on by grace to such a high ascent, drawn into that heaven of ignorance in the joyful life with the unseen beloved, as iron is drawn to the magnet. [Lines 7–10]

The final metallurgical simile, which Jacopone has used to describe the transformation of the soul in divine love is like that of Richard of St. Victor, who compares the transcendent event with the fusion of iron in a furnace. "It is thus that the soul, absorbed in this fiery furnace by the embrace of divine love which penetrates it and surrounded by the flames of eternal desires, finally melts and is completely fused with its former state."[43]

Jacopone goes on to describe the ignorant mind with its dependence on human reason and, in contrast, the "wise ignorance" that had led him miraculously to the indescribable country where he is "demented" in divine love (Lines 11–22). Though he is both describing his own unique experience and fashioning it into a poetical statement of new power, he could find that the concept of holy madness had a long and honorable history in Christian mysticism. The statement of Paul, when he attacked the gnostics of Corinth for their belief that salvation depended on some body of special knowledge, is seminal: "Let no man deceive himself. If any man among you seemeth to be wise in this world, let him become a fool, that he may be wise. For the wisdom of this world is foolishness with God. . . . We are fools for Christ's sake, but ye are wise in Christ. . . ." (1 Corinthians 3:18–19, 4:10). The doctrine had been given philosophical substance by Pseudo-Dionysius and subsequently entered into the mainstream of medieval mysticism. Among those who may have had a direct influence on Jacopone was Hugh of St. Victor, who wrote that the soul is "freed from all matter, deprived of form and overcomes all limitations. . . . transported by the excessive sweetness of the taste of God."[44] Also Richard of St. Victor explored with subtle analysis the "alienatio mentis" following upon the "excessus" of the love of God. A third Victorine, Thomas of Vercelli, took the doctrine even further when he insisted on the total denial of reason—"the emptying of the mind as a condition of union with God."[45] Even confirmed rationalists like Bonaventure wrote: "If this passing over is to be perfect, all intellectual operations must be given up, and the sharp point of our desire must be entirely directed toward God and transformed in Him."[46] And the greatest rationalist of them all, Thomas Aquinas, whom Jacopone almost certainly did not read, said on his deathbed: "The end of my writing has come, for such things have been revealed to me that all that I have written and taught seems to me very little. . . ."[47]

Jacopone was living through the abandonment of both the mind and the will, and the climax of his *lauda* is reached in a short dialogue with his soul:

"O alma nobilissima, - dimme que cosa vide!
"Veggo un tal non veggio - che onne cosa me ride;
la lengua m'è mozata - e lo pensier m'ascide,
miraculosa side - vive nel suo adorato."
    "Que frutti reducene - de esta tua visione?
"Vita ordinata veiome - en onne nazione;
lo cor ch'era immondissimo, - enferno inferiore,
de trinità magione - letto santificato."

"O most noble soul, tell me what you see!" "I see what I cannot see and everything smiles at me; my tongue is cut out, my thought cut off; the miraculous rests in its living adoration."
"What fruits do you bring back from this your vision?" "I see an ordered life in every nation, and the heart that was most filthy, lower than hell, is now the mansion and holy resting place of the Trinity." [Lines 23–30]

With this statement, Jacopone returns to the theme of the all-embracing goodness of God, applying not only to himself but also to all men. He races to his conclusion, for as always, he is in a hurry to get on with his spiritual growth. Just as his penitential *laude* are full of the urgency to reform and his *laude* on the Virgin and on Christ equally charged with the urgency of taking in their message, so that *lauda* ends with the poet's complaint that he has wasted his time before making this discovery and that now there is so little time left to him.

And so Jacopone presses on. The next two *laude* in the Buonaccorsi edition are extended dialogues in which he explores the meaning of love for his own inner life. He makes the "affectus" of the philosophers a part of his own experience, this theme of "tenderness and compassion" for Christ. He enters upon that "new type of ardent and effusive self-disclosure" characteristic of the piety of the late Middle Ages.[48]

Then, in *Lauda* LXXXII, the poem has a new insight—the realization that the entire world of the senses has been transformed for him, because he is looking at it from another point of view:

> O amor, divino amore, - perchè m'hai assediato?
> Pare de me empazato, - non puoi de me posare.
>   Da cinque parte veggio - che m'hai assediato:
> audito, viso, gusto, - tatto ed odorato;
> se esco, so pigliato, - non me te po' occultare.

> O love, divine love, why have you beseiged me? It seems as though you have driven me crazy and will not let me go.
>   I see that you have beseiged me on five sides: hearing, sight, taste, touch, and smell. If I go out, I am seized and cannot hide myself from you. [*Lauda* LXXXII, lines 1–5]

How far he has come from the asceticism of his early days, when the five senses were a source of guilt and horror! Now when he goes out into nature, he perceives through all his senses the magnificence of the world created out of the infinite goodness of God, and directs a standing reproof to those puritans of all ages with their belief in limitation and lack—even unto the environmentalists of our own time. The world becomes for him full of God, and he is hooked:

> Amor, divino amore, - amor pieno di brama;
> amor preso m'hai a l'ama - per poter in me regnare.

> Love, divine love, full of desire, you have caught me with a fishhook, in order to be able to reign in me. [Lines 13–14]

Jacopone is following in the footsteps of Francis, whose love for the created world as the expression of God found voice in the thrilling Thanksgiving hymn, the *Canticle to the Sun*.

Seeing God everywhere, Francis lived in a forest of symbols. In this symbolic world neither he nor Jacopone differed from a host of other medieval mystics. Pseudo-Dionysius had given the original impetus to what became the firm habit of the medieval mind—to see the immanence of God in all areas of creation and thus to look upon external reality not as a thing in itself but only as a symbol of true or divine reality. Hugh of St.

Victor expressed the concept succinctly: "Every being conceals divine thought. The world is an immense book written by the hand of God, in which each being is a page full of significance."[49] In the same way, the symbolism of the entire *Divine Comedy*, as Dante explains in *Paradiso*, iv, 40–48, serves to illustrate the working of God's will in the external, visible created world.

At the end of this *lauda*, Jacopone comes to another new conclusion: he is so transformed by love that he can no longer take the position of a moralist condemning the actions of others.

> S'io veggio ad omo male - o defetto o tentato,
> trasformome entro lui - e face 'l mio cor penato. . . .

> If I see evil or defects or temptations in a man, I enter into him and sorrow in my heart. . . . [Lines 24–25]

Though Jacopone does not deny the existence of evil, either in himself or in others, "measureless love," especially as shown in the sufferings and death of Jesus, has not only overcome and cured him, but also extended through him to others. Evil all men have, but they also have divine love. Love is the "ocean of light" that George Fox saw flowing over the "ocean of darkness."[50]

In *Lauda* LXXXVII, the vision carries Jacopone still further—to his total absorption in divine love and his complete transcendence over the physical universe.

> O audito senza audito, - che en te non hai clamore
> entelletto senza viso - hai anegato onne valore;
> non hai en te possessore, - da altri non èi posseduto,
> onne atto sì t'è renduto, - si sta l'amore affissato.
> L'odorato t'è renduto, - non sai dir que è delettare,
> lo sapore è fatto muto, - non sai dir più que è gustare;
> lo silenzio ce appare, - chè gli è tolto onne lenguaio;
> allor par già quietaio, - vive en sè ben roborato.
> Tutti gli atti vecchi e novi - en un nichilo son fondate,
> son formati senza forma, - non han termen nè quantitate,
> uniti con la veritate; - coronato sta l'affetto,
> quietato lo 'ntelletto, - nell'amore trasformato.

> O hearing without hearing, there is no sound in you. Intellect without sight has drowned all values. You possess nothing and are not possessed by others, since your every act has been renounced and you are fixed in love.
> Your sense of smell is given up, and you do not know how to say what delights you; your sense of taste is quieted, and you do not know how to say what tastes. Silence appears, for there is no need for speech. Then you are at peace and live strengthened within yourself.

All your acts, both old and new, are founded on nothingness, are formed
without form, have no ending or number, are united with truth. Transformed by love, your emotion is crowned and your intellect quieted. [*Lauda*
LXXXVII, lines 27–38]

Jacopone has reached the last stages in the development of the soul, as
they were described by his friend, Giovanni de la Verna: "The fourth
[stage] is in peace; and then man is taken from the world and the body,
and is placed on the cross and rests in God. . . . The fifth is glory; and this
is when man begins to be glorified and manifests in himself visions of
glory; and through this the creature is raised to that celestial glory in
which he sees the state of the angels . . . and then returns to revelation
and praise."[51] In the throes of such ecstasies, Giovanni was seized with
holy madness, reported by an eye-witness in the *Fioretti*,[52] the same holy
madness that seized Jacopone.

The nucleus of such ecstasies lies in the abandonment of the individual
will, united with truth and founded on nothingness, as Jacopone expresses it in this *lauda*. Here again the poet could find support in the
words of Paul: "Ye are not your own" (I Corinthians 6:19) . . . For it is
God which worketh in you both to will and to do of his good pleasure"
(Philippians 2:13). Furthermore, the abandonment of the individual will
to God was a cardinal doctrine of the Victorines, and Jacopone seems in
this *lauda* almost to be quoting Hugh of St. Victor, who said: "The very
mind conceives of God in fire and through fire knows God. For unless it
burns, it may not see or know, since this fire is delight and this delight is
knowledge . . . Love itself is knowledge and is feeling and is wisdom."[53]

With such a revelation in his heart, Jacopone must speak out. He is
driven like the prophet who said: "The Lord God hath spoken, who can
but prophesy?" (Amos 3:8). Neither fear of insensitive outsiders nor
discretion about the propriety of his emotion—feelings that he describes
in *Lauda* LXXXVIII—can contain the explosive force of the love of God. It
is much bigger than he. He must burst into song—which is far different
from merely describing rationally the nature of his experience. The result
is the masterpiece of his last period. "There does not exist in all our
literature, and not in ours alone," wrote the most profound of the modern
critics, "a poem more significant than the *lauda* 'Amor de caritate,' in
which the mystical experience can be said to have been captured in
action."[54]

Like a drowning man who sees all his past life in final review, Jacopone
has concentrated in this one great *lauda* all the strands of his mystical
experience and tightly woven them together into a tapestry of unsur-
passed richness. It is his great song of holy madness—but also a song
supported, in the finest Italic tradition, by an inner structure of architectural order. The poem is divided into three parts: the first, lines 1–146, an

autobiographical review of his long journey; the second, lines 147–242, a dialogue with Christ defining and ordering their relationship; and the third, lines 243–290, a pure love song capturing in action the "excessus mentis" of the Victorine philosophers. Each part builds on its predecessor, like the three acts of a drama, to reach a breathtaking climax; each part is about one third shorter than its predecessor, increasing proportionately in both precision and intensity.

Mad though it seems on the surface, the poem is cast into a metrical scheme almost as rigid as the *terzina*, the three-verse stanza of Dante. Jacopone has chosen the eight-verse stanza, the prototype of the classic Tuscan *ottava rima* of the Renaissance and a form that, as we have seen, he preferred to the medieval ballad for the expression of august emotion.[55] The *ottava rima* is in itself a circular construction, each stanza closing its own circle with a rhymed couplet (abababcc); but Jacopone has emphasized its circularity by rhyming the final verse of each stanza with the "amore" at the end of the *incipit*, thus tying all thirty-six stanzas into an enormous circle encompassing the three parts—a universe of love. It is almost as though he were acting out Coleridge's vision of the mad poet:

> Weave a circle around him thrice,
> And close your eyes with holy dread,
> For he on honey-dew hath fed,
> And drunk the milk of paradise.[56]

Yet it would be a mistake to think of Jacopone as a mad poet in the sense that Romantics like Manzoni understood a mad poet. Such a concept would be false not because it were anachronistic, as Jacopone might well have learned of mad poets from the Latin classics, but because Jacopone did not think of himself as a poet at all. He has none of the humanist sense of "onore," the consciousness of one's own individual powers so powerfully shown by Dante in his colloquy with Virgil, Homer, Horace, Ovid, and Lucan (*Inferno*, iv, 70–105). In fact Jacopone had rejected such earthly considerations during his penitential period and by now had completely outgrown them. His madness was that of a saint, that of Francis.[57]

The order and circularity of Jacopone's vision prefigure the architectural unity of Brunelleschi's dome in Florence, the glorification of the circle as a mystic symbol by the Florentine Neoplatonist philosophers, the medallion Madonnas of Michaelangelo and Raphael— and eventually the round monstrosity of a church which baroque architects built in the sixteenth century outside the walls of Todi. Thus circularity progressed through the splendors of the Renaissance to these baroque architects, for whom it has become mere mechanical repetition, the entombment of a dead idea in monumental gray stone. For Jacopone, as for Leonardo da

Vinci, circularity is a natural and easy form through which ideas and passions flow. The verses are full of echoes from the New Testament; the lively words of Jesus and Paul speak again through the experience of Jacopone. Gone is the tortured syntax of the earlier periods, gone the knotty dialect, and the poem hardly needs a gloss to be understood in modern Italian. With Paul, Jacopone stands on the summit of divine love: "For we know in part, and we prophesy in part. But when that which is perfect is come, then that which is in part shall be done away. . . . For now we see through a glass, darkly; but then face to face: now I know in part; but then shall I know even as also I am known" (I Corinthians 13:9, 10, 12).

> Amor de caritate, - perchè m'hai sì ferito?
> lo cor tutt'ho partito - ed arde per amore.
>   Arde ed incende, nulla trova loco,
> non può fugir però ched è legato,
> sì se consuma como cera a foco;
> vivendo mor, languisce stemperato,
> demanda de poter fugire un poco,
> ed en fornace tròvase locato;
> oimè, do' so menato? - A sì forte languire?
> Vivendo sì, è morire, - tanto monta l'ardore! . . .
>   Aggio perduto el core e senno tutto,
> voglia e piacere e tutto sentimento,
> onne belleza me par loto brutto,
> delize con riccheze perdimento;
> un arbore d'amor con grande frutto,
> en cor piantato, me dà pascimento,
> che fe' tal mutamento - en me senza demora,
> gettando tutto fòra, - voglia, senno e vigore.

Love of love, why have you so wounded me? I have split my heart and burn for love. My heart burns and flames and finds no place for me to flee, since I am tied to it; it burns itself up like wax in fire. Living, it dies; it languishes intemperately; it seeks to flee a little and find a place for itself in the furnace. Alas, whither am I led? To such strong languishing? To live is indeed to die, so high does my ardor mount! . . .

I have lost my heart and my whole mind, my will, pleasure, and all my feeling. Every beauty seems ugly to me; delights are lost riches. A tree of love with great fruits has been planted in my heart and gives me sustenance, which makes such a change in me, ceaselessly, as to expel completely will, mind and energy. [Lauda XC, lines 1–10, 19–26]

Looking back on his life, Jacopone has summarized in these few lines the burden of several earlier *laude*, notably LXXV, LXXXII, and LXXXIX.[58] He goes on in the next two stanzas to describe the completeness of his conversion and how he was thought mad for his excess of emotion.[59] He is approaching the complete unity of his soul with God:

> Fuoco nè ferro non li può partire,
> non se divide cosa tanto unita;
> pena nè morte già non può salire
> a quella alteza dove sta rapita;
> sotto sè vede tutte cose gire
> ed essa sopra tutte sta gradita;
> alma, co se' salita - a posseder tal bene?
> Cristo, da cui te vene, - abraccial con dolzore.

> Neither fire nor sword can separate them; a thing so united cannot be divided. Neither pain nor death can ascend to that height where it [the soul] has been swept. Below it is seen all the things that move and it is blessed above all. O my soul, how have you risen to possess such good? Embrace Christ, from whom you come, with sweetness. [Lines 43–50]

Here the Pauline echo is again heard: "Neither death, nor life, nor angels, nor principalities, nor powers, nor things present, nor things to come, nor height, nor depth, nor any other creature, shall be able to separate us from the love of God, which is in Christ Jesus our Lord" (Romans 8:38–39). It is as though Jacopone had joined Chaucer's Troilus in the empyraean and looked down on

> This litel spot of erthe, that with the se
> embraced is, and fully gan despise
> this wrecched world, and held al vanite
> to respect of the pleyn felicite
> that is in hevene above . . .[60]

Again following the lead of Paul, Jacopone finds, in the next lines (51–58), that all creation, including the shining sun and the even more resplendent cherubim and seraphim, pales in the presence of the Creator. Then, through the recognition of love in all creation, the soul of Jacopone is completely united with Christ:

> En Cristo trasformata, quasi è Cristo;
> con Dio gionta tutta sta divina;
> sopr'onne altura è sì grande acquisto
> de Cristo e tutto lo suo star regina;
> or donqua co potesse star più tristo
> de colpa demandando medicina
> nulla c'è più sentina; - dove trovi peccato,
> lo vecchio m'è mozato, - purgato onne fetore.
>   En Cristo è nata nova creatura,

spogliato lo vechio, om fatto novello;
ma tanto l'amor monta con ardura,
lo cor par che se fenda con coltello,
mente con senno tolle tal calura,
Cristo me trae tutto, tanto è bello!
Abracciome con ello - e per amor sì chiamo:
"Amor, cui tanto bramo, - famme morir d'amore!"

Transformed in Christ, it almost is Christ; joined with God, everything is divine. Such a great gain is above every height, and the soul rules with Christ and all of his. So how can one be sad any more and ask medicine for his faults? Wickedness, where sin is to be found, exists no more; the old man is destroyed, purged of every filth.

In Christ the new creature is born; the new man has cast off the old. But so high has the ardor of love risen that the heart is cut as with a knife; mind and sense cannot stand this heat; Christ has seized me completely—He is so beautiful! I embrace myself with Him and shout for love: "Love, for whom I yearn so much, make me die of love!" [Lines 99–114]

In such a state Jacopone has realized that God stands above the human world with its good and evil and that the soul in union with God finds that evil melts away. The new man "resists not evil but overcomes evil with good" (Romans 12:21; Matthew 5:39, 16:25). Jacopone presses on in his rhapsody to the final point where all the opposites of existence are resolved in unity:

Sappi parlare, or so fatto muto;
vedea, mò so cieco deventato;
sì grande abisso non fo mai veduto:
tacendo, parlo, fugo e so legato,
scendendo salgo, tengo e so tenuto,
de fuor so dentro, caccio e so cacciato;
amor esmesurato, - perchè me fai impazire,
en fornace morire - de sì forte calore?

I knew how to speak and now have been silenced. I saw and now I have become blind. Such a great abyss has never been seen: in silence I speak, I flee and am bound, descending I arise, I hold and I am held; I am inside and outside, I hunt and am hunted. O measureless love, why do you drive me mad, to die in a furnace of such great heat? [Lines 139–146]

This is the height of Franciscan ecstasy. "In this mystical union all pain becomes joy, all darkness light, all wisdom foolishness. It is an example of that reversal of all human values, that 'turning of the world upside down' which owes so much to the originality and inspiration of St. Francis."[61] The "I" and the "Thou," the subject and the object, are one.

The first part of the poem is over. There comes a stop. The stern Christ interrupts the poet:

"Ordena questo amore, tu che m'ami,
non è vertù senza ordene trovata,
poichè trovare tanto tu m'abrami
ca mente con virtute è renovata
a me amare, voglio che tu chiami
la caritate qual sia ordenata;
arbore si è provata - per l'ordene del frutto
el qual demostra tutto - de onne cosa en valore.
    "Tutte le cose qual aggio create,
sì so fatte con numero e mesura,
ad al lor fine son tutte ordenate
conservanse per orden tal valura,
e molto più ancora caritate
se è ordenata nella sua natura.
Donqua co per calura, - alma, tu se' empazita?
For d'orden tu se' uscita, - non t'è freno el fervore."

"Restrain this love, you who love me; there is no virtue without order. Since you so press to find me that your mind is renewed with the virtue of loving me, I wish that you call your love to order. The tree is known by its fruits [Matthew 7:16–20] and that is proven by everything which has value.

"Everything which I have created has been made with number and proportion, and they are all ordered to their purposes and keep their quality in this order. Hence, how have you been driven mad, o soul, through your heat? You have burst out of order and not restrained your fervor." [Lines 147–162]

Such is the harsh call back to the outside world, the categorical reminder that inner harmony must be connected with the order of the universe. In Augustine, this thought took a practical bent: "The peace, then, of the body lies in the ordered equilibrium of all its parts; the peace of the irrational soul, in the balanced adjustment of its appetites; the peace of the reasoning soul, in the harmonious correspondence of conduct and conviction; the peace of the body and soul taken together, in the well-ordered life and health of the living whole. Peace between a mortal man and his Maker consists in ordered obedience, guided by faith, under God's eternal law; peace between man and man consists in regulated fellowship."[62] The order of which Augustine speaks is to be found, of course, within the organization of the church, and no doubt, Jacopone, like most mystics of his time, looked to the same source to provide the outer framework for his ecstasies. Yet Jacopone gives Christ an argument, and here his thought verges on the heretical. Christ has so overcome him that his individuality is totally absorbed; hence, what he does is to be imputed not to him as a responsible individual, but to Christ, of whom he is the tool. His intoxicated will is wholly conformed in love to that of Christ (Lines 163–194). Furthermore, Jacopone insists that the life of Christ is in itself a supreme example of the power of love over all wisdom and discretion. How else, if not by the force of love, can one explain the Incarnation, the voluntary relinquishing of heavenly bliss for the terrible sufferings of life on earth? Then Christ gave himself up to love in his offering of the "living water" to the souls of men (John 7:37–38), in his not defending himself against the worldly power of Pilate, and at last, in his undergoing of the Crucifixion. Jacopone can see only love on the cross and neither wisdom nor discretion. He wishes to follow the example of Christ:

> La sapienza, veggio, se celava,
> solo l'amore se potea vedere;
> e la potenza già non se mostrava,
> che ere la virtute en dispiacere;
> grande era quel amor che se versava,
> altro che amore non potendo avere,
> ne l'uso e nel volere, - amor sempre legando
> en croce ed abracciando - l'omo con tanto amore.
>   Donqua, Iesù, s'io so sì enamorato,
> enebriato per sì gran dolceza,
> chè me reprende s'io vo empazato
> ed onne senno perdo con forteza?

> Wisdom, I see, is hidden; only love can be seen; and worldly power is also not shown, since you did not like that virtue. Great was the love that you poured out, not being able to have anything but love in your act and in your will—love always tied to the cross and embracing man with such great love.
>   Hence, Jesus, if I have become so in love, drunk with such great sweetness, why do you reprimand me if I go mad and lose all my sense and strength? [Lines 219–230]

From this logical structure, Jacopone launches in the third part of the *lauda*. "The drunkenness expands and brings on more drunkenness, sweeter and sharper. The mystical drama of the inner life, the conflict of activity and passivity, the urge to renounce will, reach their highest culmination. All the forces and energies of human action, curbed by the denial of individual existence, reacquire their power accompanied by the joy of sudden liberation. Passion breaks forth in phrases which succeed each other with no logical coordination."[63] It would be a mistake, however, to think of Jacopone's love song as a confused babbling, like the "speaking with tongues" that overcame the ecstatic worshipers in Paul's church at Corinth and that still overcomes ardent participants in modern evangelical services. It is anything but confused. Each of the six stanzas has a theme, each its own pattern of repeated exclamation. One scholar has even suggested that the song was derived from a popular Tuscan secular song of the period—a not unlikely phenomenon, not only because Jacopone always felt close linguistically to the common people but also because religious emotion frequently has been expressed in secular forms from the very earliest times down to *Godspell*. [64] In any case, these stanzas represent the emotional climax of Jacopone's life experience, and the music flows in pure lyricism through the constantly repeated rhythms of the tumbling verses.

Amore, amore che sì m'hai ferito,
altro che amore non posso gridare;
amore, amore, teco so unito,
altro non posso che te abracciare;
amore, amore forte m'hai rapito,
lo cor sempre se spande per amare;
per te voglio pasmare, - amor, ch'io teco sia,
amor, per cortesia, - famme morir d'amore.
    Amor, amor Iesù, so gionto a porto,
amor, amor, Iesù, tu m'hai menato;
amor, amor, Iesù, damme conforto,
amor, amor, Iesù, sì m'hai enflammato;
amor, amor, Iesù, più non lo porto,
fammete star, amor, sempre abracciato,
con teco trasformato - en vera caritate,
en somma veritate - de trasformato amore.
    Amor, amore grida tutto 'l mondo,
amor, amore, onne cosa clama;
amor, amore, tanto se' profondo,
chi più t'abracia sempre più t'abrama.
Amor, amor tu se' cerchio rotondo,
con tutto 'l cor chi c'entra sempre t'ama,
chè tu se' stame e trama - chi t'ama per vestire
con sì dolce sentire, - che sempre grida amore.
    Amore, amore, tanto tu me fai,
amor, amore, non posso patire;
amor, amore, tanto me te dai,
amor, amore, ben credo morire;
amor, amore, tanto preso m'hai,
amor, amore, famme en te transire;
amor, dolce languire, - amor mio desioso,
amor, mio delettoso, - anegame en amore.
    Amor, amor, lo cor sì me se speza,
amor, amore, tal sento ferita;
amor, amor, tramme la tua belleza,
amor, amor, per te sì so rapita;

amor, amore, vivere despreza,
amor, amore, l'alma teco unita;
amor, tu se' sua vita: - già non se può partire;
perchè la fai languire - tanto stregnendo, amore?
    Amor, amor, Iesù desideroso,
amor voglio morire te abracciando;
amor, amor Iesù, dolce mio sposo,
amor, amor, la morte t'ademando;
amor, amor, Iesù sì delettoso,
tu me t'arendi en te me trasformando,
pensa ch'io vo pasmando, - Amor, non so o'me sia,
Iesù, speranza mia, - abissame en amore.

Love, love, who has so wounded me, I cannot shout anything but love. Love, love, I am united with you; I can do naught but embrace you. Love, love, you have seized me firmly; my heart always expands with love. Love, I wish to be wracked with pain in order to be with you. Love, I beg you, make me die of love.

Love, love, Jesus, I have come to port. Love, love, Jesus, you have guided me. Love, love, Jesus, give me comfort. Love, love, Jesus, you have so enflamed me. Love, love, Jesus, I cannot stand it any more. Love, make me always be embraced, transformed by you in true charity, in highest truth and in transformed love.

Love, love, the whole world shouts. Love, love, everything yells. Love, love, you are so deep that the more I embrace you, the more I yearn. Love, love, you are a round circle, within which every one who enters always loves you; for you are the warp and woof to clothe him who loves you with such a sweet feeling that always shouts love.

Love, love, you do so much for me. Love, love, I cannot bear it. Love, love, you give me so much; love, love, that I truly think I shall die. Love, love, you have so held me; love, love, make me pass over to eternal life in you. Love, sweet languishing, love, my desire, love, my delight, drown me in love.

Love, love, my heart is so broken; love, love, I am so wounded. Love, love, your beauty draws me to you; love, love, I am fully enwrapped in you. Love, love, I disdain to live; love, love, my spirit is united with you. Love, you are its life and it cannot be separated from you. Love, why do you make it languish, hugging you so?

Love, love, desired Jesus, I want to die embracing you. Love, love, Jesus, my sweet spouse; love, love, I ask death of you. Love, love, Jesus so delightful, you give yourself to me, transforming me into you. I think I will faint. Love, I don't know where I am. Jesus, my hope, cast me into the abyss of love. [Lines 243–290]

Such is the apotheosis of the fool of God.

It would seem that Jacopone has finally come to port, that he has entered into the "round circle" of divine love, and that no further journeyings are necessary for his soul. But the end has not yet come. Two *laude* were placed after the "Amor de caritate" in the Buonaccorsi collection—and with good reason. These two poems, *Lauda* XCI "Sopr'onne lengua amore," and *Lauda* XCII "La fede e la speranza," show in Jacopone a new sense of peace and a new spirit of calm confidence beyond the violent emotion of the "Amor de caritate." He becomes accustomed to the love of God and accepts it in almost a matter-of-fact manner. He is so steeped in meditation, and the love of God has become so much a part of him as to drive out all other considerations.

> La guerra è terminata, - de le virtù battaglia,
> de la mente travaglia, - cosa nulla contende.
> La mente è renovata, - vestita a tal entaglia,
> de tal ferro è la maglia, - feruta no l'offende.
> Al lume sempre intende - nulla vuol più figura,
> però che questa altura - non cher lume de fuore.

> The war is over—the battle of virtue against vice, the travail of the mind. Nothing is in contention. The mind is renewed, clothed in such a fashion with a coat of mail that no wound can be inflicted. It hearkens only to the light and wishes to see no other image, for at this height there is no other light from outside. [*Lauda* XCI, lines 129–134]

In this last state as well, Jacopone can turn to the philosophers for support and can read in them the confirmation of his own experience. Hugh of St. Victor had written: "The soul is fully illuminated by the splendor of the eternal light . . . it rejects the world completely, renounces itself and turns fully to God. . . . freed from matter, deprived of form, and exceeding all limitation."[65] The perception of God as light shining from within the soul has been one of the most common experiences in Christian mysticism and finds expression throughout Christian history from Augustine and Bonaventure down to the Quakers, who think of themselves as "children of the Light."[66] The end of the journey for both Jacopone and Dante is in the realm of light. For both it is a great circle course, just as the beam from a distant star bends ever so slightly to form a small segment of an immense circle in the mind of God. Dante expresses this cosmic circularity by ending each of the parts of the *Divine Comedy* with the word, "stelle," his last line, in the realm of light, being: "l'amor che move il sole e l'altre stelle [love that moves the sun and the other stars]."

Like Dante, Jacopone was in the end blessed with perfect peace and cosmic objectivity. Like Dante, Jacopone found the intellectual structure for his vision in Pseudo-Dionysius, either directly or through the interpretation of Bernard or Bonaventure.[67]

> Sopra lo fermamento - lo qual si è stellato.
> d'ogne virtute ornato - e sopra al cristallino

ha fatto salimento, - puritate ha passato,
terza ciel ha trovato, - ardor de serafino.
Lume tanto divino - non se può maculare
nè per colpa abassare - nè en sè sentir fetore.
    Onne fede sì cessa, - chè gli è dato vedere,
speranza, per tenere - colui che procacciava.
Desider non s'appressa - nè forza de volere,
temor de permanere - ha più che non amava. . . .
E già non può errare, - cadere en tenebria,
la notte è fatta dia, - defetto grande amore.

Above the firmament that is full of stars and adorned with all the virtues, and above the crystalline heaven that contains purity, I have arisen and passed. I have found the third heaven, the flame of the seraphim. Such a divine light cannot be sullied or abased with sin or know filth in itself.

All faith ceases, for it has been granted to see; all hope, for it holds what it has sought. Desire does not urge on, nor the power of will nor the fear of losing that for which one has yearned. . . . And now one can no longer err, fall into darkness; the night has been made day in perfect love. [Lines 135–144, 151–152]

Quite clearly, Jacopone is describing the Third Heaven of Pseudo-Dionysius; as he continues the train of thought, he makes clear that he has understood the resolution of all opposites in divine being. He has realized "high nothingness," "willing, he no longer wills," "possessing, he is possessed" (Lines 165, 171, 195). These are the same paradoxes with which Pseudo-Dionysius illustrates the futility of dialectics in the presence of God: "There is no word for it, no name, no knowledge. There is no darkness, nor light, neither error nor truth. There is absolutely neither affirmation nor negation; we do not affirm it nor deny it."[68] And behind Pseudo-Dionysius stands the soaring thought of the pagan Plotinus, with its recognition of the "One" as pure being.

In such a context, death has no meaning—the death and damnation that started Jacopone on his spiritual journey:

Tu hai passata morte, - se' posta en vera vita,
nè non temi ferita - nè cosa che t'offenda.
Nulla cosa t'è forte, - da te po' t'èi partita,
en Dio stai enfinita, - non è chi te contenda.

You [my soul] have passed death and are in the true life. You fear neither wounds nor anything that can hurt you. Nothing is strong against you, for you are now parted from yourself. In God you are infinite, and no one fights you. [Lines 201–204]

As Paul said, "Death is swallowed up in victory. O death, where is thy sting? O grave, where is thy victory?" (I Corinthians 15:54–55).

Jacopone has transcended the bounds of his historical context. As Underhill has wisely pointed out: "We cannot honestly say that there is any wide difference between the Brahmin, Sufi or Christian mystic at their best."[69] Such a statement reveals the true nature of ecumenism, which is not the attempt to reduce the differences of religious practice to the least common denominator of homogenized mediocrity, but rather the recognition that many ways lead to God and that it is impious to try to impose limitations on the will of God through human reason and human institutions. But it is also at this point that the charges of heresy against Jacopone blare forth.[70] Denying the freedom of the individual will and disdaining the hunger for salvation, he is said consequently to deny the validity of the sacraments. He did no such thing. There is no reason to suppose that the comfort of the sacraments, for which he yearned during his imprisonment, ever became meaningless for him; nor is there any evidence that he was disobedient either to his order or to the church in general. On the contrary, the orthodox religious symbolism of his time find their way into his poetry up to the very end.

Jacopone passed from this life to the next in 1306, perhaps at Christmas. The *Franceschina* tells a lovely story about his death. It is very much like the story told of Francis, who also put off the moment of his death until he had received the expected last visit from his dear friend, Giacomina di Settesoli.[71] Because of the similarity of the stories, some have concluded that the friars invented the story for Jacopone in order to surround his memory with the glow of prophetic vision and hasten him on to sainthood. On the other hand, it can be sensed in Jacopone's later *laude* that he approached very closely to the spirit of Francis and had a spiritual life of deep intensity. The credibility of the story itself, as told both about Francis and about Jacopone, rests on two assumptions: first, that people with highly developed and sensitive souls can communicate with each other without words and over long distances; second, that such people can, within limits, choose the time of their leaving this life. In the end, those who can accept such assumptions because of their own observation or experience, will accept the story. Here it is:

> And the brothers told him that whatever he might think, it was necessary for him to receive the sacraments of the church, but he answered that he was waiting for his dearest friend, Giovanni de la Verna, because he wanted to receive them from his holy hands. However, because that place, called Collazzone where Jacopone lay ill, was a long way from Alverna, where brother Giovanni was, the brothers almost joked about it, thinking that it was impossible that brother Giovanni could come there—and especially because brother Giovanni did not know through human channels of his sickness. Hence, they were very upset, thinking that brother Jacopone would die without the sacraments of the church. And so they urged him in every way, but he, who was always with the true sacrament of Jesus Christ, began to sing a *lauda* with much sweetness and joy. . . .

When he had finished the *lauda,* one brother, looking toward the plain, saw two strangers coming; and as they approached, he recognized that it was the holy brother, Giovanni de la Verna, who by divine revelation had come to console the servant of God, brother Jacopone. And seeing this stupendous miracle, the brothers realized through true experience that brother Jacopone had the spirit of God. And once brother Giovanni had arrived, he went straight in to visit the blessed one; and enjoying themselves together with the greatest spiritual consolation, the blessed brother Jacopone received all the sacraments of the church with great reverence from the hands of brother Giovanni, as he had prophesied. And so comforted in the Lord, he began a beautiful and holy *lauda* with such great joy that it seemed that he was no longer sick. . . .

Having finished this *lauda,* he turned to the brothers who were standing around him and all crying with love, to see that glorious servant of God pass from this miserable life, where he had undergone and suffered so much in his body and where he had passed through the furnace of the great fervor and fire of the love of God, in which he had been refined more than ever was gold or silver. Finally raising his eyes, hands, and mind to his Creator and to the loving Jesus Christ, of whom he always spoke, saying: "In your hands, Lord, I commend my spirit," this happy soul passed on to the realms of eternal glory. His body was then taken honorably to the city of Todi, where not only those of the city honor him, but he is venerated and honored in all Italy as a saint. Amen.

VII ∞ The Poet as Prophet

The prophet is one who penetrates so deeply into the truth of his own time and his own experience that future generations recognize in him a precursor—certainly not one who foresees the future in some magical way. Poets and artists, as well as thinkers, become prophets when their intuitive insights are such that they prefigure the developments of later centuries. In this sense Jacopone's work was prophetic of religious attitudes and practices that were to become widespread in the fourteenth and fifteenth centuries. And yet one would not think of him as avant-garde, for that word would imply that he was ahead of his time, was not understood by his contemporaries, and was accepted only by a small coterie of adepts—clearly not the case.

His fame was surely local. In the first place, he wrote in Italian and was consequently not available to the wide audiences beyond the Alps reached by the Latin writers. Furthermore, the patterns of religious development in the fourteenth century were strongly marked by localism as mystics and worshipers tended more and more to value their immediate experience and as the universal church began to lose its spiritual leadership.[1] Yet his fame, though local, was not narrow, but rather coterminous with the wide world of the Italian communes.[2] As we have seen, some of his penitential *laude* were adopted and spread by the *disciplinati*, and his "Donna del paradiso" was one of the roots of the Italian sacred drama. In both of these forms, Jacopone's influence is evidenced by the fact that he had many anonymous imitators, but what is even more significant is that these imitators were also attracted by the mystical poems of his last period and composed a number of poems of divine love that were later attributed to Jacopone. The collection of *laude* at Urbino indicates one of the earliest centers of artistic production in the manner of Jacopone, and throughout the fourteenth century other anonymous poets continued to create Jacoponian poems so that a substantial body of work collected about his name. Numerous manuscripts of *laude* came into existence for devotional purposes, many of them thought to be by Jacopone, and eventually in the seventeenth century the process reached its maximum development when the Franciscan editor, Francesco Tresatti, brought out an enormous collection of *The Spiritual Poems of the Blessed Jacopone da Todi, Minorite Brother—Including Many Others of his Newly Discovered Songs. . . .* Of these about one third are genuine, one third of questionable authenticity, and one third definitely later accretions.[3]

In the years immediately after his death, Jacopone's influence was strongest among the radical Franciscans. It is most clearly seen in the work of the Tuscan Ugo Panziera, whose emphasis on humility and whose struggle for perfection in divine love follow Jacoponian patterns.[4] The persecution of the spirituals set in motion by the decrees of John XXII certainly limited the spread of his work, but Jacopone's *laude* were treasured among the followers of Angelo Clareno, the "fraticelli de paupere vita," and probably also among the heretical fraticelli and other rebels who abounded both at Todi and in central Italy in general.[5] It is worth noting, however, that Jacopone's anticlerical polemics were the only category of his work of which no imitations have been found.

In the long run, Jacopone's espousal of the spiritual cause was prophetic in that the strict interpretation of the Franciscan rule eventually triumphed in the Observantist movement, founded by Paolo de' Trinci in Umbria during the 1360s and 1370s. Appropriately enough, Jacopone's relics were found at this time and transferred to Todi, where they became an object of local veneration. At the same time, his poetry was rediscovered, and for the Observantists he became a hero of the order, instead of an outcast. Bartolomeus da Pisa praised him as a saintly man and included his *Detti* in the *De conformitate* of 1390, that encyclopedic mine of early Franciscan traditions.[6] Both the Franciscans and the new order of the Gesuati took up Jacopone's *laude* and spread the knowledge of them not only in central but also in northern Italy. Among the Gesuati, the Sienese Bianco di Santi wrote *laude* of sacred love on the model of the "Amor de caritate," if not of comparable poetic power.[7] Yet the Observantists were those who most highly valued Jacopone's work, and through them it was most widely spread. The great Observantist preachers of the fifteenth century, Bernardino da Siena, Giovanni da Capistrano, and Giacomo della Marca, admired his work, and in the ever widening circles of Observantist influence, used his *laude* to inspire the faithful. This development is evidenced by a note on the title page of the Jacoponian manuscript of Bergamo, the one used as the text for the second printed edition of his work, that of Brescia in 1495: "This book was found at the church of Santa Maria della Grazia in Bergamo and should be kept in the room of the seculars so that they may read it. . . . Here begin the *laude* which the holy brother Jacopo da Todi of the Friars

Minor made for the use and consolation of all those desiring to follow in the way of the cross and of the virtue of the Lord."

Further evidence of renewed interest in Jacopone toward the end of the fifteenth century is to be found in the fact that the biographies were set down at this time: the collection of traditions in the *Franceschina* and the life by the Franciscan chronicler, Mariano da Firenze.[8]

Important as this local fame in Italy may be, the prophetic nature of Jacopone's message is far more significantly apparent in the close parallels between his experience and that of the fourteenth- and fifteenth-century mystics beyond the Alps, on whom he had no influence whatever. The great German, French, and English mystics surely did not read his poetry and probably did not even know of him; but the fact that they had in common a broad spectrum of basic attitudes indicates the existence of a new type of spirituality that was to grow and survive into the modern world through the Anabaptists and the Quakers, as well as through more orthodox mystics.

The heretical potentialities in some of the ideas of Jacopone's last poems were illustrated in the life of Marguerite Porete, the French heretic whose book, *The Mirror of Simple Souls,* was widely read in the later Middle Ages. The book was not recognized as heretical in itself. Like Jacopone (in *Lauda* XXXIX) and, indeed, Richard of St. Victor, Marguerite envisioned the soul as a mirror of divine light and experienced a sense of union with God so profound as to engulf all human will and individuality—again like Jacopone and the most orthodox Caesarius of Heisterbach. But she committed acts that were considered immoral and thus fell foul of the Inquisition: she associated with Beguines, whose independent, though harmless, ways were exciting the concern of the hierarchy; she dabbled in necromancy. At her trial in 1310, her defense was that she knew the truths of divine love through experience (as did Jacopone), but the inquisitors dismissed such a plea as excessively individualistic and as an anarchistic threat to social order. She was burned.[9]

Parallels between Jacopone's mysticism and that of the more orthodox Rhenish Dominican school of Meister Eckhardt, Heinrich Suso, and Johann Tauler are equally close. The idea of God as nothingness appears in Jacopone as "alto nichilitade" and in Eckhardt as "nihte," and it is significant that Eckhardt made his boldest statements of the union of the individual with God—those which were condemned as heretical by John XXII—when he spoke his true mind in plain German, just as Jacopone's thought could only flow in plain Italian.[10] Suso felt as deeply and expressed as emotionally as Jacopone his sense of divine love, and the uselessness of reason in meditation was carried to the limit of divine folly by both Tauler and Jacopone. The Netherlander, Jan van Ruysbroeck, thought in Jacoponian terms (and in Dutch) of the three stages of divine love and of the final resolution of all polarities in the union with God. The

Yorkshireman, Richard Rolle, felt the same fire and song as did Jacopone and wrote of it in plain, vigorous English.[11]

Such a brief scanning of the patterns of religious feeling in the fourteenth century all over northern Europe is enough to show the consistency of the new spirituality—more personal, more intimate, more emotional, more individual, more local, and more filled with the power of God. It is not too much to say that Jacopone would have felt at home among the Friends of God in the Rhineland and among the Brethren of the Common Life in the Netherlands, and that he would have recognized his holy madness in the garb of Stultitia in Erasmus' *Praise of Folly*.[12] These worshipers were fully conscious of the nature of their spirituality, calling it the "devotio moderna." Their simple piety and mysticism survived during the next two centuries of religious conflict, not only in odd corners of the combative institutions of Protestantism and Catholicism but also among the Anabaptists and Quakers, for whom it was the core of religious practice.[13] In the end, "an identical consciousness of close communion with God is obtained by the non-sacramental Quaker in his silence and by the sacramental Catholic in the Eucharist."[14]

Can it be that the ancient prophecy of Joachim of Fiore is right: that mankind in its slow evolution approaches ever more closely to the realization of the will of God? The contemporary thought of Teilhard de Chardin affirms no less. If that is so, those who lead in the evolution are the glorious company of saints. Such was Jacopone.

Notes

Preface

1. Emilio Pasquini, "La Lauda" in *La letteratura italiana—storia e testi,* ed. by Carlo Muscetta, vol. I, part I, *Il duecento* (Bari: Laterza, 1970), p. 542. See also Maria Sticco, "Jacopone da Todi," *Letteratura Italiana–i minori* (Milan: Marzorati, 1961), p. 156.

2. Publications of the Modern Language Association of America, *Bibliography,* vols. 77–85 (1962–1970) passim. These bibliographies, covering the years 1960 to 1969, contain extensive listings of book and periodical titles in the major European languages, organized by country, period, and subject. There are 2203 listings for Dante and 24 for Jacopone.

3. Iacopone da Todi, *Laude,* ed. by Franco Mancini (Scrittori d'Italia no. 257, Bari: Laterza, 1974). This scholarly edition with its extensive notes, bibliography, apparatus, and glossary, is based on an exhaustive study of the known Jacoponian manuscripts and will probably remain the standard edition for years to come. It effectively supersedes its most notable scholarly predecessor, Jacopone da Todi, *Laudi, trattati e detti,* ed. by Franca Ageno (Florence: Le Monnier, 1953), reprinted in Bologna in 1971.

However, the texts quoted in this book are, unless otherwise indicated, not from the Mancini edition, but from that of Luigi Fallacara: Jacopone da Todi, *Le laudi* (Florence: Libreria Editrice Fiorentina, 1955). For the general reader this handsome edition is much easier to use because of its more modern orthography and convenient glossorial notes. It also presents the poems in the order that reflects the growth of Jacopone's inner life and hence probably the order of their composition. This order, with its accompanying numbering system, is that used by an early anonymous editor. It was adopted in the first printed edition (1490) and used in all modern editions except that of Mancini. In the interests of scholarly accuracy, the latter uses the haphazard order of the earliest manuscript collections and their orthography, which reflects more clearly the sounds of the Todian dialect.

The most penetrating stylistic analysis of Jacopone's work is that of Rosanna Bettarini in *Jacopone e il laudario urbinate* (Florence: Sanzoni, 1969). This monumental work has changed the shape of Jacoponian studies, just as the edition of Ageno did before it. The author posits the addition of fourteen *laude* to the Jacoponian corpus by first establishing the age and authenticity of the Santa Croce manuscript, on which the book is based, then comparing its texts with those of many other manuscripts, analyzing with unprecedented thoroughness the many stylistic peculiarities of the poet, and finally attributing its contents either to Jacopone or to a near contemporary "school of Jacopone." Though aware of the contribution of Bettarini, Mancini excludes all but one of these *laude* on the grounds that they do not appear in the early Todian manuscripts.

A further treatment of these problems is to be found in the Bibliographical Note and the Index of *Laude.*

4. Salvatore Quasimodo, *Il poeta e il politico e altri saggi* (Milan: Schwartz, 1960), p. 124.

5. Luke Wadding, "Scriptores Ordinis Minorum," *Analecta Franciscana* (Vol. IV, Quaracchi [Florence], 1906), p. 122.

6. Villemain as quoted in Agostino Barolo, *Jacopone da Todi* (Turin: Bocca, 1929), p. 164.

7. Eugenio Donadoni, *A History of Italian Literature* (New York: New York University Press, 1969), p. 14. This is a translation of the fifth Italian edition, published in 1963.

8. Ernest Hatch Wilkins, *A History of Italian Literature* (Cambridge: Harvard University Press, 1954), p. 33.

9. Quoted in Franco Maccarini, *Jacopone da Todi e i suoi critici* (Milan: Gastaldi Editori, 1952), p. 155.

10. Sticco, "Jacopone," pp. 154, 156.

11. Ernst Robert Curtius, *European Literature and the Latin Middle Ages,* trans. by Willard R. Trask (New York: Pantheon Books, 1932), p. 597.

12. Evelyn Underhill, *Jacopone da Todi, Poet and Mystic, a spiritual biography with a selection of the spiritual songs, the Italian texts translated into English verse by Mrs. Theodore Beck* (London and Toronto: J. M. Dent & Sons, 1919). The effort to put Italian verse into English rhymes results, as is often the case, in artistic disaster, and so the translations in this present work have been done by the author in the most liteal prose attainable. The strength of Miss Underhill's work lies in her clear understanding of the mystical experience as reflected in such works as: *The Essentials of Mysticism and Other Essays* (London: J. M. Dent & Sons, 1920); *The Mystic Way—a psychological study in Christian origins* (London: J. M. Dent & Sons, 1929); and *The Fruits of the Spirit* (London: Longmans Green, 1945).

13. John Moorman, *A History of the Franciscan Order from its origins to the year 1517* (Oxford: The Clarendon Press, 1968), pp. 265–271. This account is based entirely on Underhill, which is surprising considering the amount of more recent work.

14. Mario Casella, "Jacopone da Todi," *Archivum Romanicum,* vol. IV, nos. 3–4 (July–December, 1920), p. 321. See also Natalino Sapegno, *Frate Jacopone* (Naples: Libreria Scientifica Editrice, 1969), pp. 5–9. This is a reprint of the first edition of 1926. See also Maccarini, *Jacopone da Todi,* pp. 32–33.

15. Benedetto Croce, *Poesia popolare e poesia d'arte* (2nd ed., Bari: Laterza, 1946), p. 164.

16. Luigi Russo, "Jacopone da Todi mistico-poeta," *Ritratti e disegni storici,* ser. 3, *Studi sul due e trecento* (Bari: Laterza, 1951), p. 47. "Apply the logic of Crocean aesthetics to Jacopone, and you exile his work not only from the literature of mysticism but also from the history of poetry. This is precisely the result of the researches of Sapegno, in whom I can only admire his tenacious fidelity to the humanistic concept of poetry and his ceaseless efforts of a man of taste to dig out some flower or gem from the Jacoponian *laude*. Even when the critic's language becomes positive in admiration for Jacoponian poetry, how many reservations he has, how many warnings, how many distinctions and 'ifs' and 'buts'!" This attitude toward the separation of mysticism and poetry is shared by Mario Apollonio, *Jacopone da Todi e la poetica delle confraternite religiose nella cultura preumanistica* (Milan: "Vita e Pensiero," 1946), p. 31.

17. M. D. Lambert, *Franciscan Poverty—the doctrine of the absolute poverty of Christ and the apostles in the Franciscan Order, 1210–1323* (London: S.P.C.K., 1961).

18. Émile Durkheim, *The Fundamental Forms of the Religious Life*, trans. by Joseph Ward Swain (Glencoe: The Free Press, 1974), pp. 415–430.

19. F. C. Happold, *Mysticism, a study and an anthology* (Harmondsworth: Penguin Books, 1963), pp. 18–21. For an earlier and somewhat eccentric study and anthology of mysticism, see Richard Maurice Bucke, *Cosmic Consciousness, a study in the evolution of the human mind* (London: Innes & Co., 1901; paperback reprint, New York: E. P. Dutton & Co., 1969). The most important recent study of the mystical dimension in Jacopone is that of Alvaro Bizziccarri, "L'amore mistico nel canzoniere di Jacopone," *Italica*, vol. XLV, no. 1 (March, 1968).

Chapter I

1. The date of 1236 seems the most likely, though it is by no means certain. Only one precise date from a contemporary document referring to Jacopo's life has come down to us—May 10, 1297, when he signed the Longhezza manifesto against Boniface VIII. From this can be deduced with high probability the date of his marriage, 1267, and of his conversion, 1268. One early life states: "Jacopo, son of Ser Benedettone of the ancient and honored family of the Benedetti or Benedettoni" died at the age of seventy in 1306, thus indicating a birth year of 1236; "Vita del beato Jacopone de l'ordine di San Francesco cavata da antico libro scritto a penna, conservato nel Monastero di Monte Christo," ed. by N. Dal Gal, O.F.M., *La Verna*, vol. IV (December, 1906), pp. 385, 392 (hereafter referred to as "Monte Christo vita"). In addition, *Lauda* XCVI, line 34, states: "degli anni ben trenta e doi - bussai per farte gran dono [For a full thirty-two years I knocked to give you (Jesus) a great gift]." This shows that he was thirty-two at the time of his conversion in 1268. However, this *lauda* is not considered genuine by Ageno, *Laudi*, p. xxii. Underhill, *Jacopone*, uses the date 1228 without giving sources or reasons, and it seems too early. Others use 1230, again without substantial sources: D. Elio Margaritelli, *Messer Jacopo Benedetti dalla nascità (1230) al matrimonio (1267)* (Todi: Tipografia Tuderte, 1938); Alma Novella Marani, *Jacopone da Todi* (La Plata: Universitad Nacional de la Plata, 1964), p. 7.

2. The birthdate of Boniface VIII like many other facets of his life has been the subject of controversy. Though often thought to have been 1220, it was probably about 1235, in which case he would have arrived in Todi at about the age of sixteen—just the time to begin his studies of grammar and canon law. See Heinrich Finke, *Aus den Tagen Bonifaz VIII* (Munich: Aschendorff, 1902), pp. 1–7; and T. S. R. Boase, *Boniface VIII* (London: Constable and Co., 1933), pp. 6–7. However, some continue to use the earlier date: Giorgio Falco, "Sulla formazione e la costituzione della signoria dei Caetani," *Rivista Storica Italiana*, vol. XLV (1928), p. 230.

3. Statistics on infant and childhood mortality have not been found for periods prior to the seventeenth century, but the environmental and medical conditions in towns probably did not change very much over this long period. Hence, there is relevance in the study of Franco Saba, "Una parrochia milanese agli inizi del XVII secolo: San Lorenzo Maggiore—materiali per una storia demografica," *Nuova Rivista Storica*, vol. LIX, nos. 3–4 (May–August, 1975), pp. 407–457. In this study, mortality through the age of five ranged from a low of 35 percent for the period of 1620 to 1629 to a high of 55 percent for the period of 1607 to 1609.

Mortality up to the age of ten ranged in the same periods from a low of 42 percent to a high of 62 percent. See also E. A. Wrigley, *Population and History* (New York: McGraw Hill, 1969) and D. V. Glass and D. E. C. Eversley, *Population in History* (Chicago: Aldine Press, 1965).

4. These statistics are from a study of the population of Pistoia of a later date (1427). David Herlihy, *Mediaeval and Renaissance Pistoia, the social history of an Italian town, 1200–1430* (New Haven: Yale University Press, 1967), pp. 79–101.

5. Gianfranco Contini, *Poeti del duecento* (2 vols., Milan and Naples: Ricciardi, 1960), I, 145–148; Antonio Enzo Quaglio, "I poeti della 'Magna Curia' siciliana," *La letteratura italiana*, p. 217. Unless otherwise noted, all translations are by the author.

6. The most easily available translation into fourteenth-century Italian, though it contains only Book I, is to be found in Arrigo Levasti, *Mistici del duecento e del trecento* (Milan and Rome: Rizzoli, 1935), pp. 81–105. The Latin text is to be found in Jacques Paul Migne, *Patrologiae cursus completus . . . latinus* (vol. CCXVII, Paris, 1855). Jakob Huizinga pictures vividly the morbid aspects of late medieval culture, especially after the Black Death, and cites Jacopone as a precursor, attributing to him erroneously the hymn "Cur mundus militat"; *Le déclin du moyen âge* (Paris: Payot, 1932), pp. 164–180. The English translation for some reason does not contain the passage on Jacopone but does devote attention to Innocent III; *The Waning of the Middle Ages* (London: Edward Arnold & Co., 1924), pp. 124–135.

7. The Florentine chronicler Giovanni Villani listed in 1338, 550 to 600 students of grammar and logic on a child population estimated at 5,500 to 6,000; Paul C. Ruggiers, *Florence in the Age of Dante* (Norman: University of Oklahoma Press, 1964), pp. 102–103, 174.

8. Vitale, prior of San Egidio in the commune of San Gemini, a dependency of Todi, reported in the early years of the next century that he had studied in Todi around 1260 with Filippo, while Benedetto Gaetani (see Chapter III) was studying canon law with Filippo's brother Bartolo; Getulio Ceci, *Todi nel medio evo* (vol. I, Todi: Trombetti, 1897), p. 353; Finke, *Aus den Tagen Bonifaz VIII*, pp. 4–7. Lay teachers were not uncommon in Italian communes of this period and frequently went from town to town in the practice of their profession. Their earnings were rather meager, about twice that of a common laborer; John Larner, *The Lords of the Romagna* (New York: Macmillan Co., 1965), pp. 130–131. In Prato, a town half the size of Todi, there were nine teachers in 1339; Enrico Fiumi, *Demografia, movimento urbanistico e classi sociali in Prato* (Florence: Olschki, 1968), pp. 78–79.

9. Marc Bloch, *Feudal Society*, trans. by L. A. Manyon (2 vols., Chicago: University of Chicago Press, 1961), I, 75–78.

10. Curtius, *European Literature*, pp. 42–45; Leslie G. Whitbread, "Conrad of Hirsau as Literary Critic," *Speculum*, vol. XLVII, no. 2 (April, 1972), pp. 237–245.

11. The authenticity of both *Trattato* and *Detti*, which are printed in Ageno, *Laudi*, pp. 404–427, has been questioned by Ageno, ibid., p. xxiv, and by Sapegno, *Frate Jacopone*, p. 124. The former writes that "their authenticity is considered very doubtful by most authoritative recent students, but that they can illuminate the significance of the laude." Following this line of thought, Casella, "Jacopone da Todi," p. 311, thinks highly of them as a tool for interpreting the poems, as they were written by someone very close to Jacopone, if not by

Jacopone himself. The first mention of them comes from Alvarez de Pelayo, a Spanish Franciscan who visited Assisi in the early 1300s and quoted from the *Detti* in his work, *De planctu ecclesiae* of 1330; so some at least were probably in existence during the lifetime of Jacopone. The first full text of the *Detti* is to be found in Bartolomaeus da Pisa, "De conformitate vitae b. Francisci ad vitam divi Jesu. . . ," *Analecta Franciscana* (vol. IV, Quaracchi [Florence], 1906), pp. 235–239. This work has been thoroughly analyzed in a recent study: Carolly Erickson, "Bartholomew of Pisa; Francis Exalted: *De Conformitate*," *Medieval Studies*, vol. XXXIV (1972), 253–275.

12. Angelo Monteverdi, "Jacopone poeta," *Jacopone e il suo tempo* (Todi: Accademia Tudertina, 1959), p. 44; Bettarini, *Il laudario urbinate*, p. 228.

13. Though for many years Jacopone's main claim to fame was as the author of the great Latin hymn "Stabat mater," its attribution to him must be rejected. The hymn that was later incorporated into the ritual of the Roman Catholic Church and became the text for well-known cantatas by Pergolesi, Verdi, and others is probably of Franciscan origin. Sapegno, *Frate Jacopone*, p. 123, accepts both the "Stabat mater" and the "Cur mundus militat" as genuine Jacopone. These two and seven others were printed as being by Jacopone for the first time in the Brescian edition of 1495, and were not included by Buonaccorsi in the first, or Florentine, edition of 1490; Giuseppe Mazza, *Il laudatario jacoponico—Delta-VII-15 della Biblioteca Civica "Angelo Maj" di Bergamo* (Bergamo: San Marco, 1960), pp. xxvii–xxviii. Why Sapegno accepts the two great hymns as being by Jacopone and rejects the seven others is not made clear.

The earliest attribution of the "Stabat mater" to Jacopone dates only from a fifteenth-century Florentine manuscript; most recent critics have rejected it from the Jacoponian corpus, partly on the grounds that the earliest sources speak only of his poems in the *volgare*, and partly for the reason that the august style of the "Stabat mater" is not like that of Jacopone; Gianfranco Contini, "Per l'edizione critica di Jacopone," *Rassegna della Letteratura Italiana*, vol. LVII (1953), pp. 310–318; *Letteratura italiana delle origini* (Florence: Sanzoni, 1970), pp. 200–201. See also Hélène Nolthénius, *Duecento, the late middle ages in Italy* (New York: McGraw-Hill, 1968), p. 212.

14. This life of Jacopone was set down sometime around 1485 by Fr. Oddi; *La Franceschina, testo volgare umbro del secolo XV scritto dal P. G. Oddi di Perugia*, ed. by N. Cavanna (vol. II, Florence: Olschki, 1931), p. 85. Other accounts of about the same period are almost identical to the *Franceschina* text: "Vita inedita di Fra Jacopone da Fra Mariano da Firenze," ed. by Livario Oliger, *Luce e amore*, vol. IV (1907), pp. 419–426; and the "Monte Christo vita." All other later biographies down to those of this century follow the early legend and add little to it; Ageno, *Laudi*, p. vii.

15. Ibid., p. viii; Alessandro d'Ancona, *Jacopone da Todi—giullare di Dio* (2nd ed., Todi: Atanor, 1914), pp. 15–21; Underhill, *Jacopone*, pp. 34–36.

16. *La Franceschina*, p. 85.

17. Notaries have been the subject of much recent research, well summarized in William J. Bowsma, "Lawyers and Early Modern Culture," *American Historical Review*, vol. LXXVIII, no. 2 (April, 1973), pp. 303–327. An early study is Francesco Novati, *Freschi e minii del dugento* (Milan: Cogliati, 1908), pp. 301–328. Notarial chartularies provide a rich source of primary evidence that is beginning to be

used; see David Herlihy, *Pisa in the Early Renaissance* (New Haven: Yale University Press, 1953), pp. 1–19. The social position of notaries has been studied in J. K. Hyde, *Padua in the Age of Dante* (Manchester: University of Manchester Press, 1966), pp. 154–157, and Larner, *Lords of the Romagna*, pp. 148–151. Valuable for a later period is Lauro Martines, *Lawyers and Statecraft in Renaissance Florence* (Princeton: Princeton University Press, 1968). In addition, the statutes of the guilds of notaries and judges have in some cases survived as well as lists of members; see Santi Calleri, *L'arte dei giudici e notai di Firenze nel età communale e nel suo statuto del 1344* (Milan: Giuffrè, 1966); R. Abbondanza, ed., *Il notariato a Perugia* (Rome-Perugia: Volumnia Editore, 1973); Francesco Briganti, *L'Umbria nella storia del notariato italiano* (Perugia: Grafica del Labor, 1958); XV Congresso Nazionale del Notariato, *Il notariato veronese attraverso i secoli* (Verona: Collegio Notarile, 1966). It has been possible to compose biographies of more than fifty notaries active before and during the life of Jacopo: Consiglio Nazionale del Notariato, *Il notariato nella civiltà italiana—biografie notarili dal VIII al XX secolo* (Milan: Giuffrè, 1961).

18. Getulio Ceci, *Alla ricerca di Fra Jacopone—notizie biografiche inedite e saggio de edizione critica* (Todi: Tipografia Tuderte, 1932), pp. 7–8. See also Ceci, *Todi nel medio evo*, pp. 106–108.

19. Mancini, *Laude*, p. 345.

20. Herlihy has calculated that there was about one notary for every 165 people at Pisa, *Pisa*, p. 36; and Todi had a population of about 11,000.

21. Notaries were usually trained locally, according to Larner, *Lords of the Romagna*, p. 149, though Florentines often went to Bologna, see Calleri, *L'arte dei giudici e notai*, pp. 41–42. For Perugia, see Briganti, *L'Umbria nella storia del notariato*, pp. 37–38. Underhill, *Jacopone*, pp. 40–42, supposes that Jacopo went to Bologna, where he became acquainted with the work of Re Enzo and Guinicelli, on the basis of line 15, *Lauda* LXXXIV: "ia non vada più a Bologna - a 'mparar altra mastria." But this line is not autobiographical and should be translated: "So don't go to Bologna any more to learn other mastery." See Chapter IV.

22. "Monte Christo vita," p. 335–336.

23. The nobility of a family was not fixed by anything other than public opinion, based usually on the length of time during which a family had been in possession of a fief. Marriages most often took place between equals, but there would be money adjustments if there were inequalities of status; Hyde, *Padua*, pp. 57–60. For a slightly later period see Gene A. Brucker, *Florentine Politics and Society, 1343–1378* (Princeton: Princeton University Press, 1962), pp. 27–49. On the Collemedio family, see Ceci, *Alla ricerca di Fra Jacopone*, pp. 27–35; Ceci, *Todi nel medio evo*, p. 268. Casella, "Jacopone da Todi," p. 318, thinks that the Collemedio were Guibellines, but the weight of local evidence uncovered by Ceci seems decisive.

24. *La Franceschina*, pp. 85–86. The "Vita di Fra Jacopone . . . da Fra Mariano da Firenze," pp. 419–420, follows the *Franceschina* almost word for word. Some new details are added by the "Monte Christo vita," pp. 335–336. Though they were written down as much as 150 years later, these accounts are accepted here as substantially true, mainly because they contain so much individual material. So many specific details are given that are supported by what we know of Jacopone through his writings that a basis in fact seems likely, even though the form used

and the sentiments expressed follow Franciscan patterns and suggest pious invention. Such is the attitude of Casella, "Jacopone da Todi," pp. 303–308; and of Underhill, *Jacopone,* pp. 16, 46–52. Giuliotti considers the whole story of Donna Vanna to be an invention, and Sapegno doubts its importance in Jacopo's conversion; Domenico Giuliotti, *Jacopone da Todi* (Florence: Vallecchi, 1939), pp. 33–39; Sapegno, *Frate Jacopone,* pp. 14–21.

25. "Monte Christo vita," pp. 335–336.

Chapter II

1. Marvin Becker, *Florence in Transition,* vol. I, *The Decline of the Commune* (Baltimore: Johns Hopkins Press, 1967), pp. 11–41; John Larner, *Culture and Society in Italy, 1290–1420* (New York: Scribners', 1971), pp. 1, 14–17; Daniel Waley, *The Italian City Republics* (New York: McGraw-Hill, 1969), pp. 7–11.

2. Getulio Ceci, "Goti, greci e longobardi a Todi," *Bollettino della Deputazione di Storia Patria per l'Umbria,* vol. V (Perugia, 1899), pp. 60–70; Ceci, *Todi nel medio evo,* p. 291; Gabriele Pepe, *Il medio evo barbarico d'Italia* (3rd ed., Turin: Einaudi, 1945), pp. 66–72.

3. Daniel Waley, *The Papal State in the Thirteenth Century* (London: Macmillan & Co., 1961), p. xiii. This author recognizes the virtual independence of the communes and the failure of papal efforts at centralization; but since he is writing a history of the papal states as a whole, he frequently refers to the general conditions of anarchy within this larger unit; see for example pp. 120–121, 162, 189–190, and 209–210. See also Walter Ullmann, *The Growth of Papal Government in the Middle Ages* (3rd ed., New York: Barnes & Noble, 1970), and Peter Partner, *The Lands of St. Peter, the papal state in the Middle Ages and the early Renaissance* (Berkeley: University of California Press, 1972), pp. 257–296. The latter writer has a tendency to overstate the extent of papal power.

4. Conrad von Urslingen, duke of Spoleto and count of Assisi and Nocera, succeeded in uniting the whole duchy from his headquarters in Spoleto during the last two decades of the twelfth century; Waley, *Papal State,* p. 85. See also Franco Valsecchi, *Commune e corporazione nel medio evo italiano* (Milan: La Goliardica, 1949), pp. 163–166.

5. The building of the new walls permits an estimate of the size of Todi during this period; Ceci, *Todi nel medio evo,* pp. 121–146.

6. Todi did not participate in the Guelph league against Conrad. When Manfred sent Percivalle Doria in 1259 to conquer Tuscany and Umbria, Todi achieved neutrality in all but name; Ceci, *Todi nel medio evo,* p. 149. Since Orvieto was heavily involved with Florence in resistance to Doria, her natural enemies, Todi and Perugia, stood aside; William Heywood, *A History of Perugia* (London: Methuen & Co., 1910), pp. 70–77; and Daniel Waley, *Medieval Orvieto, the political history of an Italian city state, 1157–1334* (Cambridge: Cambridge University Press, 1952), pp. 42–47.

The great victory of the Guibelline Sienese over the Florentines and Orvietans at Montaperti assured their independence for centuries; Ferdinand Schevill, *Siena—the history of a medieval commune* (New York: Scribners', 1909), pp. 172–184. A useful paperback edition of this work is by William Bowsky (New York: Harper & Row, 1964). The large loss of life greatly impressed contemporaries;

Orvieto alone lost 1,300 men or about 10 percent of its population. Horror at the battle was expressed fifty years later by Dante in his conversation with the shade of the Guibelline commander, Farinata degli Uberti (*Inferno*, X, 19–51).

Contemporary chroniclers were equally shocked, for example, the famous Franciscan chronicler, Salimbene de Adam, *La Cronaca*, ed., by Giuseppe Tonna (Milan: Garzanti, 1964), pp. 299–302. This edition is a good modern one of a translation into medieval Italian. The original Latin is to be found in Oswaldus Holder-Egger, ed., *Cronica Fratris Salimbene de Adam O.M.*, in *Monumenta Germaniae Historica—Scriptores* (vol. XXXII, Hannover and Leipzig, 1905–1913). There is a partial English translation that is also heavily interpreted by G. G. Coulton, *From Saint Francis to Dante, a translation of all that is of primary interest in the chronicle of the Franciscan Salimbene* (London: Nutt & Co., 1906). Coulton's occasional remarks on Jacopone provide some mildly amusing Victoriana.

Other contemporary chroniclers thought that the battle was the predicted Armageddon of the Apocalypse and that it was one of the causes of the outbreak of the Flagellant movement; Raffaello Morghen, "Rainieri Fasani e il movimento dei disciplinati nel 1260," in Deputazione di Storia Patria per l'Umbria, *Il movimento dei disciplinati nel settimo centenario dal suo inizio* (Perugia, 1962), pp. 36–37. See Chapter III.

7. In the latter half of the century allied communes often provided podestà for each other as well as sending arbitrators in times of special tension; Ceci, *Todi nel medio evo*, pp. 156–166; Heywood, *Perugia*, pp. 87–89.

8. The Florentine experience is analyzed in Brunetto Quilici, "La chiesa di Firenze dal governo del 'Primo Populo' alla restaurazione guelfa, 1250–1266," *Archivio Storico Italiano*, vol. CXXVII, nos. 463–464 (Rome, 1969), pp. 323–337. A general picture of the alliances of rebellious subjects and heretics is in Gioacchino Volpe, *Movimenti religiosi e sette ereticali nella società medioevale italiana* (2nd ed., Florence: Vallecchi, 1926), pp. 126–159.

9. Ceci, *Todi nel medio evo*, pp. 183–184; Heywood, *Perugia*, pp. 87–89.

10. Ceci, *Todi nel medio evo*, gives the genealogy of the Monte Marte family, p. 64, and covers the difficulties with the rector, pp. 113–114, 138, 189–190. For the wars with Orvieto, see Waley, *Orvieto*, pp. 16–20, 70; and Waley, *Papal State*, pp. 65, 153–162.

11. This survey, which amounts to a census, is given in Ceci, *Todi nel medio evo*, pp. 320–326. The map of the contado of Todi (see Chapter II) is based on this survey and on the 1:250,000 *Carta d'Italia del Touring Club Italiano*: sheets 23 Perugia, 24 Macerata, 25 Civita Vecchia, and 28 Roma. On the map printed in Waley, *Orvieto*, a large slice of the contado of Todi lying between Marsciano and Titignano is mistakenly shown as Orvietan territory. Also shown as Orvietan are such feudal estates as Marsciano, Titignano, Alviano, and Lugnano, over which it is doubtful that either commune had much control.

12. Larner, *Lords of the Romagna*, pp. 5–20. The power and independence of the Romagnuol lords were much greater than that of the Umbrian feudality, so they dominated the life of the communes. On the other hand, the towers of San Gimignano are monuments to the aggressive and sometimes violent spirit of the communal nobility; Enrico Fiumi, *Storia economica e sociale di San Gimignano* (Florence: Olschki, 1961), pp. 91–92.

13. Armando Sapori, *The Italian Merchant in the Middle Ages* (New York: W. W. Norton, 1970), p. 11.

14. For the story of Ugolino, see Dante Alighieri, *La divina commedia, testo critico della Società Dantesca Italiana* (16th ed., Milan: Hoepli, 1955), *Inferno*, XXXIII, 1–90. Niccolò Machiavelli, *Il principe*, ed. by Gennaro Sasso (Florence: La Nuova Italia, 1963), chapter v. The translation used here is from *The Prince and the Discourses*, ed. by Max Lerner (New York: The Modern Library, 1950).

15. A full study of the podestà of Todi, including a list of all of them for the thirteenth century, is to be found in Getulio Ceci, "Podestà, capitani, e giudici a Todi nel secolo XIII," *Bollettino della Deputazione di Storia Patria per l'Umbria*, vol. III (Perugia, 1897), pp. 336, 339. See also Getulio Ceci and Giulio Pensi, *Statuto di Todi del 1275* (Todi: Trombetta, 1897), passim; Oscar Sclavanti, "Lo statuto di Todi del 1275," *Bollettino della Deputazione di Storia Patria per l'Umbria*, vol. III (Perugia, 1897), pp. 303–317. Usually most of the official family came from the home town of the podestà, though some communes like Bologna excluded compatriots of the chief executive for fear of excessive partisan interest. For the administrative arrangements of other communes, see Henry Dwight Sedgewick, *Italy in the Thirteenth Century* (2nd ed., Boston and New York: Houghton Mifflin Co., 1933), pp. 194–197. A good review of the current literature on communal institutions is that of Giorgio Chittolini, "Città e contado nella tarda età communale," *Nuova Rivista Storica*, vol. LIII (1969), pp. 706–719. For individual communes, see: Heywood, *Perugia*, pp. 30–46; Waley, *Orvieto*, pp. xxi–xxv, 10–12, 38–41, 53–55, 78–83, 145–148; Herlihy, *Pistoia*, pp. 214–221; Herlihy, *Pisa*, pp. 54–67; Hyde, *Padua*, pp. 4–5, 23–25, 29–56, 121–153; Larner, *Lords of the Romagna*, pp. 12–17; Fiumi, *San Gimignano*, pp. 23–37, 51–53; Gaetano Salvemini, *Magnati e popolani in Firenze dal 1280 al 1295*, followed by *La dignità cavalleresca nel commune di Firenze*, ed. by Ernesto Sestan (2nd ed., Turin: Einaudi, 1960), pp. 127–135, 193–198, 313–317; Nicola Ottokar, *Il commune di Firenze alla fine del duecento* (2nd ed., Turin: Einaudi, 1962), pp. 3–32.

16. For example, in the strong Guelph reaction after the death of Frederick, when the Primo Populo flourished in Florence under the leadership of a *capitano del popolo*, a host of smaller towns introduced the same official: Orvieto in 1251, Perugia and Todi in 1255, Terni in 1258, Narni in 1261, and Gubbio in 1263. Todi kept electing *capitani del popolo* in an off-and-on manner for the rest of the century, but the office seems to have had but little function, as Todi scarcely had a "popolo" in the Florentine sense. Waley, *Italian City Republics*, pp. 7–11.

17. Ceci, *Todi nel medio evo*, pp. 105–160.

18. William Bowsky, "The mediaeval commune and internal violence: police power and public safety in Siena, 1287–1335," *American Historical Review*, vol. LXXIII, no. 1 (October, 1967), pp. 1–17. Lauro Martines, ed., *Violence and Civil Disorder in Italian Cities* (Berkeley: University of California Press, 1972) is a collection of studies that explore the problem in depth.

19. Quoted in Waley, *Italian City Republics*, p. 54. See also Herlihy, *Pistoia*, pp. 1–6.

20. Emilio Sereni, *Storia del paesaggio agrario italiano* (Bari: Laterza, 1962), pp. 83–112. For an excellent synthesis, see Georges Duby, *L'économie rurale et la vie des campagnes dans l'Occident médiévale* (Paris: Aubier, 1962). For agricultural patterns and class structure in other areas, see Herlihy, *Pistoia*, pp. 31–51, 121–147, 186–212; and Fiumi, *San Gimignano*, pp. 112–159. The property assessment for Orvieto in 1292, showing a large group of owners of small plots of land, is to be found in Waley, *Italian City Republics*, p. 28.

21. Ceci and Pensi, eds., *Statuto di Todi*. For millers, see Book I, paragraphs 40, 43, 45. Agricultural workers, Book I, 13, 78, 81; Book II, 13, 116. Bakers, Book I, 62. Markets, Book I, 62; Book II, 26, 84, 85. Inns, Book I, 1. Butchers, Book I, 53; Book II, 134. Depredations of animals, Book II, 56, 107, 112.

22. Hyde, *Padua*, pp. 15–17; Larner, *Lords of the Romagna*, pp. 16–17, 99–100.

23. Rosario Romeo, *Il commune di Origgio nel secolo XIII* (2nd ed., Assisi: Carucci, 1970), pp. 69–93. Herlihy, *Pistoia*, pp. 121–147.

24. Henri Pirenne, *Medieval Cities, their origins and the revival of trade*, trans. by Frank D. Halsey (Princeton: Princeton University Press, 1925).

25. Josiah Cox Russell, *Mediaeval Regions and their Cities* (Bloomington: University of Indiana Press, 1972), pp. 5–52. G. Tabacco, "Fief et seigneurie dans l'Italie communale," *Le Moyen Âge*, vol. LXXV (1969). For the structure of Todi's region, see map in Chapter II.

26. That Todi was not primarily an animal-raising community is shown not only by the nature of the land but also by the provisions of the *statuto* protecting agriculture from the depredations of animals; see above n. 21.

27. One of the more surprising revelations about San Gimignano was the extraordinarily wide range of its long-distance trade, not only throughout western Europe but also to northern Africa and the Levant; Fiumi, *San Gimignano*, pp. 54–85.

28. A list of the bankers at Todi at the end of the thirteenth century is given in Ceci, *Todi nel medio evo*, pp. 335–343.

29. Robert Brentano, *Two Churches—England and Italy in the Thirteenth Century* (Princeton: Princeton University Press, 1968), p. 183. See also Fiumi, *San Gimignano*, pp. 86–89; Quilici, "La chiesa di Firenze," pp. 431–433.

30. Niccolò Rodolico and Giuseppe Marchini, *I palazzi del popolo nei communi italiani del medio evo* (Milan: Electa Editrice, 1962).

31. Ceci and Pensi, eds., *Statuto di Todi*. For the regulation against committing nuisances near the church of St. John and St. Paul, see Book II, paragraph 103; the same provision was made for the piazza in front of the old church of San Fortunato, Book I, 59. Very extensive regulations were made for the protection of streets and the control of building: Book I, 15, 55, 80, 122; Book II, 9, 29, 95, 115, 127, 139.

32. One of the ways of estimating town population is to multiply the number of oath-takers, or citizens, by a coefficient of 3.5. When Manfred was defeated by Charles of Anjou, the Guibellines were driven from Todi and forced to take refuge in Acquasparta. Following up his advantage, Pope Clement IV forced 2,080 citizens of Todi in 1268 to swear allegiance both to him and to the rector of the Patrimony. This figure would indicate a total town population of only 7,280. However, as soon as possible, the town affected a reconciliation of the parties, for despite the theoretical allegiances of the parties to pope or emperor, all Todians stood together when it became a question of conferring real power on the pope's representative at the expense of the commune. Todi claimed that the oath was invalid, since only half the citizens (Guelphs) had taken the oath and the other half (Guibellines) were out of town. No doubt the claim was exaggerated, since a resulting population of 14,560 would certainly be too large for a town of only 82 acres in extent. In the same period San Gimignano, the walls of which were two-thirds as long as those of Todi, had a population of 5,900. So the estimate of

11,000 for Todi may not be far off the mark. See Fiumi, *San Gimignano*, pp. 147–155; Herlihy, *Pistoia*, pp. 72–77; Herlihy, *Pisa*, pp. 35–43, and Fiumi, *Prato*, pp. 25–47.

33. Population in the countryside was more dense at Todi than at Pistoia, since half the territory of the latter lay in the thinly settled high Appennines. On the other hand, San Gimignano achieved its remarkable density of population, which is almost exactly what it is today, because of the commercial production of saffron and wine. In estimating population from number of hearths, Fiumi uses a coefficient of 4 for the town and 5 for the countryside, while Herlihy uses 4.65 for the countryside. The latter coefficient has been used here. For comparisons of the size of cities, see Russell, *Mediaeval Regions*, pp. 41, 131.

A general decline in population set in after 1340, largely but not exclusively due to the plague; and the diocese of Todi, which was the same size as the medieval contado, fell in population to a low of 14,435 in 1588, about one-third of its thirteenth-century size. Karl Julius Beloch, *Die Bevölkerungsgeschichte Italiens*, vol. II, *Die Bevölkerung des Kirchenstaates, Toscanas, und die Herzogtümer am Po* (Berlin: Walter de Gruyter, 1940), pp. 62–74. Today the commune of Todi, which includes only the core of the medieval contado, has a population of 19,713; while the entire contado (i.e., the modern communes of Acquasparta, Collazzone, Fratta Todina, Massa Martana, Montecastello di Vibio, Montecchio, and Todi, the total lands of which about cover the medieval contado) has a population of 39,884; Istituto Centrale di Statistica, *10° Censimento Generale*, vol. I, *Dati riassuntivi* (Rome, 1963), pp. 112–113.

34. Consiglio Nazionale del Notariato, *Il notariato nella civiltà italiana*, pp. 436–439; 475–477; Giulio Bertoni, *Il duecento* (Milan: Vallardi, 1930), pp. 220–228.

35. Herlihy, *Pisa*, pp. 3–10; XV Congresso Nazionale del Notariato, *Il notariato veronese*, pp. xix–xxix.

36. Hyde, *Padua*, pp. 49, 154. See also Fiumi, *Prato*, pp. 78–79.

37. Briganti, *L'Umbria nella storia del notariato*, pp. 54–55; Ceci, *Todi nel medio evo*, pp. 204–222; Sclavanti, "Lo statuto di Todi," pp. 336–344.

38. Calleri, *L'arte die giudici e notai a Firenze*, pp. 25–96, covers in great detail the guild regulations of the *statuto* of 1344. The same sort of information is available for Verona in XV Congresso Nazionale del Notariato, *Il notariato veronese*, pp. 3–21. In general the communes of Umbria did not have guilds of notaries until the next century; Briganti, *L'Umbria nella storia del notariato*, pp. 66–69. Municipal control of notaries at Spoleto was much like that at Todi; Giovanni Antonelli, ed., *Statuto di Spoleto del 1296* (Florence: Olschki, 1962), Book I, sections 2, 3, 21, 24, 29, 44, 55; Book II, section 3.

39. Bettarini, *Il laudario urbinate*, pp. 223–224; Mancini, *Laude*, p. 365.

40. Larner, *Culture and Society*, pp. 201–206. A convenient list of chronicles by notaries, which have been printed, appears in Consiglio Nazionale del Notariato, *Il notariato nella civiltà italiana*, p. 555. See also Bertoni, *Il duecento*, pp. 228–231; Hans Baron, *The Crisis of the Early Italian Renaissance* (Princeton: Princeton University Press, 1966), pp. 100–118, 146–166.

41. Hyde, *Padua*, p. 169.

42. For example, Jacopone's contemporary, Tommaso di Armannino of Bologna was in the process of amassing a considerable fortune in every sort of

mercantile investment. There were also Chello Baldovini of Florence, the successor of Brunetto Latini as chancellor-dictator; Bartolommeo Scriba of Genoa, who
was both a chronicler and a man with a lucrative private practice; and Guglielmo
Cassinese, also of Genoa, who profited mightily by taking shares in sea voyages;
Consiglio Nazionale del Notariato, *Il notariato nella civiltà italiana*, pp. 67, 75, 325,
536–537. See also Larner, *Lords of the Romagna*, pp. 133–141.

43. Hyde, *Padua*, pp. 49–50, 181–190; Carlo Carrà, *Giotto, la capella dei
Scrovegni* (Milan: Collezione Silvana, Edizioni d'Arte Amilcare Pizzi, 1944). For
the sociological background of the building of the chapel, see Michael Thomas,
"Contributi alla storia della Cappella degli Scrovegni a Padova," *Nuova Rivista
Storica,* vol. LVII (January–April, 1973), pp. 111–128.

44. Lester K. Little, "Pride Goes before Avarice: social change and the vices in
Latin Christendom," *American Historical Review,* vol. LXXVI, no. 1 (February,
1971), pp. 16–49.

45. The original Latin text is in Consiglio Nazionale del Notariato, *Il notariato
nella civiltà italiana,* p. 438. A translation into medieval Italian is in Mario Marti,
"La prosa," *Storia della letteratura italiana,* vol. I, *Le origini e il duecento* (Milan:
Garzanti, 1960), p. 532.

46. d'Ancona, *Jacopone da Todi,* pp. 80–81. This view has been contested by
Casella, "Jacopone da Todi," p. 456; Francesco Grisi, *La protesta di Jacopone da
Todi* (Rome: Trevi, 1969), p. 41.

47. In 1322 there were at Orvieto, which was slightly larger than Todi, 27 noble
families in the town and 21 in the contado; Waley, *Orvieto,* p. 38. At Todi there
were probably not more than 80 men of law—about 65 notaries, 3 judges, several
arbitrators, and a few canon lawyers; Ceci, *Todi nel medio evo,* pp. 204–220;
Sclavanti, "Statuto di Todi," pp. 336–345.

48. Henry the Poet as quoted by Brentano, *Two Churches,* p. 28. See also Ceci,
Todi nel medio evo, pp. 353–355; Waley, *Papal State,* pp. 101–109; Falco, "Signoria
dei Caetani," pp. 231–244.

49. For the portraits, see Giorgio Petrocchi, "La letteratura religiosa," *Storia
della letteratura italiana,* p. 669; *Letteratura italiana,* ed. by Muscetta, vol. I, part II,
656; Boase, *Boniface VIII,* frontispiece and pp. 4–5. Examples of long cardinalates
are those of Matteo Rosso Orsini (1262–1305) and Napoleone Orsini (1288–1342);
Waley, *Papal State,* p. 224.

50. Waley, *Orvieto,* p. 61.

51. Established in 1249 and administered by the Franciscans, this hospital or
orphanage was the pride of Todi. The hospital, unlike most charitable institutions, was owned and carefully supervised by the commune; Ceci and Pensi,
eds., *Statuto di Todi,* Book I, paragraphs 102, 103, 105; Book II, 108, 119; Ceci, *Todi
nel medio evo,* pp. 270–271, 328–344.

52. Salimbene, *La Cronaca,* p. 335. See also d'Ancona, *Jacopone da Todi,*
pp. 79–80; Natalino Sapegno, "Appunti intorno alla vita di frate Jacopone—il
papa e il fraticello," *Archivum Romanicum,* vol. VIII (Geneva, 1924), p. 416.

53. G. Mignini, "I codici del commune di San Fortunato a Todi," *Archivio
Storico per le Marche e per l'Umbria,* vol. III (Foligno, 1886), pp. 523–530.

54. Salimbene, *La Cronaca,* p. 335. See also Brentano, *Two Churches,* pp. 64–85;
Ceci, *Todi nel medio evo,* pp. 274–278.

55. Paul Sabatier, *Life of St. Francis of Assisi,* trans. by Louis Seymour

Houghton (London: Hodder & Stoughton, 1899), pp. 5–6; Casella, "Jacopone da Todi," p. 291.

56. Pasquini, "Letteratura delle origini," *Letteratura italiana*, pp. 117–120. On the general influence of the French language in Italy see the excellent bibliography, ibid., pp. 163–164; also Wilkins, *History of Italian Literature*, pp. 6–12; Antonio Viscardi, *Le origini* (2nd ed., Milan: Vallardi, 1950), pp. 494–515.

57. Marti, "La prosa," *Storia della letteratura italiana*, p. 606; Pasquini, "Letteratura delle origini," *Letteratura italiana*, pp. 110–111; Dante Alighieri, *De vulgari eloquentia*, ed. by Bruno Pamini (Palermo: Ando, 1968), p. 71.

58. Ernst Kantorowicz, *Frederick II*, trans. by E. O. Lorimer (London: Constable & Co., 1931), pp. 486–488; Ceci, *Todi nel medio evo*, pp. 133–134.

59. Dante, *De vulgari eloquentia*, Book I, chapter XIII, 4.

60. F. Dietz, *Die Poesie der Troubadours*, quoted in Gianfranco Folena, "Cultura e poesia dei Siciliani," *Storia della letteratura italiana*, p. 315.

61. Piero Cudini, "Contributo ad uno studio di fonti siciliane nelle laude di Jacopone da Todi," *Giornale Storico della Letteratura Italiana*, vol. CXLV, no. 452 (1968), pp. 561–572; Mancini, *Laude*, pp. 357–358.

62. Lines 13–19 of "Ancor che l'aigua per lo foco lassi"; Contini, *Poeti del duecento*, I, 107–110.

63. Lines 24–31 of "Madonna, dir vo voglio"; ibid., pp. 51–54.

64. Cudini, "Fonti siciliane," p. 564.

65. Lines 7–11 of "A l'aire claro ho vista ploggia dare"; Contini, *Poeti del duecento*, I, 78.

66. Lines 43–48 of "Per fin' amore vao sì allegramente"; ibid., pp. 111–114.

67. Lines 1–4; ibid., pp. 99–101.

68. Luigi Russo, ed., *I classici italiani*, vol. I, *Dal duecento al quattrocento* (Florence: Sanzoni, 1948), pp. 37–40.

69. Achille Tartaro, "Guittone e i rimatori siculo-toscani," *Storia della letteratura italiana*, pp. 351–425.

70. Contini, *Poeti del duecento*, I, 230–231.

71. See Chapter VI. On the influence of Guittone on Jacopone, see Mancini, *Laude*, pp. 359–360.

72. Salimbene, *La Cronaca*, pp. 306–309.

73. Contini, *Poeti del duecento*, I, 200–205, 222–226.

74. d'Ancona, *Jacopone da Todi*, pp. 36, 46; Barolo, *Jacopone da Todi*, p. 161. G. Latini, *Dante e Jacopone e loro contatti di pensiero e di forma* (Todi: Trombetta, 1906), fails to make a convincing case.

75. Francesco de Sanctis, *Storia della letteratura italiana* (2 vols., Milan: A. Barion, 1938), I, 33. This work was originally published in 1872 and has been translated by Joan Redfern (2 vols., New York: Barnes & Noble, 1968). Since de Sanctis wrote before the corpus of Jacopone's work was clearly defined and so quotes several selections that are not by Jacopone, it is to be expected that some of his judgments are quite far off the mark; what is surprising, rather, is that many of his basic conceptions have stood the test of time so well.

76. Waley, *Italian City Republics*, pp. 42–43; Ceci, *Todi nel medio evo*, p. 340; Heywood, *Perugia*, pp. 358–359.

77. Bertoni, *Il duecento*, pp. 181–184.

78. Ibid.

79. Aldo Rossi, "Poesia didattica e poesia popolare del Nord," *Storia della letteratura italiana*, pp. 488–490.

80. Letteria di Francia, ed., *Novellino* (Turin: UTET, 1945), pp. v–xviii. An English translation is by Edward Storer, *Il novellino* (London: "Broadway Translations," n.d.). For the origins of the *Novellino*, see Angelo Monteverdi, *Studi e saggi sulla letteratura italiana dei primi secoli* (Milan and Naples: Ricciardi, 1954), pp. 95–110.

81. Salimbene, *La Cronaca*, p. 53.

82. It has been suggested that the brevity of these stories is to be accounted for by thinking of them as mere sketches to which the cantastorie added his own details, but even so this story must have been pretty thin if its point had not been considered ludicrous in itself.

83. Bertoni, *Il duecento*, pp. 235–238; see also Helen Waddell, *The Wandering Scholars* (7th ed., London: Constable & Co., 1934), pp. 123–194.

84. Ernst Buschor, ed., *Carmina Burana—Benedictbeurer Lieder, lateinisch und deutsch* (Wiesbaden: Insel-Verlag, 1955), p. 120. An English translation is that of John Addington Symonds, *Wine, Women, and Song: Mediaeval Latin student songs now first translated into English verse* (London: Chatto & Windus, 1907), p. 152. This translation is, however, by the author.

85. Sedgewick, *Italy in the Thirteenth Century*, pp. 204–209. Games of a later period are described in Lillian M. C. Randall, "Games and the Passion in Pucelle's Hours of Jeanne d'Evreux," *Speculum*, vol. XLVIII, no. 2 (April, 1972), pp. 246–256.

86. Artusi and Gabrielli, *Early Florence and the historic game of calcio* (Florence: Sanzoni, 1972).

87. Heywood, *Perugia*, pp. 382–384; Ruggiers, *Florence*, pp. 118–120.

88. Bettarini, *Il laudario urbinate*, pp. 225–226, cites instances where Jacopone uses the language and manner of minstrels and refers to dances, songs, dice games, and chess.

89. Ceci, *Todi nel medio evo*, pp. 344–345; Fiumi, *San Gimignano*, pp. 29–32.

Chapter III

1. *Detti*, iii; Ageno, *Laudi*, p. 416. On the authenticity of the *Detti* and *Trattato*, see above, Chapter I, n. 11. There is, of course, nothing very original about this description of the growth of the inner life. Similar stages of mystical progress had been described by the Victorines, Bernard of Clairvaux, Bonaventure, and others. They were later to be almost canonically defined as the stages of purgation, illumination, and union, and it is this progress that forms the central theme of both the *laude* and the life of Jacopone. See Underhill, *Essentials of Mysticism*, pp. 7–11; Rudolph Otto, *Mysticism East and West*, trans. by Bertha L. Bracey and Richenda C. Payne (New York: Macmillan Co., 1932), pp. 63–72; *The Life of Teresa of Jesus—the Autobiography of St. Teresa of Avila*, ed. and trans. by E. Allison Peers (Garden City, N.Y.: Doubleday Image Books, 1960), chapters xi–xxi; George Peck, *The Triple Way* (Pendle Hill Pamphlet no. 216, Wallingford, Pa., 1977).

2. *La Franceschina*, p. 86.

3. Sabatier, *Life of St. Francis*, pp. 18–25, 54–56. The story of Bernardo da Quintavalle is in the *Fioretti*, of which one of the best scholarly editions is that of

Mario Casella, *I fioretti di San Francesco* (Florence: Sanzoni, 1926). A good translation is that of Serge Hughes, *The Little Flowers of St. Francis and other Franciscan Writings* (New York: Mentor-Omega Books, 1964), pp. 48–51.

4. "Monte Christo vita," p. 386.

5. Most scholars have pictured Jacopone's conversion as gradual and as the direct outgrowth of the death of Donna Vanna; see Casella, "Jacopone da Todi," p. 310; Underhill, *Jacopone*, pp. 57–60; Ceci, *Alla ricerca di Fra Jacopone*, p. 39. How little we really know about the conversion is emphasized by Ageno, *Laudi*, p. ix, and Sapegno, *Frate Jacopone*, pp. 16–23.

6. Ibid., pp. 61–63. It is evident that Donadoni shares his opinion; see Introduction. Interestingly enough, Francesco de Sanctis, writing more than 100 years ago, manages to make Jacopone's vulgarity seem attractive. He refers to Jacopone's intuitive grace and freshness: "prayers, hatreds, follies of love, fantasies, ecstasies, visions—all you will find in Jacopone, naturally and coming from within—whatever is most simple and moving, most strange and common." De Sanctis is not repelled when he finds the "plebian, indecent, and disgusting mixed with the most gentle effects." De Sanctis, *Storia della letteratura italiana*, I, 34, 38.

7. Quasimodo, *Il poeta e il politico*, p. 125. Such recent critics as Emilio Pasquini point out the futility of applying Crocean aesthetics to Jacopone; "La lauda," *Letteratura italiana—Il duecento*, I, 504. Luigi Russo dismisses Sapegno's criticism as "abstract" and "judgemental"; see Maccarini, *Jacopone da Todi*, pp. 34–36.

8. *La Franceschina*, pp. 86–87. Some critics, notably Ageno, *Laudi*, p. vii, have greatly devalued the Franceschina account, since it contains so many parallels in Franciscan lore. However, while clearly recognizing such parallels, Casella, "Jacopone da Todi," pp. 303–308, indicates that the account may still be essentially true, since it contains many colorful and individual details about Jacopone and so departs from the commonplaces of hagiographical lore. It is also possible that Jacopone had Franciscan models in mind and consciously expressed his tensions in traditional patterns.

9. Thomas of Celano, *St. Francis of Assisi, First and Second Life of St. Francis with selections from Treatise on the Miracles of beloved Francis*, trans. by Placid Hermann (Chicago: Franciscan Herald Press, 1962), *First Life*, Book I, chapter 6. See also *Scripta Leonis, Ruffini, et Angeli sociorum S. Francisci*, ed. and trans. by Rosalind B. Brooke (New York: Harpers, 1970), chapter vi. Of particular value for the student of Francis is Théophile Desbonnets and Damien Vorreux, eds. and trans., *Saint François d'Assise, Documents: Écrits et premières biographies* (Paris: Éditions Franciscaines, 1968), which contains a detailed concordance for tracing the incidents of Francis's life in the various sources.

10. Hughes, *Franciscan Writings*, p. 107. See also pp. 20–21, 51, 192–193.

11. The signature on the manifesto of Longhezza is shown by d'Ancona, *Jacopone da Todi*, p. 65. Some chroniclers referring to Jacopone are: Luke Wadding, *Annales Minorum* (3rd ed., Quaracchi [Florence], 1931), V, 364; Wadding, "Scriptores Ordinis Minorum," p. 122; and Bartolomaeus da Pisa, "De conformitate," IV, 235. The meaning of the name, Jacopone, has been variously interpreted; the authors of the fifteenth-century lives, Wadding, and d'Ancona thought that it expressed contempt. Annibale Tenneroni put forward the thesis that it was merely another form of the name Jacopo, like Guittone for Guido,

Benedettone for Benedetto, etc.; but this interpretation does not seem likely, as both forms of the name would not have been used at the same time. That Jacopone was tall was discovered by Tenneroni when he exhumed the bones of Jacopone during a search for his portrait and found that the tibia was very long; Annibale Tenneroni, "Un ritratto di Fra Jacopone da Todi," *Bollettino della Deputazione di Storia Patria per l'Umbria,* vol. XIII (Perugia, 1907), p. 634. Ceci, *Alla ricerca di Fra Jacopone,* p. 12, believed that the name grew up primarily because of Jacopone's tallness and implied no contempt.

12. For the rejection of his mother and brothers, see Matthew 12:46-50; Mark 3:31-35. In Luke 11:27-28, Jesus specifically denied that any special reverence should be accorded to his mother—obviously an unacceptable stand in a world so deeply involved in mariolatry as the thirteenth century. The rejection of Jesus in Nazareth is reported in Luke 4:16-30.

13. Matthew 8:19-22; Luke 9:57-62. The incident of the rich young ruler is found in Matthew 19:16-22; Mark 10:17-22; and Luke 18:18-23.

14. *Scripta sociorum,* chapter viii, paragraph 5. The first of Francis's texts is from the incident of the rich ruler as written in Matthew. The second is drawn from Jesus' instructions to his disciples in Matthew 10:5-10; Mark 6:7-9; and Luke 9:1-3. The third is in Luke 9:23-27.

15. *La Franceschina,* pp. 86-87.

16. This detail is added in the "Monte Christo vita," p. 387, where the account of the incident varies somewhat: "Once, Messer Ranaldo, the brother of the said Messer Jacopo, presented a wedding reception for his wife; while all the relations were at the party, the said Messer Jacopo came right into the party all covered with honey and with feathers stuck into it. His appearance caused such displeasure and horror that some left for shame, others for annoyance, and others for compassion. Still others made fun of him, calling him crazy, struck him with their fists, and drove him from the house with insults. The children and common people followed him with whistling and taunts, throwing water and refuse on his back. He internally rejoiced in these persecutions and showed himself most happy about them. From that time on people began calling him Jacopone in derision."

17. Hughes, *Franciscan Writings,* pp. 186-201. This is the "Life of Brother Juniper," which was often written down with the *Fioretti* and probably reflects Franciscan traditions dating back to the last quarter of the thirteenth century.

18. Salimbene, *La Cronaca,* pp. 22-24. The chronicler has caught the flavor of the scene in such a lively and realistic manner that it is well worth reading.

19. This is *Lauda* XII of the "Recuperi jacoponici" in Bettarini, *Il laudario urbinate,* pp. 527-528. Finding it here indicates Jacopone's close relationship to the penitential activities of these *disciplinati.*

20. Sidney Raymond Packard, *Europe and the Church under Innocent III* (New York: Russell & Russell, 1968), contains a good up-to-date bibliography of the work on Innocent III. A number of English translations of the *De contemptu mundi* are available, two dating from the sixteenth century.

21. Book I, chapter 1, "On the miserable beginning of the human condition"; Levasti, *Mistici del duecento,* pp. 81-82.

22. Casella, "Jacopone da Todi," pp. 305-306; Sapegno, *Frate Jacopone,* p. 15.

23. *La Franceschina,* pp. 87-88.

24. A large painting, probably by Andrea Polinori (1593-1648), shows

Jacopone among several saints with the chickens at his feet; Tenneroni, "Un ritratto di Fra Jacopone," pp. 632–634. In the house of Count Giuseppe Pongelli at Todi, there was a set of twelve small pictures illustrating incidents from the *Franceschina* account; Giulio Pensi, *Documenti e ricordi iacoponici a Todi* (Todi: Tip. Tuderte, 1930), p. 21. For the practical jokes, see Salimbene, *La Cronaca*, pp. 46–53; Giovanni Boccaccio, *Il decameron*, ed. by Carlo Salinari (Bari: Laterza, 1963), 8th Day, stories 3 and 6; 9th Day, story 5; Poggio Bracciolini, fiorentino, *Facezie* (Milan: Dall'Olio, 1950), passim; Carlo Levi, *Cristo si è fermato a Eboli* (Turin: Einaudi, 1946), passim.

25. St. Peter Damian inaugurated the practice of flagellation in the reformed Benedictine houses of the mid-eleventh century; Gilles Meersseman, "Disciplinati e penitenti nel duecento," *Il movimento dei disciplinati*, pp. 50–51. Meersseman makes a distinction between the flagellants who followed a regular program of flagellation and the *disciplinati* who only occasionally followed the practice. For the origns of the *lauda*, see Pasquini, "Letteratura delle origini," "La lauda," *Letteratura italiana*, I, 49–53, 131–137, 144–154, 481–493; Aurelio Roncaglia, "Le origini," Petrocchi, "Letteratura religiosa," *Storia della letteratura italiana*, I, 213–221, 627–666.

26. A recent thorough study, relating the Italian poem to Francis's Latin works, is that of Giovanni Getto, "Francesco d'Assisi e il cantico di frate Sole," *Pubblicazioni della Facoltà di Lettere e Filosofia*, vol. VIII, no. 2 (University of Turin, 1956). An English translation with notes on the sources is to be found in *The Writings of St. Francis of Assisi*, trans. by Benen Fahy and ed. by Placid Hermann (Chicago: Franciscan Herald Press, 1964), pp. 127–131.

27. Salimbene, *La Cronaca*, pp. 43–45.

28. Ibid. See also Coulton, *From Saint Francis to Dante*, pp. 21–25.

29. The Bolognese chronicle is quoted in Emilio Ardù, "Frater Raynerius Faxanus de Perusio," *Il movimento dei disciplinati*, pp. 93–98; see also Morghen, "Rainieri Fasani e il movimento dei disciplinati," ibid., pp. 32–39, 46–47.

30. E. Randolph Daniel, "A Re-examination of the Origins of Franciscan Joachimism," *Speculum*, vol. XLIII, no. 3 (October, 1969), pp. 671–676; E. Randolph Daniel, "The Role of Franciscan Spirituality in the Franciscan Spirituals," paper American Historical Association Meeting (December, 1971). See also Luigi Salvatorelli, "Movimento francescano e gioacchimismo," *Relazione del X Congresso Internazionale di Scienze Storiche*, vol. III (Florence: Sanzoni, 1955), pp. 403–448. A recent collection containing some of the above works as well as many others is Delno C. West, ed., *Joachim of Fiore in Christian Thought, Essays on the Influence of the Calabrian Prophet* (New York: Burt Franklin, 1975). See also Coulton, *From Saint Francis to Dante*, pp. 152, 158–159.

31. Salimbene, *La Cronaca*, p. 305.

32. Norman Cohn, *The Pursuit of the Millennium, revolutionary millenarians and mystical anarchists of the Middle Ages* (2nd ed., New York: Oxford University Press, 1970), pp. 99–107, 161–165. For a fuller discussion, see Chapter IV.

33. Salimbene, *La Cronaca*, p. 89.

34. The *Annales S. Justinae Patavini* are quoted in Morghen, "Ranieri Fasani," *Il movimento dei disciplinati*, p. 33.

35. The disturbances in the Romagna are reported in Salimbene, *La Cronaca*, pp. 303–304.

36. Meersseman, "Disciplinati e penitenti," *Il movimento dei disciplinati*, p. 67.

37. Bertoni, *Il duecento*, p. 200. Despite much recent work, this relatively old account of the development of the *lauda* is still authoritative. See also Casella, "Jacopone da Todi," pp. 292–293.

38. Pasquini, "La lauda," *Letteratura italiana*, pp. 492–493; Petrocchi, "La letteratura religiosa," *Storia della letteratura italiana*, pp. 656–657; Ignazio Baldelli, "La lauda e i disciplinati," *Il movimento dei disciplinati*, pp. 341–342.

39. *Annales S. Justinae Patavini*, quoted in Morghen, "Rainieri Fasani," ibid., p. 37. The chronicler's estimate of 70,000 combatants and 25,000 casualties is too high, as the military and political technology of the time could not produce slaughter on this scale; John Beeler, *Warfare in Feudal Europe, 730–1200* (Ithaca and London: Cornell University Press, 1971), pp. 185–214, 249–251. Also see above, Chapter II, n. 6.

40. "But is it not possible that Ser Jacopone was moved, even though he was a noble and a learned man, by the spectacle of the Flagellants . . . in his very own city of Todi? It may well be that he poked fun at them with the other sophisticates, but inside himself was there not perhaps born a thought, a suspicion, a beginning of remorse?" Jacopone da Todi, *Le laude, ristampa integrale della prima edizione (1490) con prefazione di Giovanni Papini* (Florence: Lib. Ed. Fiorentina, 1923), p. xii.

41. Meersseman, "Disciplinati e penitenti," *Il movimento dei disciplinati*, p. 55; Barolo, *Jacopone da Todi*, pp. 55–56; Ageno, *Laudi*, p. 443.

42. Especially the afore-mentioned studies of Morghen, Meersseman, and Baldelli, plus: Franco Mancini, "I disciplinati di Porta Fratta in Todi e il loro primo statuto," pp. 269–277; and Mario Pericoli, "La matricola dei disciplinati della fraternità di Santa Maria Maggiore a Todi," *Il movimento dei disciplinati*, pp. 290–298.

43. Erik Schöne Staaff, *Sur une lauda de Jacopone da Todi: Quando t'alegri, homo de altura* (Uppsala: Almquist & Wikoells, 1927), pp. 21–23. The contrast between the profundity of Jacopone's poetry and the commonplace nature of most of the hymns of the *disciplinati* is clearly shown in Franca Ageno, "Modi stilistici delle laudi di Jacopone da Todi," *La Rassegna d'Italia*, vol. I, no. 5 (May, 1946), p. 21.

44. Fernando Liuzzi, *La lauda e i primordi della melodia italiana* (2 vols., Rome: Libreria dello Stato, 1935), contains musical settings for about 140 *laude*, of which a few are by Jacopone. See also Fernando Liuzzi, "Profilo musicale di Jacopone," *Nuova Antologia*, vol. CCCLVI (September, 1931), pp. 171–192; Nolthénius, *Duecento*, p. 206.

45. Monteverdi, *Studi e saggi*, p. 15. Among the prominent early scholars who emphasized the role of Jacopone as a popular singer were de Sanctis, *Storia della letteratura italiana*, I, 33–36; and d'Ancona, *Jacopone da Todi*, pp. 6–8. The first substantial revision is that of Novati, *Freschi e minii del duecento*, pp. 185–190; his interpretation has been refined and deepened by Casella, "Jacopone da Todi," pp. 292–296; and Maccarini, *Jacopone da Todi*, pp. 25–32, 43–52.

46. "De contemptu mundi," Book I, chapter 26; Levasti, *Mistici del duecento*, p. 102.

47. Salinari edition, pp. 8–17.

48. "De contemptu mundi," Book I, chapter 10; Levasti, *Mistici del duecento*, p. 88. Innocent elaborates: "But if any one should reach old age, his heart is afflicted, his head shakes, his spirit languishes, his breath stinks, his face is

wrinkled, his form is bent, his eyes are blinded, his knuckles tremble, his nose drips, his hair falls out, his touch fades, his movements fails, his teeth blacken, and his ears become deaf. The old man is easily moved to anger and is hard to placate . . . believes quickly and doubts rarely . . . he is tenacious, greedy, melancholy, and complaining . . . he is quick to speak and slow to listen . . . praises the ancients and condemns the moderns . . . curses the present and recommends the past . . . he sighs and is anxious, lazy, and sick." Jacopone's picture is just as black and just as concise.

49. Paolo Toschi, *Il valore attuale ed eterno della poesia di Jacopone* (Todi, "Res Tudertinae," no. 4, 1964), pp. 43–45.

50. Scholars of fifty years ago were intent on characterizing Jacopone according to various formulas, especially d'Ancona, Brugnoli, Novati, Parodi, and Sapegno; see Bizziccarri, "L'amore mistico," pp. 2–5; Maccarini, *Jacopone da Todi*, pp. 26–37. It is Underhill's *Jacopone*, pp. 90–98, 107–120, which gives the clearest picture of the stages of development of Jacopone's soul.

51. *Le speculum perfectionis*, ed. by Paul Sabatier (2 vols., Manchester: University of Manchester Press, 1928–1931), chapter 3. A recent translation is by Leo Sherley-Price, *St. Francis of Assisi, his life and writings* (New York: Harpers, 1960).

52. *Trattato*, paragraph 1; Ageno, *Laudi*, p. 405.

53. Irene Steiger, *Jacopone da Todi, Welthass und Gottesliebe* (Zürich: Akeret, 1945), pp. 12–17.

54. Underhill, *Jacopone*, pp. 89–90.

55. Morton W. Bloomfield, *The Seven Deadly Sins* (Lansing: Michigan State University Press, 1952 and 1967), pp. 72–73, 123–140. See also Little, "Pride Goes before Avarice," pp. 17–31.

56. See the comments of Sapegno, *Frate Jacopone*, pp. 69–71, who also includes many of Jacopone's didactic poems in his criticism.

57. Machiavelli, *The Prince*, chapter 17. It might be added here that *Lauda* V, "Cinque sensi," is another of these uninspired poems and deals with the limitations of sensuous gratification.

58. This saying was set down as having been heard at Assisi in the early fourteenth century by Alvarez de Pelayo and is the earliest reference to the *Detti*—an argument in favor of their authenticity. See above, Chapter I, n. 11.

59. Julia O'Faolain and Lauro Martines, *Not in God's Image* (New York: Harper & Row, 1973), pp. 74–83, 96–106, 132–160.

60. "De contemptu mundi," Book I, chapters 4–5; Levasti, *Mistici del duecento*, pp. 85–86. For an interesting article on the position of women and children in the renaissance, see Richard A. Goldthwaite, "The Florentine Palace as Domestic Architecture," *American Historical Review*, vol. LXXVII, no. 4 (October, 1972), pp. 1009–1011.

61. Aldo Rossi, "Poesia didattica e poesia popolare del Nord," *Storia della letteratura italiana*, I, 435–436; Emilio Pasquini, "La letteratura didattica e allegorica," *Letteratura italiana, Il duecento*, I, ii, 13–15, 44–45.

62. Buschor, ed., *Carmina Burana*, p. 135.

63. Celano, *St. Francis of Assisi*, First Life, chapter 2, paragraph 2; chapter 5, paragraph 1.

64. Livario Oliger, "Verba fratris Johannis de Alverna," *Studi Francescani*, vol. XII (Arezzo, 1914), pp. 314–316. An Italian translation is "I gradi dell'anima" in

Levasti, *Mistici del duecento,* p. 269. The fact that Giovanni was a close friend of Jacopone is attested by *Lauda* LXIII, which is a letter to him. See also the biographical note on Giovanni, ibid., p. 991.

65. M. L. von Franz, "The process of individuation," in Carl G. Jung, ed., *Man and his Symbols* (Garden City: Doubleday, 1964), pp. 184–188.

66. See Chapter III, above.

67. Ceci, *Todi nel medio evo,* pp. 230–266. For provisions of the commune of Todi regarding the Franciscan order, see *Statuto di Todi,* ed. by Ceci and Pensi, Book I, paragraphs 40, 43, 45, 81, 83, 102, 103, 105, 108; Book II, paragraphs 24, 38, 80, 81, 100, 108, 119.

68. This story seems to be an elaboration of the ass story in the *Franceschina* and may be a later invention. It appears in Cornelius a Lapide, *Commentarium in Ecclesiasticum* (Venice, 1717), quoted by Underhill, *Jacopone,* p. 61.

69. *La Franceschina,* p. 88.

Chapter IV

1. Quoted from the *De planctu ecclesiae,* Book II, chapter lxxiii, written in about 1330, by Underhill, *Jacopone,* p. 7, and by Novella Marani, *Jacopone da Todi,* p. 8.

2. "Monte Christo vita," pp. 388–389.

3. See the excellent summary in Sapegno, *Frate Jacopone,* pp. 37–39.

4. Lambert, *Franciscan Poverty,* pp. 89–93; Moorman, *Franciscan Order,* pp. 99–108; Gratien of Paris, *Histoire de la fondation et de l'évolution des Frères Mineurs au xiiie siècle* (Paris: J. Duculot, 1928), pp. 140–160; Rosalind B. Brooke, *Early Franciscan Government—Elias to Bonaventure* (Cambridge: Cambridge University Press, 1959), pp. 7–9, 60–125; Cajetan Esser, *Origins of the Franciscan Order,* trans. by Aedan Daly and Irini Lynch (Chicago: Franciscan Herald Press, 1970), pp. 137–185.

5. *La Franceschina,* pp. 111–112.

6. Underhill, *Jacopone,* p. 114.

7. Lambert, *Franciscan Poverty,* pp. 32–36.

8. *Sacrum commercium S. Francisci cum domina paupertate* (Quaracchi [Florence], 1929); English translation by H. D. Rawnsley (London: J. M. Dent & Sons, 1926); Italian translation in Levasti, *Mistici del duecento,* pp. 339–372. This work dates from as early as 1227; see Moorman, *Franciscan Order,* p. 278. Giotto's painting and its inspiration are described in Heinrich Thode, *Franz von Assisi und die Anfänge der Renaissance in Italien* (2 vols., Berlin, 1885), II, 208–212; French translation by Gaston Lefèvre (Paris, 1908).

9. Paragraph vi; see also paragraphs iv and v on money and begging. "Opuscula S. Patris Francisci," ed. by Leonhardt Lemmens, O.F.M., *Biblioteca Franciscana Ascetica* (vol. I, Quaracchi [Florence], 1904); English translation in Hughes, *Franciscan Writings,* pp. 212–220; Italian translation in Levasti, *Mistici del duecento,* pp. 109–120.

10. These incidents are all reported in Celano, *St. Francis,* First Life, Book I, chapters iv, vi, ix, xvi, xix, xxviii; Second Life, Book I, chapters ix, xii; Book II, chapters xxv–xlvii. Some of these incidents and other similar ones are reported in the *Speculum perfectionis,* the *Scripta sociorum,* and the *Fioretti.* For the relative authenticity of these sources, see Lambert, *Franciscan Poverty,* pp. 1–30.

11. Aegidius of Assisi, *Dicta* (Quaracchi [Florence], 1939), chapters vii; English translation by Ivo O'Sullivan, *Golden Words* (Chicago: Franciscan Herald Press, 1966); Italian translation in Levasti, *Mistici del duecento*, pp. 123–159.

12. *Testamentum*, paragraph v; Hughes, *Franciscan Writings*, p. 219.

13. Gratien, *Histoire des Frères Mineurs*, p. 374.

14. Celano, *St. Francis*, Second Life, Book II, chapter civ.

15. Esser, *Origins of the Franciscan Order*, pp. 137–201.

16. Lambert, *Franciscan Poverty*, p. 69.

17. Quoted by Edmund G. Gardner, *Dante and the Mystics* (2nd ed., New York: Octagon Books, 1968), p. 209.

18. So he was called by Bonaventure; he also referred to himself by these same words; Moorman, *Franciscan Order*, p. 258.

19. "Verba fratris Conradi," ed. by Paul Sabatier, *Opuscules de critique historique* (vol. I, Paris, 1903), pp. 370–405.

20. The most complete treatment of the growth of the spirituals is Decima Douie, *The Nature and Effect of the Heresy of the Fraticelli* (Manchester: Manchester University Press, 1932). A well-written essay, though now somewhat dated, is David Saville Muzzey, *The Spiritual Franciscans* (reprint, Washington: American Historical Association, 1914). A very important recent study is Marjorie Reeves, *The Influence of Prophecy in the Later Middle Ages: A study of Joachimism* (New York: Oxford University Press, 1969), pp. 175–213.

21. Franz Ehrle, "Petrus Iohannis Olivi, sein Leben und seine Schriften," *Archiv für Literatur und Kirchengeschichte* (vol. III, Berlin, 1887), p. 465. The works on poverty are described on pp. 505–515. A recent study is in Gordon Leff, *Heresy in the Later Middle Ages* (2 vols., Manchester: Manchester University Press, 1967), I, 100–139.

22. The basic work on Ubertino is still that of Ernst Knoth, *Ubertino von Casale* (Marburg: Elwert'sche Verlag, 1903).

23. Gratien, *Histoire des Frères Mineurs*, p. 361.

24. On the properties at Todi, see Ceci, *Todi nel medio evo*, pp. 238–266. On the regulations for the friars from the constitutions of Narbonne (1260) and of Paris (1292), see Lambert, *Franciscan Poverty*, pp. 160–165; Moorman, *Franciscan Order*, pp. 183–194; Gratien, *Histoire des Frères Mineurs*, pp. 365–377.

25. Douie, *Heresy of the Fraticelli*, p. vii. Because of this attitude Douie devotes scant attention to Jacopone's role, and the same is true of most other writers on the spirituals.

26. Leone Bracaloni, O.F.M., "La spiritualità francescana ascetica e mistica," *Studi Francescani* (vol. XII, Florence, 1940), pp. 7–31. See also Sapegno, *Frate Jacopone*, pp. 33–35; Underhill, *Jacopone*, pp. 136–139.

27. Huizinga, *Waning of the Middle Ages*, pp. 235–242.

28. Celano, *St. Francis*, Second Life, Book II, chapter lxxiii. Other passages in Celano relating to learning and preaching are: First Life, Book I, chapters x, xii, xviii, xx, xxii, xxvii; Book II, chapter v; Second Life, Book II, chapters xxxii, lviii, lxviii, lxix, cxxii, cxlii, cxliv, and cxlvii. See also Moorman, *Franciscan Order*, pp. 54–58; Sabatier, *Life of St. Francis*, pp. 39–50, 204–215; Gratien, *Histoire des Frères Mineurs*, pp. 110–135.

29. *Speculum perfectionis*, chapter iv. See also chapters v, xxxviii, lxviii, and lxxii.

30. Étienne Gilson, *The Philosophy of St. Bonaventure,* trans. by Illtyd Tretho-wan and Frank J. Sheed (Paterson: St. Anthony Guild Press, 1965), p. 71. See also pp. 44–49; J. Guy Bougerol, *Introduction to the Works of Bonaventure,* trans. by Jose de Vinck (Paterson: St. Anthony's Guild Press, 1961), pp. 123–134, 156–160; *The Works of Bonaventure—mystical opuscula,* trans. by Jose de Vinck (vol. I, Paterson: St. Anthony's Guild Press, 1960), passim.

31. Douie, *Heresy of the Fraticelli,* pp. 95–103; Leff, *Heresy in the Later Middle Ages,* I, 119–120; Ehrle, "Olivi Leben und Schriften," pp. 413–435; Reeves, *Influence of Prophecy,* pp. 194–197.

32. *Commentary on the Apocalypse,* quoted by Sabatier, *Life of St. Francis,* p. 51. For a survey of the recent work on Joachim, see Morton W. Bloomfield, "Joachim of Flora," *Traditio* (vol. XIII, New York: Fordham University Press, 1957), pp. 249–307.

33. The "Responsio," written in 1312 at the time of the Council of Vienne and printed in Franz Ehrle, "Die Spiritualen, ihr Verhältniss zum Franciskanerorden und zu den Fraticellen," *Archiv für Literatur und Kirchengeschichte* (vol. III, Berlin, 1887), p. 73. See also Knoth, *Ubertino von Casale,* pp. 3–20, 52–69.

34. "Historia septem tribulationum Ordinis Minorum," printed in Ehrle, "Die Spiritualen," II, 305.

35. Daniel, "Franciscan Spirituality."

36. Casella, "Jacopone da Todi," p. 450; see also Maccarini, *Jacopone da Todi,* pp. 21–22, 128–129.

37. Grisi, *La protesta di Jacopone,* p. 40; Biordo Brugnoli, *Fra Jacopone da Todi e l'epopea francescana* (Assisi: Metastasio, 1907), pp. 26–32. The latter's edition of the "satires" of Jacopone is so dated that it is no longer of much use: Biordo Brugnoli, *Le satire . . .* (Florence: L. S. Olschki, 1914).

38. See above, Chapter III. See also the neat little study: Mario Pericoli, *Escatologia nella lauda jacoponica* (Todi: Accademia Tudertina, 1962), pp. 9–11.

39. Francesco Tresatti, the seventeenth-century historian and editor of Jacopone's poems, as quoted by Franco Mancini, "Due postille jacoponiche," *Convivium* (1952), p. 459.

40. See above, Chapter III. For the history of the hospital, see Ceci, *Todi nel medio evo,* pp. 270, 328–334.

41. See above, Chapter III, For a commentary on *Lauda* L, see Franca Ageno (Brambilla), "Sull' invettiva di Jacopone da Todi contro Bonifazio VIII," *Cultura Neolatina,* vol. XVI, no. 4 (Florence, 1964), pp. 413–414. The position that Jacopone was not strongly influenced by Joachimism, as expressed in Maccarini, *Jacopone da Todi,* pp. 57–59, is no longer tenable.

42. For example, the *Liber de Flore* was discovered in 1386 in Calabria by Telesphorus of Cosenza; Herbert Grundmann, " 'Liber de Flore', eine Schrift der Franciskaner-Spiritualen aus dem Anfang des 14 Jahrhunderts," *Historisches Jahrbuch,* vol. XLIX (Munich, 1929), pp. 33–91.

43. The pseudo-Joachimist *Commentary on Jeremiah* has been dated 1249; ibid., pp. 33–35; see also Daniel, "Origins of Franciscan Joachimism," pp. 671–676.

44. Bloomfield, "Joachim of Flora," p. 261. It might be said that Henri Bergson and Pierre Teilhard de Chardin modernized this view.

45. Reeves, *Influence of Prophecy,* p. 181.

46. Douie, *Heresy of the Fraticelli,* p. 133; see also Knoth, *Ubertino von Casale,* pp. 4–7, 14–20, 30–42; Reeves, *Influence of Prophecy,* pp. 207–209.

47. Ibid., p. 198. Author's translation. See also Ehrle, "Petrus Iohannis Olivi," pp. 492–497.

48. Waley, *Papal State*, pp. 71–73, 87–90, 221–224. Baldelli developed the thesis that there was a strong difference in the character of the *disciplinati* in those parts of Umbria and the Marches influenced by communal civilization and those still in feudal conditions; Ignazio Baldelli, "La lauda e i disciplinati," *Il movimento dei disciplinati*, pp. 354–358. The Marches were also the center of some heretical activity, especially that of the Apostles; Volpe, *Movimenti religiosi*, pp. 118–160; Leff, *Heresy in the Later Middle Ages*, I, 168–172.

49. "Historia septem tribulationum," in Ehrle, "Die Spiritualen," III, 304; see also Douie, *Heresy of the Fraticelli*, p. 54.

50. Contini, *Poeti del duecento*, II, 625–652; see also Moorman, *Franciscan Order*, p. 270.

51. Amadeo Amato, "La teologia di Fra Jacopone da Todi," *Bollettino della Deputazione di Storia Patria per l'Umbria*, vol. XIX (Perugia, 1915), pp. 50–59.

52. Marjorie Reeves and Beatrice Hirsch-Reich, *The "Figurae" of Joachim of Fiore* [Oxford Warburg Studies, Oxford: Clarendon Press, 1972). See also Reeves, *Influence of Prophecy*, p. 27; Bloomfield, "Joachim of Flora," p. 257.

53. "The Journey of the Mind to God," *Works of Bonaventure*, ed. by de Vinck, I, 5–6.

54. Celano, *St. Francis*, First Life, Book II, chapter ix; Second Life, Book II, chapters xcviii–c; *Scripta Sociorum*, chapter xvii; Hughes, *Franciscan Writings*, pp. 149–185.

55. Mignini, "I codici del commune di San Fortunato," pp. 523–530.

56. There is a record of an episcopal visitation of the seventeenth century, in which the friars were reprimanded for not keeping Jacopone's cell in good condition. Though the house at Pantanelli is now only a ruin, Jacopone's cell was pointed out to visitors as late as 1880. Pensi, *Documenti iacoponici a Todi*, p. 25. There exists an account of the house, which the writer has not been able to obtain: Livario Oliger, *Pantanelli presso Orvieto—romitorio dei tempi di San Francesco* (Rome, 1932).

57. The text here is from Ageno, *Laudi*, p. 260, which also contains the letter in the original Latin.

58. "I gradi dell'anima," Levasti, *Mistici del duecento*, p. 268. The *Fioretti* account of Giovanni is in Hughes, *Franciscan Writings*, pp. 138–148.

59. Waley, *Orvieto*, p. 59.

60. *Detti*, II a; Ageno, *Laudi*, pp. 414–415.

61. Bernard Barbiche, "Les 'scriptores' de la chancellerie apostolique sous le pontificat de Boniface VIII," *Bibliothèque de l'École des Chartres*, vol. CXXVIII (Paris, 1970), pp. 115–187.

62. Salimbene, *La Cronaca*, p. 169.

63. The only historical study devoted to Pietro da Morrone which I have found is: Hans Schulz, "Peter von Murrhone as Pabst Cölestin V," *Zeitschrift für Kirchengeschichte*, vol. XVII (Gotha, 1897), pp. 363–397, 477–507. See also Boase, *Boniface VIII*, pp. 29–50; Ferdinand Gregorovius, *History of the City of Rome in the Middle Ages*, trans. by Anne Hamilton (vol. IV, London: George Bell, 1897), pp. 516–527. By far the most interesting work on Celestine V is not a history at all but a historical play: Ignazio Silone, *L'avventura di un povero cristiano* (Milan: Mondadori, 1968), trans. by William Weaver as *The Story of a Humble Christian*

(New York: Harper & Row, 1970). Rarely departing from historical accuracy, Silone has captured the spirit of Celestine and related it to the simple piety and peasant culture of the Abruzzi, which he knows so well. The work is an outstanding example of the genre—"Se non è vero, è ben trovato [If it is not true, it should have been]." However, the extent of the lack of understanding of Jacopone among cultured Italians of today is shown by Silone's note: "His *Laude* clearly drew on the Franciscan tradition; rather than the lyrical expression of personal feelings, they were texts meant to edify, a complement to preaching." Ibid., p. 200.

64. "De ecclesiae potentia," Book III, chapter ii. The most complete accounts are based on Stefaneschi: Schulz, "Peter von Murrhone," pp. 367–380; Boase, *Boniface VIII*, pp. 42–43.

65. "Historia septem tribulationum"; Ehrle, "Die Spiritualen," III, 308. Author's translation.

66. For a study of this *lauda*, see Mario Martelli, "Per l'interpretazione di una lauda jacoponica," *Belfagor*, vol. XVIII (July, 1963), pp. 381–402.

67. "Epistola excusatoria," Ehrle, "Die Spiritualen," I, 525.

68. There is no evidence for this, but it is possible; Sapegno, *Frate Jacopone*, p. 42; "Appunti intorno a Jacopone," p. 415.

69. These are the words of Tommaso d'Aversa, the Inquisitor General of Naples, who imprisoned Clareno and Liberato on their return to Italy in 1303. After investigation he released them, but the persecutions of the spirituals continued. "Epistola excusatoria," Ehrle, "Die Spiritualen," I, 531.

70. Quoted in Boase, *Boniface VIII*, p. 45.

71. Boys used to tease Brother Giles by calling out to him "Paradiso! Paradiso!" and then watching him go into a trance; Moorman, *Franciscan Order*, p. 257. The author knows of an incident that took place about thirty years ago at the Convento di San Antonio in Tricarico (Matera). An eccentric old man used to spend nights there in prayer; one night some boys hid in the gallery and intoned at him, imitating the voice of God; and for a while the old man was taken in.

72. It is astonishing that some modern writers of a certain generation had little sympathy for Celestine V; he was called "a peasant of the Abruzzi, a narrow-minded fanatic" by Émile Gebhardt, *Mystics and Heretics in Italy*, trans. by E. M. Hulme (New York: A. A. Knopf, 1922), p. 213. The depth of the veneration accorded to him in his time is shown by the lovely Abruzzese *lauda* printed by Vincenzo de Bartholomaeis, *Laude drammatiche e rappresentazioni sacre* (3 vols., Florence: Le Monnier, 1943), II, 3–6.

73. Gebhardt, *Mystics and Heretics*, p. 216.

74. Reeves, *Influence of Prophecy*, pp. 401–405; Douie, *Heresy of the Fraticelli*, pp. 41–43, 138–139.

75. Gregorovius, *History of Rome*, p. 527.

76. Gratien, *Histoire des Frères Mineurs*, pp. 351–352.

77. Clareno, "Epistola excusatoria," Ehrle, "Die Spiritualen," I, 528.

78. Clareno, "Historia septem tribulationum," ibid., III, 296.

79. Sapegno, "Appunti intorno a Jacopone," p. 416.

80. See above, Chapter II.

81. Boase, *Boniface VIII*, p. 160.

82. Ignatius Jeiler, "Ein inedirte Briefe des P. Olivi," *Historisches Jahrbuch*, vol.

III (Münster, 1882), pp. 648–659; Livarius Oliger, "Petri Iohannis Olivi de renuntiatione papae Celestini V," *Archivum Franciscum Historicum*, vol. XI (Quaracchi [Florence], 1918), pp. 308–339; Ehrle, "Petrus Iohannis Olivi," p. 438.

83. For the attack on the simoniacal clergy in this *lauda*, see above, Chapter II.

84. Boase, *Boniface VIII*, pp. 169–180; Gratien, *Histoire des Frères Mineurs*, pp. 421–423, 628–634.

85. Heinrich Denifle, "Die Denkschriften der Colonna gegen Bonifaz VIII und die Cardinäle gegen die Colonna," *Archiv für Literatur und Kirchengeschichte*, vol. V (Freiburg, 1889), p. 510.

86. This work has been lost; Sapegno, "Appunti intorno a Jacopone," p. 418; Ageno (Brambilla), "Sull' invettiva di Jacopone," p. 375.

87. A tract of 1308, "De recuperatione terrae sanctae," attributed to a French lawyer, Philip of Blois, developed arguments for the confiscation of church lands; Volpe, *Movimenti religiosi*, p. 165.

88. The interpretation of this poem is based on Ageno (Brambilla), "Sull' invettiva di Jacopone," pp. 373–390, who has cleared up most of the problems connected with it. Before her writing, there were those who dated the poem in 1297 or 1298, before the prison poems *Laude* LV, LVI, and LVII, since it shows an intransigence against Boniface that does not square with his change of heart in prison; others dated it after 1303, since lines 43–66 clearly refer to events after 1298, including the capture of Boniface at Anagni. Ageno has shown conclusively that these latter lines were added later and also believes that they were not even written by Jacopone. Her interpretation has been followed by Pasquini, "La Lauda," *Letteratura italiana—Il duecento*, pp. 495–498.

89. Underhill, *Jacopone*, p. 188; Sapegno, *Frate Jacopone*, p. 46.

90. It is placed at the head of the selections from Jacopone by Pasquini, "La Lauda," pp. 495–498 and Petrocchi, "La letteratura religiosa," *Storia della letteratura italiana*, pp. 667–668. See also Contini, *Poeti del duecento*, II, 105–108.

91. Grisi, *La protesta di Jacopone*, p. 40.

92. Leff, *Heresy in the Later Middle Ages*, I, 168–195, 308–315.

93. In the *Inferno*, XXVII, 73–91. Dante tells the story of Guido da Montefeltro, who was absolved ahead of time by Boniface, the "prince of the Pharisees," for the betrayal of Palestrina. Even Francis (Guido had become a Franciscan in his old age) could not save him from lying in the eighth ditch of Malebolge with the other evil counselors.

94. It is not known where Jacopone was imprisoned. Franco Mancini has tried to show that it was at San Fortunato in Todi, thinking that the Fra Gentile, who was to carry Jacopone's plea in the last line of *Lauda* LVII, was Gentile Bentivenga d'Acquasparta, the Dominican penitentiary of Todi, rather than the Franciscan Cardinal Gentile da Montefiore, the papal penitentiary in those years. The argument runs that Jacopone would have known the Todian Gentile and so was imprisoned there and would not have known the more important papal official. It does not seem convincing, since Jacopone not only had many connections at the curia, especially Franciscan ones, but also he could have been in any papal prison under the supervision of the penitentiary. See Franco Mancini, "La prigionia di Jacopone e 'l'empiasto' di Fra Gentile," *Rassegna della Letteratura Italiana*, vol. LXIV, no. 1 (January–April, 1960), pp. 47–49; Mancini, "Due postille iacoponiche," pp. 456–458.

95. The ms. picture is reproduced in Petrocchi, "La letteratura religiosa," *Storia della letteratura italiana,* p. 671. The Prato portrait is famous; Tenneroni, "Un ritratto di Fra Jacopone a Todi," p. 635. A rather complete list of representations of Jacopone is to be found in Giulio Pensi, *Documenti e ricordi iacoponici a Todi* (Todi: Tipografia Tuderte, 1930), pp. 20–33.

96. Giovanni Getto, "Il realismo di Jacopone da Todi," *Letteratura religiosa dal due al novecento* (vol. I, Florence: Sanzoni, 1967), pp. 89–95, 119.

97. Statements on contemporary conditions in prisons are based on the author's experience.

98. Boase, *Boniface VIII,* p. 189.

99. Philippe Soupault, *Le temps des assassins, histoire du dètenu no. 1234* (New York: Éditions de la Maison Française, 1945).

100. *Testamentum;* Hughes, *Franciscan Writings,* p. 218.

101. Gratien, *Histoire des Frères Mineurs,* pp. 408–418; Douie, *Heresy of the Fraticelli,* pp. 43–44, 77, 139–141; Lambert, *Franciscan Poverty,* pp. 173–182; Knoth, *Ubertino von Casale,* pp. 43–92; Reeves, *Influence of Prophecy,* pp. 206–212, 408–413; Grundmann, "Liber de Flore," pp. 80–91.

102. Sapegno, *Frate Jacopone,* pp. 48–50.

103. This is one of the two *laude* to be selected for readings by contemporary actors (the other being *Lauda* LXXVI "O iubilo del core") in the series *I 30 discolibri della letteratura italiana; Da San Francesco a Cecco Angiolieri,* ed. by Ettore Mazzali (Milan: Nuova Accademia Editrice, 1963). The radio artist, Tino Carraro, has caught the extraordinary melodic beauty of the poem.

104. Gregorovius, *History of Rome,* pp. 595–596.

Chapter V

1. The standard text for many years included only this poem and an excerpt from the prison poem, "Que farai, Fra Iacovone?"; Mario Sterzi, *Manuale della letteratura italiana ad uso dei licei* . . . (vol. I, Florence: Barbera, 1938), pp. 64–72.

2. Alessandro d'Ancona, *Origini del teatro in Italia* (2 vols., reprint 2nd ed., Rome: Bardi, 1966), p. 156. He cites as especially dramatic dialogues the *Laude* XIX, XXV, XLII, and XLVII.

3. In *Lauda* XXI, see above, Chapter III. The relationship of the "Donna del paradiso" to the rise of the drama is succinctly stated by Contini, *Letteratura italiana delle origini,* p. 201.

4. Vincenzo de Bartholomaeis, *Le origini della poesia drammatica italiana* (Bologna: Zanichelli, 1924), p. 249. See also Apollonio, *Jacopone da Todi,* p. 34.

5. Ferri and Caramella, eds., *Le laude,* pp. 4, 155.

6. Sapegno, *Frate Jacopone,* pp. 108–115; Underhill, *Jacopone,* pp. 202–204, 220–221; Barolo, *Jacopone da Todi,* pp. 136–143; Maccarini, *Jacopone,* pp. 115–117; Giuliotti, *Jacopone da Todi,* pp. 179–183, 205–215. All these writers treat the "Donna del paradiso" together with the mystical poems of the last period. The one great exception is, as usual, Casella, "Jacopone da Todi," p. 335, who deals with the poem as part of Jacopone's "ascetic life."

7. Some critics have even suggested that the "Donna del paradiso" should be read rather as a lyrical and personal expression than as a dramatic poem; Apollonio, *Jacopone da Todi,* p. 101; Maccarini, *Jacopone,* pp. 115–117.

8. d'Ancona, *Origini del teatro,* pp. 116–117.

9. Liuzzi considered this *lauda* to be a suitable song text, basing his opinion on the fact that the similar *Lauda* XLI was set to music, *La Lauda*, I, 142. He is the only researcher who has seriously attempted the very difficult job of transcribing the musical notation of the hymnbooks into modern notation, and his work has been seriously criticized by Nolthénius, *Duecento*, p. 206. Despite the promise of its title, the following work has little to offer, since its author is equally ignorant of Italian scholarship and musicology: M. Cyrilla Barr, "The popular hymnody of mediaeval Italy and its relationship to the pious and penitential confraternities," *Studies in Mediaeval Culture*, vol. III (The Medieval Institute, Western Michigan University, 1970), pp. 151–158.

10. For an excellent up-to-date study of the French chansons, see Henrik van der Werf, *The chansons of the troubadours and trouvères: a study of the melodies and their relation to the poems* (Utrecht: Oosthoek, 1972). However, the independent origin of the music for the Italian *laude* has been maintained both by Liuzzi and by Raffaello Monterosso, "Il linguaggio musicale della lauda dugentesca," *Il movimento dei disciplinati*, pp. 476–479.

11. The *laude* with musical accompaniment are the following: Jacopone XLI, "O Cristo omnipotente," the Urbino *Lauda* XI, "Voi ch'amate lo Creatore," and these six pseudo-Jacoponian *laude*: *Lauda* CI, "Troppo perde il tempo," "Oi me lasso e freddo il mio core," "Lamentomi e sospiro," "Tutor dicendo," "Dolce Vergine Maria," and "Vergen puzella per merce." Liuzzi, *La lauda*, I, 143–144, 394, 409; II, 40, 46, 70, 96, 160, 166; Bettarini, *Il laudario urbinate*, pp. 122–138, 265–267.

12. Liuzzi has collected a number of Jacopone's references to song, *La lauda*, I, 141–142; but he makes no distinction between Jacopone's various attitudes toward music. Sometimes both song and dance are thought of in a pejorative sense: the "bad song" of Celestine in *Lauda* LIV, the inappropriate dancing and singing during Holy Week in *Lauda* LVIII, the dance to keep warm in prison in *Lauda* LV, and the singing and dancing of the worldly young people in *Lauda* XXI. At other times, Jacopone thinks of song as an expression of divine love, as in the Nativity *laude* and in the great hymn to joy, *Lauda* LXXVI, see Chapter VI.

13. See above, Chapter III.

14. See above, Chapter III. For a different interpretation of *Lauda* II, see Mario Martelli, "Cielo e terra in una lauda di Jacopone da Todi," *Giornale Storico della Letteratura Italiana*, vol. CXLI, no. 434 (1964), pp. 161–185.

15. de Bartholomaeis, *Origini della poesia drammatica*, p. 145; Martin Franzbach, "Die Planctus Maria Virginis von Gonzalo de Berceo und Jacopone da Todi," *Cultura Neolatina*, vol. XXVII (Rome, 1957), pp. 95–96.

16. Printed in Ernesto Monaci, *Crestomazia italiana dei primi secoli* (2nd ed., Rome: Soc. Ed. Dante Alighieri, 1955), pp. 17–18. See above, Chapter III.

17. Baldelli, "La lauda e i disciplinati," *Il movimento dei disciplinati*, pp. 340–343.

18. Printed in Monaci, *Crestomazia*, pp. 504–509. Selections of *laude* from Bergamo, Piedmont, and Pieve di Cadore are also given; ibid., pp. 509–515, 525–526. See also de Bartholomaeis, *Origini della poesia drammatica*, pp. 539–541.

19. Monaci, *Crestomazia*, pp. 514–515. For analyses of the *laudario* of Cortona, see Petrocchi, "La letteratura religiosa," *Storia della Letteratura italiana*, I, 660–662; Pasquini, "La Lauda," *Letteratura italiana*, I, 488–493.

20. Bettarini, *Il laudario urbinate*, pp. 247–307.

21. *Meditations on the Life of Christ, an illustrated manuscript of the fourteenth century*, trans. by Isa Ragusa and ed. by Ragusa and Rosalie B. Green (Princeton: Princeton University Press, 1961). The original Latin is to be found in *Meditaciones de passione Christi olim Sancti Bonaventurae attributae*, ed. by M. Jordan Stallings (Washington: Catholic University of America Press, 1965). For the authorship of the work, see Petrocchi, "La letteratura religiosa," *Storia della Letteratura italiana*, I, 652–653.

22. *Meditations*, pp. xxviii, 5, 96.

23. Ibid., pp. 308–309. See also d'Ancona, *Origini del teatro*, pp. 124–131; de Bartholomaeis, *Origini della poesia drammatica*, p. 250.

24. For a good recent study, see Ruth Ellis Messenger, *The Mediaeval Latin Hymn* (Washington: The Capital Press, 1953), pp. 108–110.

25. *Meditations*, pp. 333, 335.

26. For an analysis of the *laudario* of Urbino from the point of view of its place in the rise of religious drama, see de Bartholomaeis, *Origini della poesia drammatica*, pp. 250–255. The texts quoted below are taken from Bettarini, *Il laudario urbinate*, pp. 486–504. Detailed analyses of these selections are to be found in the same work, pp. 267–276, 289–292, 294–307.

27. On the Goliardic poets, see above, Chapter II. For *Lauda* LIX, see above, Chapter IV; for *Lauda* XC, see Chapter VI.

28. de Bartholomaeis, *Laude drammatiche*, I, 4.

29. Mario Apollonio, *Storia del teatro italiano* (vol. I, Florence: Sanzoni, 1958), pp. 188–190. See also Apollonio, *Jacopone da Todi*, p. 101.

30. d'Ancona, *Origini del teatro*, pp. 152–162. Other analyses of the poem are to be found in Sapegno, *Frate Jacopone*, pp. 108–115; Franzbach, "Die Planctus," pp. 97–103. Underhill dismisses the poem as an "appeal to crude emotion, which falls far below the level of thought and feeling achieved in Jacopone's best work"—another indication of how far the "Donna del paradiso" is in style from the mystical poems, which Underhill understands so well; see Underhill, *Jacopone*, pp. 220–221.

31. The picture is reminiscent of an incident said to have occurred during World War II, when a Tuscan peasant woman was accused by the Nazis of harboring a Canadian flyer. Upon being pressed by the military court as to the reason for her helping the enemy, the woman silently searched her heart and finally answered: "Non era anche lui figlio di mamma? [Was not he too the son of a mother?]"

32. Franzbach, "Die Planctus," p. 97.

33. See above Chapter I, n. 13.

34. de Bartholomaeis, *Laude drammatiche*, p. 3; see also Apollonio, *Teatro italiano*, pp. 189–193.

35. Mazza, *Il laudatario jacoponico*, pp. vii–xi.

36. Mario Apollonio, "Lauda drammatica umbra e methodi per l'indagine critica delle forme drammatiche," *Il movimento dei disciplinati*, pp. 395–404; Angela Maria Terrugia, "In quale momento i disciplinati hanno dato origine al loro teatro," ibid., pp. 434–447.

37. de Bartholomaeis, *Origini della poesia drammatica*, p. 260; for the texts of many of the Perugian *laude*, see de Bartholomaeis, *Laude drammatiche*, I, 35–328.

38. Vincenzo de Bartholomaeis, *Il teatro abruzzese del medio evo* (Bologna: Zanichelli, 1924), pp. 16–20, 24–31.

39. Two are printed in Monaci, *Crestomazia*, pp. 516–524. See also de Bartholomaeis, *Laude drammatiche*, pp. 321–328; Apollonio, *Teatro italiano*, pp. 161–185.

40. Toschi, *Il valore attuale di Jacopone*, p. 10.

41. de Bartholomaeis, *Origini della poesia drammatica*, p. 372.

Chapter VI

1. Livario Oliger, *Dove è morto il beato Jacopone da Todi?* (Quaracchi [Florence], 1907), pp. 1–16; Pensi, *Ricordi jacoponici*, pp. 8–39; Mancini, "La prigionia di Jacopone," pp. 47–49.

2. Luigi Russo, "Jacopone da Todi mistico-poeta," p. 45.

3. Such is the interpretation of Sapegno, *Frate Jacopone*, pp. 33–36, 109; see also Natalino Sapegno, "La 'santa pazzia' di Frate Jacopone e le dottrine dei mistici medievali," *Archivum Romanicum*, vol. VII (1923), pp. 363–366. Casella implies that the mystic poems were written earlier by dealing with many of them before describing the political poems; "Jacopone da Todi," pp. 429–466. However, he does reserve the "Amor de caritate" for the end of his study, pp. 474–480. Underhill, as has been noted, develops an overly precise scheme of dating based on her knowledge of progress in mystical living. While she places most of the poems of divine love in this last period, she does relegate the "Amor de caritate" and a few others to the period 1278–1293; *Jacopone*, pp. 507–510. Giuliotti alone dates all of these poems in the last period, but then he also includes in the period lots of others, notably the Francis, the Virgin, and the Nativity poems; *Jacopone da Todi*, pp. 169–229.

4. *The Book of Saint Bernard on the Love of God*, ed. and trans. by Edmund G. Gardner (New York: E. P. Dutton & Co., 1915), chapter x. See also Étienne Gilson, *The Mystical Philosophy of Saint Bernard*, trans. by A. H. C. Downes (2nd ed., London and New York: Sheed & Ward, 1955); M. Marguerite O'Connell, *The Relation between Solitude and Social Action as Lived and Taught by Saint Bernard* (Notre Dame: Dept. of Philosophy Ph.D. thesis, 1948); Gardner, *Dante and the Mystics*, pp. 111–151; Louis Bouyer, Jean Leclerq, and François Vandenbroucke, *Histoire de la spiritualité chrétienne*, vol. II, *La spiritualité au moyen âge* (Paris: Aubier, 1961), pp. 242–248. An English translation of the last work was made by the Benedictines of Holme Eden Abbey in 1968.

5. Beginning with Novati, many writers have got stuck in Jacopone's penitential period. Novati wrote: "Between the master [Francis] and the disciple rises an insurmountable barrier. Jacopone could not . . . transform his whole nature; he was and remained a man of battle; he emerges from his poetry as very different from the seraphic father whom he proposed to exemplify. A violent and implacable fighter against sin and guilt, his poetic genius sparkles most brightly . . . when imagination assails him and anger is his guide." *Freschi e minii*, p. 243. Similar attitudes are reflected in Maccarini, *Jacopone da Todi*, pp. 75–78, and Sapegno, "La 'santa pazzia,' " pp. 368–371; Ageno, *Laudi*, pp. xv–xvii; Grisi, *La protesta di Jacopone*, pp. 17–21; and Mancini, *Laude*, pp. 351–354.

6. Giles Constable, "Twelfth Century Spirituality and the Late Middle Ages," *Mediaeval and Renaissance Studies* (no. 5, Chapel Hill: University of North Carolina Press, 1971), pp. 27–29.

7. Gilson, *Philosophy of St. Bonaventure*, p. 63.

8. Brother Lawrence, *The Practice of the Presence of God* (Mt. Vernon, N.Y.: Peter Pauper Press, 1963); Thomas R. Kelly, *A Testament of Devotion* (New York: Harper & Bros., 1941).

9. For *Lauda* XXXIX, see above, Chapter III; *Lauda* LX, see above, Chapter IV; *Lauda* LXV, see above, Chapter V; and for the prison poems, see above, Chapter IV.

10. Gervais Dumeige, *Richard de Saint-Victor et l'idée chrétienne de l'amour* (Paris: Presses Universitaires de France, 1952), p. 123.

11. Underhill, *Jacopone*, pp. 195–196. Jacopone's experience is meaningfully compared to that of St. John of the Cross.

12. Hughes, *Franciscan Writings*, pp. 149–185. Also see above, Chapter IV.

13. *Works of Bonaventure*, ed. by de Vinck, pp. 6, 97.

14. See above, Chapter III. The resolution of two of the tortured dialogues of his penitential period lies in his identification with Christ on the cross, *Lauda* XLI, lines 51–56, and *Lauda* XLII, lines 48–53; see above, Chapter III and Chapter V.

15. "Just in this so absolute and rigid contrast between the infinite wisdom of God and the vileness of the world and men, in this fundamental opposition to the civil and moral habits of the crowd reposes the central nucleus of his madness." Sapegno, "La 'santa pazzia,' " p. 363.

16. Dumeige, *Richard de Saint-Victor*, p. 6 and passim; Giovanni Maria Bertin, *I mistici medievali* (Milan: Garzanti, 1944), pp. 58–62, 205–210; Bouyer, Leclerq, and Vandenbroucke, *Histoire de la spiritualité*, pp. 282–295.

17. *The Book of Divine Consolation of the Blessed Angela of Foligno*, trans. by Mary G. Steegman (New York: Cooper Square Publishers, 1966). An interesting example of the neglect and misunderstanding of Jacopone and the higher valuation of the more conventional Angela is to be found in Bouyer, Leclerq, and Vandenbroucke, *Histoire de la spiritualité*, pp. 378–379. It is not necessary to speculate on the influence of Jacopone on Angela, since the ideas that she expressed and the symbols that were important to her were common currency among the spirituals; Underhill, *Jacopone*, pp. 129, 161, 238; Moorman, *Franciscan Order*, pp. 222–223.

18. Sapegno, "La 'santa pazzia,' " pp. 363–367, *Frate Jacopone*, pp. 26–27.

19. Ageno, *Laudi*, pp. 412–413.

20. "Monte christo vita," pp. 389–390.

21. These quotations are from the charming story in the *Fioretti*, chapter viii, "How St. Francis taught Brother Leo the meaning of perfect joy." Hughes, *Franciscan Writings*, pp. 62–63.

22. See especially Sapegno, "La 'santa pazzia,' " pp. 363–367, and *Frate Jacopone*, pp. 26–27, 32–33. It may seem carping continuously to point out differences of interpretation from Sapegno, but his work on Jacopone is among the most authoritative and the most readily available in Italy. Views similar to those of Sapegno are to be found in Maccarini, *Jacopone da Todi*, pp. 75–78; Bertin, *Mistici medievali*, p. 76; and Novati, *Freschi e minii*, p. 243. On the other hand, Underhill develops a clear picture of what she calls Jacopone's "jubilus"; *Jacopone*, pp. 76–78; and Casella relates Jacopone's joy to Francis's *Canticle to the Sun*; "Jacopone da Todi," p. 435.

23. See above, Chapter IV.

24. Dumeige, *Richard de Saint-Victor*, p. 117. See also Casella, "Jacopone da Todi," pp. 429–430; Underhill, *Jacopone*, pp. 195–196.

25. *Bernard on the Love of God*, chapter x, paragraph 27.

26. Bonaventure was sent to Todi to prevent the commune from supporting Manfred's military activity in Umbria; Ceci, *Todi nel medio evo*, p. 150.

27. Bonaventuran influences on Jacopone in his earlier periods have been traced by Michele Vinai, "Jacopone e San Bonaventura," *Cultura Neolatina*, vol. I (1941), pp. 134–142. For the last period, Bonaventure's influence has been shown by Agide Gottardi, " 'L'albero spirituale' in Jacopone da Todi," *Rassegna Critica della Letteratura Italiana*, vol. XX (1915), pp. 1–28, 84–116.

28. From "The Journey of the Mind to God," *Works of Bonaventure*, ed. by de Vinck, p. 25; see also Bougerol, *Introduction to the Works of Bonaventure*, pp. 123–126.

29. Underhill, *Jacopone*, p. 224; Sapegno, *Frate Jacopone*, p. 71; Casella, "Jacopone da Todi," p. 436.

30. Gardner, *Dante and the Mystics*, pp. 51–76, 88–110, 135–151, and 168–170.

31. Bertin, *Mistici medievali*, p. 32. See also Gilson, *Philosophy of St. Bonaventure*, pp. 74–77; Maccarini, *Jacopone da Todi*, pp. 61–63; Bouyer, Leclerq, and Vandenbroucke, *Histoire de la spiritualité*, pp. 282–288.

32. Underhill, *Essentials of Mysticism*, p. 101.

33. See above, Chapter I.

34. Quaglio, "Poeti della 'Magna Curia' siciliana," *Letteratura italiana*, pp. 220–222; see also Folena, "Poesia dei siciliani," *Storia della letteratura italiana*, pp. 325–326; Apollonio, *Jacopone da Todi*, p. 89.

35. For Calvacanti, see Quaglio, "Gli stilnovisti," *Letteratura italiana*, pp. 424–431. For Dante, see Niccolò Mineo, "Dante," ibid., vol. I, part II, 453–479, 536–546. See also Apollonio, *Jacopone da Todi*, p. 94.

36. Sonnets LXXXIV and CCLXXV; *Petrarch Sonnets and Songs*, trans. by Anna Maria Armi (New York: Grosset & Dunlap, 1968), pp. 138–139, 396–397. There can, of course, be no question of Jacopone's influence on Petrarch.

37. Sonnet XXXV, ibid., pp. 56–57.

38. The significance of this little poem has been generally overlooked by most modern critics, the notable exception being, as usual, Casella, "Jacopone da Todi," pp. 437–438.

39. For the rest of this poem, see above, Chapter IV.

40. d'Ancona, *Jacopone da Todi*, pp. 6–11. d'Ancona's misconception is shared by Gebhardt, *Mystics and Heretics*, pp. 218–223. For criticism of d'Ancona's thesis, see Maccarini, *Jacopone da Todi*, pp. 26–28; Bizziccarri, "L'amore mistico," pp. 2–5; Ernesto Giacomo Parodi, *Lingua e letteratura* (vol. I, Venice: Neri Pozza, 1957), pp. 144–148.

41. Constable, "Twelfth Century Spirituality," p. 28.

42. "The Journey of the Mind to God," *Works of Bonaventure*, ed. by de Vinck, p. 56. The total loss of individuality was an element in Plotinian Neoplatonism, which had a varied reception among Christians; see the comments of Hugh of St. Victor in Bouyer, Leclerq, and Vandenbroucke, *Histoire de la spiritualité*, p. 289. For an introduction to the thought of Plotinus, see P. V. Pistorius, *Plotinus and Neoplatonism* (Cambridge: Bowes & Bowes, 1952); *The Philosophy of Plotinus*, ed. and trans. by Joseph Katz (New York: Appleton-Century, 1950).

43. "The Four Degrees of Violent Love," quoted in Dumeige, *Richard de Saint-Victor*, pp. 144–145.

44. "On Contemplation," quoted in Bouyer, Leclerq, and Vandenbroucke, *Histoire de la spiritualité*, p. 288. For a recent review of the state of studies on Hugh, see Roger Baron, "Hughes de Saint Victor: contribution à un nouvel examen de son oeuvre," *Traditio*, vol. XV (1959), pp. 223–298.

45. Thomas wrote one of the several commentaries on Pseudo-Dionysius current in the thirteenth century; Bouyer, Leclerq, and Vandenbroucke, *Histoire de la spiritualité*, p. 297. For a thorough study of the history of the idea of "alienatio mentis," see Gerhart B. Ladner, "Homo Viator: Medieval ideas of alienation and order," *Speculum* (April, 1967), vol. XLII, 239–246.

46. "The Journey of the Mind to God," *Works of Bonaventure*, ed. by de Vinck, p. 57.

47. Quoted by Gardner, *Dante and the Mystics*, p. 5.

48. R. W. Southern, *The Making of the Middle Ages* (New Haven: Yale University Press, 1953), pp. 228–232.

49. Quoted in Bertin, *Mistici medievali*, p. 36. Pseudo-Dionysius wrote in "On the Heavenly Hierarchy": "It is not possible for our mind to be raised to that immaterial presentation and contemplation of the heavenly hierarchies without using the material guidance suitable to itself, accounting the visible beauties as reflections of the invisible comeliness." *The Works of Dionysius the Areopagite*, ed. and trans. by John Parker (vol. II, London: James Parker & Sons, 1899), p. 3.

50. "I saw that there was an ocean of darkness and death; but an infinite ocean of light and love which flowed over the ocean of darkness. In that also I saw the infinite love of God, and I had great openings." *The Journal of George Fox*, ed. by Rufus Jones (New York: Capricorn Books, 1963), p. 87.

51. "I gradi dell' anima," Levasti, *Mistici del duecento*, p. 269. Jacopone's *Lauda* LXV, "En cinque modi appareme - lo Signor en esta vita [The Lord appeared to me in five ways in this life]" is almost a paraphrase of Giovanni's words.

52. Chapters lii and liii; Hughes, *Franciscan Writings*, pp. 145–148.

53. Quoted in Gottardi, "L'albero spirituale," p. 100; see also Sapegno, "La 'santa pazzia,' " p. 369. Psychological studies of such mystical states are to be found in James H. Leuba, "Les tendences fondamentales des mystiques chrétiens," *Revue Philosophique*, vol. LIV (July–December, 1902), pp. 1–36, 441–487; and E. Murisier, "Le sentiment réligieux dans l'ecstase," *Revue Philosophique*, vol. XLIV (July–December, 1898), pp. 449–472, 607–626.

54. Casella, "Jacopone da Todi," p. 474.

55. See above, Chapter V.

56. "Kubla Khan," lines 51–54.

57. The Middle Ages knew of the concept of the mad poet through Horace and Ovid, but not through the *Phaedrus* of Plato; see "The Poet's Divine Frenzy" in Curtius, *European Literature*, pp. 474–475; and Bizziccarri, "L'amore mistico," p. 13. For the comparison of the poet and the saint as fools, see Enid Welsford, *The Fool, his social and literary history* (New York: Doubleday Anchor Books, 1961), pp. 76–112, 321–323.

58. See above, Chapter VI.

59. See above, Chapter III.

60. "Troilus and Criseyde," lines 1815–1819; *The Complete Works of Geoffrey Chaucer*, ed. by F. N. Robinson (Boston: Houghton Mifflin Co., 1933), p. 564.

61. Moorman, *Franciscan Order*, p. 264.

62. Augustine, *The City of God*, book ix, chapter 13, *an abridged version* . . ., ed. by Vernon J. Bourke (New York: Doubleday Image Books, 1958), p. 456. On the general need for order, see Underhill, *Essentials of Mysticism*, pp. 23–24; Gardner, *Dante and the Mystics*, pp. 48–64.

63. Casella, "Jacopone da Todi," p. 478.

64. Toschi, *Il valore attuale della poesia di Jacopone*, pp. 15–24. For the phenomenon of "speaking with tongues," see Acts 10:44–46; I Corinthians 14:2–14; Underhill, *Jacopone*, pp. 130–135, 235.

65. From "De contemplatione," quoted in Bouyer, Leclerq, and Vanden-broucke, *Histoire de la spiritualité*, p. 284.

66. The nature of Jacopone's divine vision is explored in Bizziccarri, "L'amore mistico," pp. 17–20; Casella, "Jacopone da Todi," pp. 432–433; Underhill, *Jacopone*, pp. 225–248; Apollonio, *Jacopone da Todi*, pp. 90–93; and Sapegno, *Frate Jacopone*, p. 88.

67. Gardner, *Dante and the Mystics*, pp. 20–22, 83–90, 312–321.

68. Bertin, *Mistici medievali*, pp. 14, 54; Pistorius, *Plotinus*, pp. 7–26.

69. Underhill, *Essentials of Mysticism*, p. 4.

70. Jacopone's theology has been called "free" and his "disdain for salvation, a novelty"; Gebhardt, *Mystics and Heretics*, p. 219. Sapegno was the first to analyze in some depth the charge of heresy; *Frate Jacopone*, pp. 26–27; "La 'santa paz-zia,' " pp. 364–366. Russo highlighted this analysis and stated: "In this sense, all profound mystics are outside the church in the act of their mysticism, and mysticism is always a potential heresy. The extreme wing of Franciscan mystics had already excommunicated themselves before they were cursed by the church"; *Ritratti storici*, p. 58. But Jacopone's heresy remained "potential," and after his imprisonment, he took no further action against the hierarchy or the order. That Jacopone's heresy was potential cannot be doubted and has been clearly defined by the Franciscan Bracaloni, see above, Chapter IV. But it re-mained only potential in that he did not commit heretical acts or associate with heretical groups; and since the church judged heresy on the evidence of moral actions, he was never accused of it. This distinction is made clear by the Catholic historian Antoine Frédéric Ozanam: "When Jacopone wishes that his soul should pass through nothingness to lead it to God, the excess of his expressions recalls Indian pantheism, proposing as the last happiness eternal apathy, the annihilation of the human personality in divine immensity. When he praises this peace, in which all fear and all hope are extinguished, when he is no longer worried over his salvation and asks for hell on the condition of bringing love there, he is very close to the quietism into which the false mystics of his time slid." Quoted in Apollonio, *Jacopone da Todi*, p. 14.

71. Celano, *Treatise on the Miracles of St. Francis*, pp. 38–39. The story of Jacopone's death is in *La Franceschina*, pp. 153–155. See also "Monte Christo vita," pp. 391–392; and "Compendium chronacharum Frati Minori scripti a P. Mariano de Florentia," Archivum Franciscanum Historicum (vol. II, Quaracchi [Florence], 1908), p. 628.

Chapter VII

1. R. W. Southern, *Western Society and the Church in the Middle Ages* (Harmondsworth: Penguin Books, 1970), pp. 300–304.

2. It is interesting to note that Jacopone's poems circulated to some extent in Spain, where evidently the linguistic barrier was not insuperable and certainly the tradition of religious poetry is much deeper than in Italy. One of the greatest Spanish historians, Ramón Menendez Pidal, advanced the intriguing thesis that some of Jacopone's metrical patterns derive from Moorish sources, "Poesie arabe e poesie europea," *Bulletin Hispanique*, vol. XL (1938), p. 423. Mancini found that about one quarter of Jacopone's poems do follow an originally Moorish metrical scheme, rather less than Menendez Pidal claimed; see *Laude*, p. 380.

3. Francesco Tresatti, ed., *Poesie spirituali del B. Jacopone da Todi frate minore, accresciute di molti altri suoi cantici nuovamente ritrovati che non erano venuti in luce. . . .* (Venice: Niccolò Misserini, 1617). The most thorough study of this edition is in Bettarini, *Il laudario urbinate*, pp. 403–482. See also Casella, "Jacopone da Todi," pp. 295–297.

4. Selections from Ugo Panziera's work are to be found in Levasti, *Mistici del duecento*, pp. 273–316, 992–993. See also Moorman, *Franciscan Order*, pp. 399–400.

5. Leff, *Heresy in the Later Middle Ages*, I, 230–255. L. Fumi, "Eretici e ribelli nell' Umbria dal 1320 al 1330," *Bollettino della Deputazione di Storia Patria per l'Umbria*, vol. III (Perugia, 1897), pp. 257–285, 419–489.

6. See above, Chapter I, n. 11.

7. Natalino Sapegno, *Il trecento* (2nd ed., Milan: Vallardi, 1960), pp. 505–525.

8. Mazza, *Il laudatario jacoponico*, pp. vii–xxi. This work contains a good summary of the various manuscript families, based on the work of such earlier scholars as G. Galli. For an exhaustive inventory of the surviving manuscripts, see Mancini, *Laude*, pp. 389–447 and Bettarini, *Il laudario urbinate*, pp. 723–727. See above, Chapter I, n. 13.

9. Robert E. Lerner, *The Heresy of the Free Spirit* (Berkeley: University of California Press, 1972), pp. 70–84; Huizinga, *Waning of the Middle Ages*, p. 261; Underhill, *Jacopone*, pp. 138–139, 230–233; Bertin, *Mistici medievali*, pp. 54–60; Constable, "Twelfth Century Spirituality," pp. 37–39.

10. See especially Sermon 28, Raymond B. Blakney, *Meister Eckhardt, a modern translation* (New York: Harper & Row, 1941), pp. 224–232. See also Lerner, *Heresey of the Free Spirit*, pp. 281–290; Leff, *Heresy in the Later Middle Ages*, pp. 260–291.

11. Bertin, *Mistici medievali*, pp. 107–112, 355–378; Underhill, *Jacopone*, pp. 124–125, 198–200; David Knowles, *The English Mystical Tradition* (New York: Harpers, 1961), pp. 1–7, 48–66.

12. Ladner, "Homo Viator," pp. 256-258; R. R. Post, *The Modern Devotion* (Leiden: Studies in Mediaeval and Renaissance Thought, no. 3, 1968).

13. The classic account is Rufus M. Jones, *Spiritual Reformers in the 16th and 17th Centuries* (reprint, Boston: The Beacon Press, 1959).

14. Underhill, *Essentials of Mysticism*, p. 18.

Bibliographical Note

This note is concerned only with those works that refer directly and importantly to Jacopone and hence does not include sources used for background materials. The latter can be found in the notes with the aid of short-title listings in the index.

The most recent and most useful bibliograhy on Jacopone can be found in Iacopone da Todi, *Laude*, edited by Franco Mancini (Scrittori d'Italia no. 257, Bari: Laterza, 1974), pp. 473–479. An earlier voluminous bibliography, containing about 1300 titles, is now virtually worthless: Vigenio Soncini, *Fonti dottrinali, storiche, e letterarie per lo studio della vita e del pensiero di Fra Jacopone da Todi* (Reggio-Emilia: Libreria Editrice Frati Francescani, 1932).

Works by Jacopone da Todi

More than any other single scholar, Franca Ageno is responsible for the fixing of the corpus of Jacopone's writings. So many accretions to his works had occurred over the centuries that it was necessary to distinguish between genuine Jacoponian products and the compositions of followers and imitators on the basis of the strictest possible definition of Jacopone's style. Franca Ageno sketched her criteria in "Modi stilistici nelle laudi di Fra Jacopone da Todi," *Rassegna d'Italia*, vol. I (1946), and then proceeded to bring out a fine scholarly edition: *Laudi, trattato e detti* (Florence: Le Monnier, 1953), reprinted in Bologna in 1971. Her preface presents a precise and accurate account of substantially all the early references to Jacopone, a brief summary of his main stylistic characteristics, and an analysis of the manuscript families and early printed editions.

Ageno's work has been admirably supplemented by Mancini's recent and authoritative edition of Iacopone da Todi, *Laude*. Mancini confirms the decisions regarding the authentic Jacoponian poems made by Ageno and bases his work on an even more exhaustive analysis of the existing manuscripts. His main contribution is that he has followed the two earliest manuscripts with fidelity, reproducing both the Todian orthography and the haphazard order of these sources. Except for these matters the Mancini edition presents a text that is substantially the same as that of Ageno. Since Mancini bases his edition exclusively on these Todian manuscripts, he has excluded all but one of the Jacoponian poems discovered by Rosanna Bettarini in *Jacopone e il laudario urbinate* (Florence: Sanzoni, 1969). The general reader will find this edition hard to use for several reasons. The orthography, which according to Mancini, reproduces more exactly the sound of the Todian dialect and avoids the Tuscan patina of the other editions, is more distant from modern Italian and thus harder to read. The order of the poems has been destroyed, and this order is important for the understanding of Jacopone's message and spiritual growth. Finally, the exhaustive glossary has been placed at the back of the book, instead of placing notes by each poem, and so the reader must continually refer to it. Still, all in all, it now appears that the Jacoponian corpus is complete and that the Mancini edition is likely to remain the standard one for many years to come.

Despite the obvious quality of the Ageno edition, the texts quoted in this book are not taken from it but from Luigi Fallacara, ed., *Le laude* (Florence: Libreria Editrice Fiorentina, 1955), since the latter uses more modern orthography, thus making the poems easier to read, and is readily available to students. The Fallacara edition is based on the work of Ageno and also earlier editions, containing, for example, nine poems excluded by the former as apocryphal; it is provided with adequate explanatory notes.

Following essentially the same procedures as Ageno—but with even greater precision and thoroughness—Rosanna Bettarini examined virtually the entire production of the Jacoponian school in *Jacopone e il laudario urbinate*. She began her work by establishing the authenticity and antiquity of the Urbino manuscript and then distinguished in it the work of Jacopone from that of his followers by close stylistic analysis. In the process she added fourteen more poems to the body of Jacopone's work. Her monumental volume includes a full consideration of practically all the poems of the Jacoponian school, including those collected and published as genuine Jacopone by Francesco Tresatti in: *Poesie spirituali del B. Jacopone da Todi . . .* (Venice: Niccolò Misserini, 1617).

Of value in establishing the influence of Jacopone in Northern Italy is Giuseppe Mazza, *Il laudatario jacoponico—Delta-VII-15 della Biblioteca Civica "Angelo Maj" di Bergamo* (Bergamo: Editrice San Marco, 1960). The author is well acquainted with hymnbooks of the *disciplinati* and the Franciscans in the Veneto and shows that the manuscript under his study was the major source of the editions printed later in Brescia and Rome. Also of interest is Francesco Ugolini, ed., *Laude di Jacopone da Todi tratte da due manocritte umbre . . .* (Turin: Istituto Editrice Gheroni, 1947).

Up until the work of Ageno, Jacopone's best editor was Francesco Buonaccorsi, who brought out the first printed edition in 1490, basing it on the best Umbrian manuscipts available to him. The order, which Buonaccorsi used in printing the poems is that which he found in a Todian manuscript of the second generation, and it follows closely the development of both Jacopone's style and his spiritual growth; it is still used in all editions except Mancini's. For several decades in this century the best Jacoponian editions were based on Buonaccorsi's: Giuseppe Ferri and S. Caramella, eds., *Le laude di Jacopone da Todi secondo la stampa fiorentina del 1490* (2nd ed., Bari: Laterza, 1930). Giovanni Papini, ed., *Le laude, ristampa integrale della prima edizione (1490)* (Florence: Libreria Editrice Fiorentina, 1923).

The following works of little value should be noted: Biordo Brugnoli, ed., *Le satire, ricostrutte nella loro più probabile lezione originaria con le varianti dei manoscritti più importanti e precedute da un saggio sulle stampe e sui codici jacoponici* (Florence: L. S. Olschki, 1914). Biordo Brugnoli, *Fra Jacopone da Todi e l'epopea francescana* (Assisi: Metastasio, 1907).

Early References to Jacopone

Perhaps the earliest reference to Jacopone is to be found in the "Historia septem tribulationum" written in the 1420s and 1430s by Angelo Clareno and printed in Franz Ehrle, "Die Spiritualen, ihr Verhältniss zum Franciskanerorden und zu den Fraticellen," *Archiv für Literatur und Kirchengeschichte*, vol. III (Berlin,

1887). In 1390 Bartolomaeus da Pisa made brief reference to Jacopone and included his *Detti* in the "De conformitate vitae b. Francisci ad vitam divi Jesu . . .," *Analecta Franciscana,* vol. IV (Quaracchi [Florence], 1906). A recent authoritative study of the latter work is that of Carolly Erickson, "Bartholomew of Pisa; Francis Exalted: *De Conformitate,*" *Medieval Studies,* vol. XXXIV (1972), 253-275.

Much use has been made in this book of the Franciscan legends surrounding Jacopone, set down in writing towards the middle of the fifteenth century, and the inclusion of such material of doubtful historicity has been justified by the thesis that folklore and mythology offer important insights. Perhaps the earliest of these "lives" of Jacopone is that found in; N. Cavanna, ed., *La Franceschina, testo volgare umbro del secolo XV scritto dal P. G. Oddi di Perugia* (2 vols., Florence: L. S. Olschki, 1931). The Franciscan chronicler, Mariano da Firenze, included Jacopone in his "Compendium chronacharum Frati Minori . . .," *Archivum Franciscanum Historicum,* vol. II (Quaracchi [Florence], 1908); and followed the Franceschina account almost word for word in his "Vita inedita di Fra Jacopone da Todi da Fra Mariano da Firenze," ed. by Livario Oliger, *Luce e Amore,* vol. IV 1907). Other interesting details are to be found in a fifteenth-century manuscript that is no longer in existence but was printed by A. Tobler, ed., "Vita del beato Jacopone da Todi," *Zeitschrift für Romanische Philologie,* vol. II, III (1878–1879). Probably of later provenance is the "Vita del beato Jacopone de l'ordine di San Francesco cavata da . . . Monastero di Monte Christo," ed. by Niccolò Dal Gal, *La Verna,* vol. IV (1906).

. The seventeenth-century Irish Franciscan chronicler, Luke Wadding, who based his work on sources that have since perished, presents some Jacoponian materials in: "Scriptores Ordinis Minorum," *Analecta Franciscana,* vol. IV (Quaracchi [Florence], 1906) and *Annales Minorum* (vol. V, 3rd ed., Quaracchi [Florence], 1931).

General Studies of Jacopone

The seminal literary critique of Jacopone in modern times is that of Mario Casella, "Jacopone da Todi," *Archivum Romanicum,* vol. IV (1920), pp. 281–329, 429–485. It has been recognized as fundamental by many of the leading literary historians, as for example: Luigi Russo, ed., *I classici italiani* (vol. I, Florence: Sanzoni, 1948), p. 383; it has been widely used in this book. Not only is Casella's interpretation of individual poems profound but also his classification of the *canzoniere* into ascetic, Franciscan, and mystical groups has been widely followed. By and large his relating of the poems to the life of Jacopone (and the legends surrounding it) is clear and complete, though he does misdate the invective against Boniface VIII (*Lauda* LVIII)—a mistake that was later corrected by Ageno.

Standing completely aside from the mainstream of Jacoponian studies is the work of Evelyn Underhill, *Jacopone da Todi, Poet and Mystic, a spiritual biography with a selection of the spiritual songs, the Italian texts translated into English verse by Mrs. Theodore Beck* (London and Toronto: J. M. Dent & Sons, 1919). The main value of the work is that Jacopone's spiritual development is projected against a background of mystical experience as expressed over the ages from the time of

Plotinus to that of Teresa of Avila; the author, herself a spiritual giant, recognized the spiritual genius of the poet. However, Underhill's interpretation has serious drawbacks. She places many of the later poems among the early penitential ones; she expurgates some of Jacopone's most pungent realism; she ignores Jacopone's invectives; she denigrates the "Donna del paradiso"; and she presents prettied-up translations, which because they have been used in English works, have blocked an appreciation of the poetry among English-speaking people.

In Italy the most influential work, until very recently, was that of Natalino Sapegno, *Frate Jacopone* (reprint, Naples: Libreria Scientifica Editrice, 1969). Based on careful scholarship and backed by a well-justified reputation as one of Italy's leading literary scholars, Sapegno's interpretation, originally published in 1926, found many followers and has been responsible for some important misconceptions. The most striking of these is Sapegno's condescension toward Jacopone as a poet; he guards the pantheon of Italian classicism against the intrusion of the vulgar, the exaggerated, the seeming formlessness, and the didacticism that he finds in the work of Jacopone. Futhermore, he has little or no appreciation of the spiritual message so well understood by Underhill. This "official" line was given additional credence by the equally influential Giulio Bertoni in *Lingua e pensiero* (Florence: L. S. Olschki, 1932); "La lingua di Jacopone," *Archivum Romanicum,* vol. XVI, no. 3 (July–September, 1932); and *Il duecento* (Milan: Vallardi, 1930). At one point at least, Ageno agreed with them, see above "Modi stilistici." Two other writers of the same period add little to our knowledge of or appreciation for Jacopone: Agostino Barolo, *Jacopone da Todi* (Turin: Fratelli Bocca, 1929) and Domenico Giuliotti, *Jacopone da Todi* (Florence: Vallecchi, 1939).

The Sapegno thesis was effectively attacked by Luigi Russo, "Jacopone da Todi mistico-poeta," *Ritratti e disegni storici,* ser. 3, *Studi sul due e trecento* (vol. I, Bari: Laterza, 1951); see also Luigi Russo, "Jacopone poeta," *Belfagor,* vol. VII (1952), 620–631. A sensitive understanding of Jacopone's style is shown in Giovanni Getto, "Il realismo di Jacopone da Todi," *Letteratura religiosa dal due al novecento* (vol. I, Florence: Sanzoni, 1967). Equally interesting artistic insights are to be found in: Angelo Monteverdi, "Jacopone poeta" in Convegno del Centro di Studi sulla Spiritualità Medievale, *Jacopone e il suo tempo* (Todi: Accademia Tudertina, 1959)—a volume that also contains studies by Raffaello Morghen, Mario Salmi, and Arsenio Frugoni; and Salvatore Quasimodo, *Il poeta e il politico e altre saggi* (Milan: Schwartz, 1960).

The whole course of Jacoponian critical studies up to the early 1950s was admirably summarized in Franco Maccarini, *Jacopone da Todi e i suoi critici* (Milan: Gastaldi Editori, 1952). Here the "discovery" of Jacopone is attributed to Antoine Frédéric Ozanam in a work that is now mainly of historical interest, *Les poètes franciscains en Italie au treizième siècle* (Paris: Le Coffre, 1852), translated and edited by A. E. Nellen and N. C. Craig as *The Franciscan Poets in Italy in the Thirteenth Century* (London: David Nutt, 1914). Maccarini further defines the early importance and the limitations of the interpretation by Alessandro d'Ancona, first published in 1880 and revised as *Jacopone da Todi—giullare di Dio* (2nd ed., Todi: Atanor, 1914). Other earlier works, though dated, are still of interest: Francesco Novati, "L'amor mistico in San Francesco d'Assisi e in Jacopone da Todi," *Freschi e minii del dugento* (Milan: Cogliati, 1908); and Ernesto G. Parodi,

"Il giullare di Dio," *Poeti antichi e moderni* (Florence: Sanzoni, 1923)—an essay that has been reprinted in *Lingua e Letteratura* (vol. I, Venice: Neri Pozza, 1957).

The religious significance of Jacopone's work is presented in an orthodox setting and illustrated by detailed analyses of his poems of divine love by Mario Apollonio, *Jacopone da Todi e la poetica delle confraternite religiose nella cultura preumanistica* (Milan: Società Editrice, "Vita e Pensiero," 1946). Two enthusiastic Jacoponians of recent times are: Maria Sticco, "Jacopone da Todi," *Letteratura Italiana—i minori* (vol. I, Milan: Marzorati, 1961) and Paolo Toschi, *Il valore attuale ed eterno della poesia di Jacopone* (Todi: "Res Tudertinae," 1964). Two doctoral theses have been carefully done and offer balanced judgments: Irene Steiger, *Jacopone da Todi, Welthass und Gottesliebe* (Zürich: Akeret, 1945); and Alma Novella-Marani, *Jacopone da Todi* (Monograph no. 5, La Plata, Argentina: Universitad Nacional de La Plata, 1964).

The most up-to-date general treatments of the work of Jacopone, which are at once extremely competent and readily available, are to be found in the encyclopedic histories of Italian literature published by Garzanti and by Laterza. The first of these in terms of publication date is that edited by Emilio Cecchi and Natalino Sapegno, *Storia della letteratura italiana*, vol. I, *Le origini e il duecento* (Milan: Garzanti, 1965). The section entitled "La letteratura religiosa" by Giorgio Petrocchi contains an able assessment of Jacopone and his position in Italian literature. Similarly, the more recent Laterza publication is outstanding: Carlo Muscetta, general editor, *La letteratura italiana—storia e testi*, vol. I, parts I and II (Bari: Laterza, 1970). Here the emphasis is rather on fine stylistic and textual analysis, and chapter V, "La Lauda" by Emilio Pasquini, contains a thorough presentation of the major Jacoponian poems, accompanied by detailed textual notes and a fine bibliography.

Both these works extensively use earlier collections of thirteenth-century texts, especially: Ernesto Monaci, *Crestomazia italiana dei primi secoli* (2nd ed., Rome: Società Editrice Dante Alighieri, 1955); and Gianfranco Contini, *Poeti del duecento* (2 vols., Milan and Naples: Ricciardi, 1960). The latter work is more valuable for the study of Jacopone, since its author is thoroughly acquainted with the problems of establishing the Jacoponian corpus; see Gianfranco Contini, "Per l'edizione critica di Jacopone," *Rassegna della Letteratura Italiana*, vol. LVII (1953). See also his treatment of Jacopone in Gianfranco Contini, *Letteratura italiana delle origini* (Florence: Sanzoni, 1970).

General Histories

In some general histories interesting references to Jacopone can be found. This is especially true of the following: Francesco de Sanctis, *Storia della letteratura italiana* (2 vols., Milan: A. Barion, 1938); trans. by Joan Redfern (New York: Barnes & Noble, 1968); Antonio Viscardi, *Le origini* (2nd ed., Milan: Vallardi, 1950); and Angelo Monteverdi, *Studi e saggi sulla letteratura italiana dei primi secoli* (Milan and Naples: Ricciardi, 1954). Other general literary and cultural histories are both superficial and contain frequent misconceptions; see for example: Eugenio Donadoni, *A History of Italian Literature*, trans. by Richard Monges (2 vols., New York: New York University Press, 1969); Joseph Spencer Kennard, *A Literary History of the Italian People* (New York: Macmillan Co., 1941); Hélène

Nolthénius, *Duecento, the late middle ages in Italy* (New York: McGraw-Hill, 1968); Ernest Hatch Wilkins, *A History of Italian Literature* (Cambridge: Harvard University Press, 1954); J. H. Whitfield, *A Short History of Italian Literature* (London: Cassell, 1960).

For general cultural background, the following is valuable: John Larner, *Culture and Society in Italy, 1290–1420* (New York: Scribners' 1971). However, the studies both of Franciscanism and of medieval heresy are notably lacking in references to Jacopone, and when he is treated, the accounts are generally based on inadequate evidence. For example, John Moorman uses the Underhill account almost exclusively in *A History of the Franciscan Order from its origns to the year 1517* (Oxford: The Clarendon Press, 1968); and Émile Gebhardt sees Jacopone largely through the eyes of d'Ancona and thus presents the aesthetic and religious attitudes of the late nineteenth century in *Mystics and Heretics in Italy*, trans. by E. M. Hulme (New York: A. A. Knopf, 1922).

Special Studies—Local History

Getulio Ceci has been the most active researcher into the local records of Todi, seeking material on Jacopone. Three of his writings contain important evidence: *Alla ricerca di Fra Jacopone . . .* (Todi: Tipografia Tuderte, 1932); *Todi nel medio evo* (Todi: Trombetta, 1897); "Podestà, capitani e giudici a Todi nel secolo XIII," *Bollettino della Deputazione di Storia Patria per l'Umbria,* vol. III (1897). In collaboration with Giulio Pensi, he edited the *Statuto di Todi del 1275* (Todi: Trombetta, 1897); and the latter gathered more Jacoponiana in *Documenti e ricordi iacoponici a Todi* (Todi: Tipografia Tuderte, 1930).

In more recent times, the director of the town library, Professor Franco Mancini, has published articles on Jacopone of uneven quality: "La prigionia di Jacopone e 'l'empiasto' di Fra Gentile," *Rassegna della Letteratura Italiana,* vol. LXIV, no. 1 (January–April, 1960); "Per una nota agiografica sul Jacopone da Todi," *Convivium* (1951), pp. 550–555; "Due postille iacoponiche," ibid., (1952), pp. 456–460; and "Prolegomeni all'identificazione di due nuove laude di Jacopone," *Bollettino di Storia Patria per l'Umbria,* vol. LXIX (1962), pp. 265–269. Incidentally, the index of the latter publication reveals articles on Jacopone and on Todi that have appeared over the last eighty years. Of special interest is the research on the several portraits of Jacopone to be found in Annibale Tenneroni, "Un ritratto di Fra Jacopone da Todi," ibid., vol. XIII (1907).

What was available for Jacopone to read at San Fortunato has been established in a study of the manuscripts held by that community by G. Mignini, "I codici del commune di San Fortunato a Todi," *Archivio Storico per le Marche e per l'Umbria,* vol. III (1886). Jacopone's relationship to the various local Franciscan houses is treated in Livario Oliger, *Dove è morto il beato Jacopone da Todi* (Quaracchi [Florence], 1907).

Several local publications appear to be of interest but have not been seen by the author, due to their rarity, namely: Livario Oliger, *Pantanelli presso Orvieto—romitorio dei tempi di San Francesco* (Rome, 1932); D. Elio Margaritelli, *Messer Jacopo Benedetti dalla nascità (1230) al matrimonio (1267)* (Todi: Tipografia Tuderte, 1938); Tommaso Biondi, "Ser Jacopo dei Benedetti, notaio di Todi," *Per la Storia del Notariato* (Perugia: G. Domini, 1954); and Pirro Alvi, *Jacopone da Todi—cenni storici* (Todi, 1906). The volume of notarial biographies contains a short life of

Jacopone as well as much material on notaries in general: Consiglio Nazionale del Notariato, *Il notariato nella civiltà italiana—biografie notarili dal VIII al XX secolo* (Milan: Giuffrè, 1961).

Special Studies—The Conflict with Boniface VIII

Jacopone's role in the spiritual group during the pontificates of Celestine V and Boniface VIII was carefully set forth in Natalino Sapegno, "Appunti intorno alla vita di frate Jacopone—il papa e il fraticello," *Archivum Romanicum*, vol. VIII (1924). His most powerful invective, *Lauda* LVIII, was minutely analyzed and securely dated in a monograph that is a model of its type: Franca Ageno (Brambilla), "Sull' invettiva di Jacopone da Todi contro Bonifazio VIII," *Cultura Neolatina*, vol. XVI (1964). Another excellent monograph is the study of *Lauda* LIV, which explores Jacopone's relation to Celestine V: Mario Martelli, "Per l'interpretazione di una lauda jacoponica," *Belfagor*, vol. XVIII (July, 1963). By contrast the literary study of Francesco Grisi is rather superficial: *La protesta di Jacopone da Todi* (Rome: Trevi, 1969). There is little to be found specifically of interest on Jacopone in such general histories of the period as T. S. R. Boase, *Boniface VIII* (London: Constable & Co., 1933).

Special Studies—Stylistic

In addition to the stylistic studies mentioned elsewhere, special notice should be given to the comparison of Jacopone's style with that of the Sicilian school in Piero Cudini, "Contributo ad uno studio di fonti siciliane nelle laude di Jacopone da Todi," *Giornale Storico della Letteratura Italiana*, vol. CXLV, no. 452 (1968). On the other hand, the attempt to relate Jacopone to Dante fails in G. Latini, *Dante e Jacopone e loro contatti di pensiero e di forma* (Todi: Trombetta, 1906). A recent study of Jacopone's style is that of Lidia Brisca-Menapace, "La poetica di Jacopone," *Contributi dell' Istituto di Filologia Moderna*, vol. I (1961).

Special Studies—Theater and Music

The work of Vincenzo de Bartholomaeis on the origins of Italian sacred drama in the *laude* of Jacopone's time has effectively superseded all earlier accounts, such as Alessandro d'Ancona, *Origini del teatro in Italia* (2 vols.; 2nd ed. reprint, Rome: Bardi, 1966); the original edition dated from 1877. Two works of de Bartholomaeis are particularly useful for the study of Jacopone: *Le origini della poesia drammatica italiana* (Bologna: Zanichelli, 1924) and *Laude drammatiche e rappresentazioni sacre* (3 vols., Florence: Le Monnier, 1943). A more recent work substantially follows the de Bartholomaeis interpretation: Mario Apollonio, *Storia del teatro italiano* (vol. I, Florence: Sanzoni, 1958).

Valuable insights into the development of the *lauda* and specifically the laments of the Virgin are given by Martin Franzbach, "Die Planctus Maria Virginis von Gonzalo de Berceo und Jacopone da Todi," *Cultura Neolatina*, vol. XXVII (1957); while a great volume of excellent material on the *disciplinati* is contained in Deputazione di Storia Patria per l'Umbria, *Il movimento dei disciplinati nel settimo centenario dal suo inizio* (Perugia, 1960, Convegno Internazionale, 1962).

Musicological investigation of thirteenth-century Italy appears to be in its infancy. The only works that I have found are entirely inadequate: Fernando Liuzzi, "Profilo musicale di Jacopone," *Nuova Antologia*, vol. CCCLVI (September, 1931) and his *La lauda e i primordi della melodia italiana* (2 vols., Rome: Libreria dello Stato, 1935). Here the author has attributed to Jacopone *laude* long since known to be spurious and has rather inaccurately transcribed the music into modern notation.

Special Studies—Religious

Jacopone's penitential period is discussed with penetration in the study of *Lauda* XXV: Erik Schöne Staaff, *Sur une lauda de Jacopone da Todi: Quando t'alegri, homo de altura* (Uppsala: Almquvist & Wikoells, 1927); and Mario Pericoli presents an excellent analysis of Joachimist tendencies in *Laude* L, LI, LII, LIII, and LIV in *Escatologia nella lauda jacoponica* (Todi: Accademia Tudertina, 1962).

When one approaches the study of Jacopone's mysticism, there are discovered varieties of interpretations deriving from the different points of view of the authors. For example, Leone Bracaloni is concerned with defending Jacopone against the charges of nihilism, pantheism, and quietism and with asserting his Franciscan orthodoxy: "La spiritualità francescana ascetica e mistica," *Studi Francescani*, vol. XII (1940). In the process, Bracaloni denies the authenticity of the "incriminating" *Lauda* LX—which is rather far-fetched—and undervalues the importance of the entire neo-Platonic tradition. Natalino Sapegno advances equally deep misconceptions of Jacopone's mysticism with great learning in "La 'santa pazzia' di Frate Jacopone e le dottrine dei mistici medievali," *Archivum Romanicum*, vol. VII (1923). Here Jacopone is pictured as always in conflict with evil and always deeply torn in his emotions; he knows not the love of God and men which Francis knew, nor the contemplative peace of Bonaventure and the Victorines. Such conclusions can only arise from misinterpreting the bulk of the later poems of mystical love.

A more balanced assessment of Jacopone's place in the literature of medieval mysticism is to be found in Arrigo Levasti, ed., *Mistici del duecento e del trecento* (Milan and Rome: Rizzoli, 1935). This competent and handy anthology contains Jacopone's *Trattato* and *Detti*, as well as other mystical writings not easily found elsewhere. Another fine study and anthology is: Giovanni Maria Bertin, *I mistici medievali* (Milan: Garzanti, 1944).

Incidentally, a collection of proverbs long attributed to Jacopone was published by Franco Mancini: "I 'proverbia moralia' . . . secondo il manoscritto 195bis della communale di Todi," *Miscellanea Franciscana*, vol. LV (1955). Later the collection was shown to have been made by one of Jacopone's followers in: V. Bigazzi, "I 'proverbia' pseudoiacoponici," *Studi di Filologia Italiana*, vol. XXI (1963).

One of the earliest explorations into the theological sources of Jacopone's thought is that of Agide Gottardi, "'L'albero spirituale' in Jacopone da Todi," *Rassegna Critica della Letteratura Italiana*, vol. XX (1915). The author concentrates on the philosophical *laude* of Jacopone, which though less interesting aesthetically, do contain strong echoes of the Victorines, Joachim of Fiore, and the whole range of Franciscan thinkers, thus indicating that Jacopone was no doubt learned. The specific links between Jacopone and Bonaventure are clarified in

Michele Vinai, "Jacopone da Todi e San Bonaventura," *Cultura Neolatina*, vol. I (1941). Also of interest is: Amadeo Amato, "La teologia di Fra Jacopone da Todi," *Bollettino della Deputazione di Storia Patria per l'Umbria*, vol. XIX (1915).

A firm grasp of Jacopone's experiences of mystical love is shown in the analysis of *Lauda* II done by Mario Martelli, "Cielo e terra in una lauda di Jacopone da Todi," *Giornale Storico della Letteratura Italiana*, vol. CXLI, no. 434 (1964). Perhaps the most comprehensive and sound recent study of Jacopone's mysticism is to be found in Alvaro Bizziccarri, "L'amore mistico nel canzoniere di Jacopone da Todi," *Italica*, vol. XLV, no. 1 (March, 1968).

Index of the Laude of Jacopone

This index presents the first lines of Jacopone's poems and the numbers of the pages on which they are mentioned or quoted in this book. The numeration in Roman numerals refers to that of the first printed edition, by Buonaccorsi in 1490, and frequently republished, e.g., by Ferri and Fallacara. Numbers XCIV through CII in those editions have been omitted as spurious.

The Ageno edition similarly omits these last poems. Otherwise it follows the Buonaccorsi numeration, except that it omits number LXXXVI; thus the Ageno LXXXVI becomes the Buonaccorsi LXXXVII and so on down to Ageno XCII = Buonaccorsi XCIII.

The new Mancini edition contains the same poems as the Ageno edition but follows an entirely different numeration. For the convenience of those using the Mancini edition, his numbers are placed in Arabic numerals in parentheses following the Roman numerals. In an appendix Mancini adds seven poems as possibly genuine but rejects all the Jacoponian works in the *Laudario Urbinate*, except VIII, which is included as A3.

Chronology of Popes

Gregory I, 590–604, the Great, 10, 77

Celestine III, 1194–1198, Giacinto Bobo

Innocent III, 1198–1216, Lothario dei Conti, 2, 11, 32, 49, 62, 70, 72, 73, 78, 99, 134, 192 (n.6)

Honorius III, 1216–1227, Curzio Savelli

Gregory IX, 1227–1241, Ugolino dei Conti, 93, 96

Celestine IV, 1241, Goffredo di Castiglione

Innocent IV, 1241–1254, Sinisbaldo dei Fieschi, 94, 140

Alexander IV, 1254–1261, Rinaldo dei Conti, 30, 85, 96

Urban IV, 1261–1264, Pantaleon Aucher

Clement IV, 1265–1268, Guy Foulkes, 200 (n.32)

Gregory X, 1271–1276, Tebaldo dei Visconti, 31

Innocent V, 1276, Pierre Tarentaise

Adrian V, 1276, Ottobuono dei Fieschi

John XXI, 1276–1277, Juan Pedro Juliani

Nicolas III, 1277–1280, Giovanni Gaetano degli Orsini, 31, 33, 94

Martin V, 1281–1285, Simon de Brie, 32, 95

Honorius IV, 1285–1287, Jacopo Savelli, 30

Nicolas IV, 1288–1292, Geronimo Maschi, 32, 69, 111–112

Celestine V, 1294, Pier da Morrone, 111, 112–117, 120, 125, 213 (n.63)

Boniface VIII, 1294–1303, Benedetto Gaetani, 1, 15, 17, 19, 22, 23, 30–33, 88, 94, 104, 112–113, 114, 116–125, 153, 155, 193 (n.2), 212 (n.41), 213 (n.61)

Benedict XI, 1303–1304, Niccolò Boccasini, 131

Clement V, 1305–1314, Bertrand de Got

John XXII, 1316–1334, Jacques Driès, 188–189

General Index